The Viability of the
Rhetorical Tradition

The Viability of the Rhetorical Tradition

edited by

Richard Graff
Arthur E. Walzer
Janet M. Atwill

STATE UNIVERSITY OF NEW YORK PRESS

Published by
State University of New York Press, Albany

For information, address State University of New York Press, Albany, NY
www.sunypress.edu

Production by Christine L. Hamel
Marketing by Susan Petrie

Library of Congress Cataloging-in-Publication Data

The viability of the rhetorical tradition / edited by Richard Graff, Arthur E. Walzer, Janet M. Atwill.
    p. cm.
    Includes bibliographical references and index.
    ISBN 978-0-7914-6285-0 (alk. paper) — 978-0-7914-6286-7 (pbk. : alk. paper)
    1. Rhetoric. I. Graff, Richard, 1968– II. Walzer, Arthur E., 1944– III. Atwill, Janet, 1955–

PN187.V53 2005
808—dc22
                                                                    2004056466

10 9 8 7 6 5 4 3 2 1

*Richard Graff dedicates his portion of the
volume to his wife, Dori Post Graff.*

*Arthur E. Walzer dedicates his portion to Casey Otis Howell,
born 26 April 2004, his first grandson.*

*Janet M. Atwill dedicates her portion of the volume to the memory
of her grandparents Noval Dawes and W. Campbell Bland.*

Contents

PART TWO
Possibilities: Contemporary Rhetorical Occasions and the Tradition(s)

Acknowledgments

The conversation captured between the covers of this book has developed over many years and, indeed, spans across generations of scholarship in rhetoric. Many of the ideas collected here were first presented at meetings of the American Society for the History of Rhetoric (ASHR). We want to thank especially the ASHR board for devoting valuable conference time—in Seattle in 2000 and in Atlanta in 2001—to early versions of the studies presented here. The lively exchanges among ASHR members at those meetings demonstrated a deep interest in the topic and encouraged us to create this collection.

We also thank our editor at State University of New York Press, Priscilla Ross, for her enthusiastic support of this project, and the Press's readers and editorial staff for their assistance in bringing it to final form. We must also acknowledge the diligence and energy of our contributors, many of whom have worked patiently through several revisions of their chapters. Finally, we would like to express our appreciation to our families and friends for their patience and support through the process of bringing this volume to completion.

Introduction

Richard Graff

Does the past that has given shape to modern rhetoric studies make us more or less able to address contemporary concerns and flourish in the modern university? The question is the basis of a compelling current debate within rhetoric studies. In addressing this question, contributors to this volume have taken the concept of 'tradition' as the central problematic. In the early stages of the development of programs of advanced study devoted to rhetorical theory, history, and criticism—in the United States, predominantly in departments of English or speech communication—reference was often made to something called "the rhetorical tradition." The title was honorific, suggesting at once a long and distinguished history, a sizeable collection of texts containing serious ideas, and a sense of unity, vitality, and purpose. Understandably, then, the term *rhetorical tradition* was regularly invoked as part of efforts to authorize or legitimize a program of study to external audiences within the academy, including those with whom rhetorical studies would need to compete for resources and recognition. And for a time, such invocations were performed without reflection. The existence of the rhetorical tradition was assumed by specialists who could be confident that at least fellow scholars in the history of rhetoric had a clear sense of what it was.

There are signs that testify indirectly to the success of such appeals to the tradition. One of these was an increase in publishing forums and academic positions in rhetorical studies in the mid- to late twentieth century. The same period witnessed a corresponding growth in numbers and strength of graduate programs, especially in rhetoric and composition. This development, in turn, created new demand for resources to facilitate such study: synoptic histories of rhetoric (like those of Kennedy or Conley), anthologies of primary texts (notably, Bizzell and Herzberg's collection, but now also Brummett), and

encyclopedias of rhetorical concepts and authors such as those edited by
Theresa Enos and Thomas Sloane. The term *tradition* figures prominently in
many of these books, often appearing in their titles (e.g., Kennedy; Conley;
Bizzell and Herzberg). Through these and other comparable sources, an
increasing number of graduate students have become acquainted with the history of the discipline. More than this, they have been encouraged to see this
history as constituting a tradition.

But the repeated evocations of 'the rhetorical tradition' had the perhaps
unintended effect of reifying the concept. This outcome has been the cause of
growing concern for scholars in both speech communication and rhetoric-composition. Several in the current generation, including many of the contributors
to the present volume, have urged us to reconsider the story of rhetoric promoted in the standard historical accounts and have raised awareness of the dangers attaching to unreflexive gestures toward "the tradition." In one view, 'the
rhetorical tradition' is acknowledged as a perhaps outmoded but still convenient
label. It performs a grouping and unifying function; it orders the immense mass
of historical materials and perspectives that may be deemed relevant to the study
of rhetoric in its various contemporary guises. In this respect, rhetoric's self-con-
ception, its self-presentation, and its intellectual autonomy have long relied on
an identification with "the tradition," a situation that becomes self-perpetuating
as invocations of the tradition become the basis for rhetoric's claim to "'hang . . .
together' as a domain of knowledge" (Charland 119).

That even this minimum of order, unity, or coherence may be artificial—
imposed rather than organic—is not cause for acute anxiety but at the same
time leaves the tradition without claim to any special reverence. For example,
one should thus be able to accept references to "the classical tradition" of
rhetoric, while at the same time recognizing that the label actually yokes
together several very distinct, often competing perspectives, each of which
may be the source of its own "tradition."[1] If some have been satisfied in sustaining this rather benign double-consciousness, others have called for more
serious interrogation of the relationship between rhetoric's past and present.
Here too the idea of tradition has figured prominently. S. Michael Halloran's
1976 essay "Tradition and Theory in Rhetoric," for example, argued that there
was a profound disconnect between classical rhetoric with its goal of
"prepar[ing] others to speak in conformity with the established conventions"
and modern inquiry focused on the construction of theory (239). While Halloran did not reject the possibility of a meaningful rapprochement between
the classical and modern, he did provide a particularly clear summary of the
inadequacy of then current conceptions of the tradition: "[I]f there is such a
thing as a rhetorical tradition, it cannot be successfully defined by either the
kind(s) of discourse it deals with or the precepts for discourse it offers. There
is just too much disagreement in these areas among the people whose writings
are supposed to articulate the tradition" (235).

If Halloran's essay unsettled the long-supposed continuity between ancient and modern rhetoric, the years following its appearance generated more caustic critique. Beginning in earnest in the late 1980s, attention turned from how to define the rhetorical tradition to consideration of the dangers of inherited definitions. The available full-scale histories and anthologies of rhetoric were together implicated in the process and politics of canon formation and, thus, opened to charges of inadequacy on several counts, exclusivity chief among them. In this view, 'the rhetorical tradition' is often employed as a synonym for a fixed set of texts, concerned with a rather limited range of discursive practices and overwhelmingly authored by white European males.[2] In the context of this debate, Hans Kellner observed that "appeals to the rhetorical tradition configure a version of that tradition in the act of calling it forth" (245)—and this particular ("canonical") conception of tradition appears to underlie much recent work in the history of rhetorical theories and practices that fall outside the received canon, notably those authored by women or by non-whites, or those having origins outside the European continent. 'The rhetorical tradition' appears regularly in titles of such works—indeed, at least as regularly as it had in the older work—but is invoked not with reverence but rather as a backdrop or, commonly, as a foil against which new scholarship can be framed.[3]

Enough has been said to suggest that even when it is not openly contested or interrogated, the concept of tradition haunts the contemporary study of rhetoric. I employ the spectral metaphor deliberately and intend it to serve as a sort of counterpoint to a slightly different image once invoked by Thomas Miller. "The rhetorical tradition," he wrote, "is a fiction that has just about outlasted its usefulness" (26). While attention is naturally drawn to the "fiction" in Miller's sentence, I would like to lay special stress on the "just about." In this spirit, readers of the current book are encouraged to read its title, *The Viability of the Rhetorical Tradition,* not as a proposition to be defended but as an opening to several problem areas addressed in the chapters that follow. The title's second "the" generates initial questions: Is there such a thing as "the" rhetorical tradition, and if so, what is it? Similarly, "viability" is an open issue—the viability of "the," or any, rhetorical tradition cannot be assumed. And so follow a number of further questions: If the rhetorical tradition is a fiction, has its usefulness finally come to an end? Might the rhetorical tradition be reconceptualized, refigured as a "better" fiction that may have considerable use in future? Might a traditionalist conception of "the" tradition still serve an important function in the current academy or outside it? Should 'the tradition' be permanently replaced with 'traditions' (plural) as Miller and others have argued? Is it preferable to conceive rhetoric's historical tradition(s) as irreducibly multiple? Is it possible to do so and still retain some minimal level of coherence deemed necessary for disciplinary recognition in the contemporary (and future) academy or for the maintenance of successful interdisciplinary alliances?

While all of the scholars in this volume take such questions seriously and critically, their answers are diverse and sometimes at odds. Because contributors were selected, in part, for the different perspectives they bring to the study of rhetoric and its tradition(s), it is hardly surprising that the chapters do not present a unified front. The chapters can, however, be grouped into two basic sorts. In part 1, five chapters address historiographical and definitional issues. Richard Graff and Michael Leff consider the various ways in which the rhetorical tradition has been shaped under the pressure of successive waves of revisionist and critical historiography in twentieth-century rhetorical studies. Beneath some subtle differences of emphasis, they note broad commonalities in the calls for new histories out of the fields of speech communication and rhetoric-composition, tracking the development of a generally "unsentimental attitude toward tradition." They contend, however, that some notion of tradition is desirable, not least for its capacity to sustain a sense of intellectual community; they then describe the history of rhetorical pedagogy and teaching practices as a tradition that resonates strongly across disciplinary divides and yet also encourages sensitivity to the particularities of specific historical moments. Where Graff and Leff emphasize a conception of tradition that aligns it with the history of teaching, Alan G. Gross's chapter argues for a view of tradition that emphasizes the development of rhetorical theory. More specifically, Gross urges rhetoricians to attend to what he calls (following W. B. Gallie) "essentially contested concepts." Following Gallie, Gross contends that such concepts provide the intellectual core of humanistic disciplines such as rhetoric. As he shows through an investigation of the concepts of 'bringing-before-the eyes,' 'vivacity,' and 'presence,' individual efforts to grapple with them can lead to theory refinement but do not presuppose or demand a single grand and continuous narrative of rhetoric's history.

Where Gross focuses on contested concepts within the realm of rhetorical theory, Leah Ceccarelli directs attention to the "ends" toward which rhetoric aims. She identifies three such ends—the aesthetic, the epistemic, and the political—and locates their sources in classical Greece. But the thrust of Ceccarelli's argument is to show that these are not merely ends for the practice of rhetoric; rather, they also provide the coordinates for the rhetorical criticism of such practice. This she demonstrates through a work of metacriticism on studies devoted to Lincoln's Gettysburg Address. Although she admits that a given critic (or rhetor) can rarely be characterized as holding to one single end to the exclusion of the others, her case models a fruitful way to account for competing interpretations of the same work. More than this, Ceccarelli's chapter suggests that the three ends, present and often competing from the very origins of Western rhetoric, are the source of a productive tension that continues to animate the study of rhetoric.

Neither Gross's discussion of bringing-before-the eyes, vivacity, and presence nor Ceccarelli's metacriticism on the Gettysburg Address takes us out of the orbit described in the older histories of rhetoric and encapsulated in the standard anthologies. Their choice of objects might thus be taken, in simplistic terms, to suggest a kind of traditionalism that tends to draw one ever back to the canon. As we have already noted, the constitution of the rhetorical canon has been the locus of especially keen dispute. In his contribution, Robert N. Gaines considers the sources of disagreement and the values and priorities evinced in this dispute. Focusing on the classical period, Gaines argues that no canon-based conception of the rhetoric of Greco-Roman antiquity will ever be sufficient and is liable to impoverish historical research on the period. He then describes a conceptual alternative to the canon—a "corpus," which he contends should include not a limited number of texts about rhetoric but rather an expansive array of objects, artifacts, and representations of rhetorical theory, pedagogy, practice, and criticism.

Like others in this collection, Janet M. Atwill maintains that interrogation of rhetoric's relationship to tradition(s) leads us to reconsider the relationships among rhetorical theory, practice, and pedagogy. In her chapter, Atwill explores the viability of classical traditions of civic rhetoric by outlining versions of civic virtue in antiquity and two contemporary conceptions of civic rhetoric. She suggests that concepts of 'virtue' and 'rhetoric,' in both eras, have been shaped by especially powerful models of political order: in classical Athens, *harmonia* and *isonomia;* in contemporary rhetorical theory, civic republicanism and liberalism. The shaping force of ideology, however, is not restricted to traditions since, as she argues, academic investigations, themselves, are also shaped by political ideology, including left political critique. Put another way, scholarship is contingent on its own traditions of research conventions.

The chapters in part 1, by and large, consider tradition in rhetoric at a rather broad conceptual level. They offer different perspectives on or visions of the concept of tradition. In Atwill's consideration of the competing models of political order, for example, or in Ceccarelli's identification of the different "ends" of rhetoric, we are encouraged to view tradition as centered on points of persistent or recurring tension or contestation. But while such acts of re-view or re-vision may enable us to "see" tradition(s) more clearly or completely, they do not necessarily seek to assess tradition's role as a living force, one that simultaneously enables and constrains. Such assessment becomes central in the chapters that make up part 2. However one defines a tradition, its vitality will be measured by its capacity to address the needs of the present. The five chapters of part 2 present varying assessments of traditional rhetoric and its ability to account for contemporary discursive practice, to address contemporary pedagogical concerns, and to enable or, alternatively, disable critique.

In her contribution, Susan C. Jarratt considers the rhetorical responses to the events of September 11, asking how materials inherited from rhetoric's past might serve us in a time of national crisis. She offers the ancient Greek practices of epideictic or funeral oratory as "resonant analogues" for the discourses of memory and mourning that followed in the wake of September 11. Although she notes the tendency of such practices to devolve into state ritual and patriotic display, Jarratt notices in the latter case a tension between a dominant nationalistic discourse and a variety of resisting rhetorics produced by a newly (re)constituted public and disseminated through virtually every available medium.

The chapters by William Hart-Davidson, James Zappen, and S. Michael Halloran and Thomas J. Kinney and Thomas P. Miller make claims bearing directly on some of the themes of part 1. Both argue that rhetoric's history of involvement in elitist institutions has, regrettably, defined it. But both insist that its long commitment to the education of citizens and to political involvement puts rhetoric and rhetoric scholars in a position to promote participatory democracy in the face of the determinative forces of technology and capitalism. Both chapters not only argue for a new conception of rhetoric but also accept the challenge of showing how this "new" rhetoric has contributed or could contribute to democratizing deliberations about new technologies. Hart-Davidson, Zappen, and Halloran and Kinney and Miller contend that if contemporary education in literacy and rhetoric is to continue to find value in traditional or canonical approaches, it must also be careful to recognize and at times correct many core assumptions attaching to rhetoric's historically dominant articulations.

In their contributions, Arthur E. Walzer and Jeanne Fahnestock argue that even canonical texts of the past still have much to teach us in the present—indeed, that they can be heard to speak very subtly to some of today's most pressing problems and interests. Walzer analyzes the circumstances and arguments of two of Isocrates' discourses, *Archidamus* and *On the Peace,* in order to assess their pedagogical status and potential relevance. Walzer discovers in Isocrates' model of education in political wisdom a purpose (to create critical citizens) and a method (that of *dissoi logoi*) that he argues can form the basis for courses in citizenship education today. Fahnestock reevaluates a specific component of traditional rhetoric, the theory of figures or schemes of style. She shows how historical-rhetorical accounts of the figures of parallelism and paronomasia shadow and in some cases prefigure insights into language currently being advanced in the field of cognitive science. Ironically, the very same figurist rhetorics that many commentators have said killed the rhetorical tradition are transformed, in Fahnestock's account, into a source of considerable vitality.

Fahnestock's comparison of the views on language within the fields of cognitive science and traditional rhetoric reintroduces the subject of disciplinary unity and division—an issue of considerable salience in rhetoric studies. As an academic discipline, rhetoric is currently housed in a number of different university departments. If the hope that this volume holds out for rhetoric is to be realized, scholars in this sometimes seemingly amorphous field will need a mutual appreciation for the different ways in which rhetoric is understood and practiced in English composition and speech communication. In the afterword, Steven Mailloux draws on the work of Hans-Georg Gadamer to reflect on how tradition defines and distinguishes rhetorical studies as an interdiscipline and on the advantages of cross-disciplinary conversation and cooperation. Because the scholars who have contributed to this volume by intention come from both communication studies and English, the editors hope that *The Viability of the Rhetorical Tradition* successfully models the type of cooperation that can assure the vitality of rhetoric well into the future.

NOTES

1. This way of approaching the rhetoric of Greece and Rome is actually quite "traditional." See, for example, Friedrich Solmsen's well-known essay wherein an Aristotelian or peripatetic "tradition" is set apart from the "Isocratean tradition." A similar tendency is evidenced in George Kennedy's tripartition of classical rhetoric's "Christian and secular tradition" into distinct "strands"—the sophistic, technical, and philosophical—or in Thomas Conley's somewhat looser division of the "European tradition" of rhetoric into "four models" he discovers in classical Greece. Compare also the treatment of Duhamel, discussed by Graff and Leff in this volume.

2. From this perspective, tradition is not uncommonly described as a binding or constraining force. As Jacqueline Jones Royster has put it, Western "traditions of theory and practice" that have dominated the study of rhetoric "have tended to function with a heavy and relentlessly constraining hand" (149).

3. See, for example, the recent collections titled *The Changing Tradition: Women in the History of Rhetoric* (Sutherland and Sutcliffe) and *Alternative Rhetorics: Challenges to the Rhetorical Tradition* (Gray-Rosendale and Gruber). The editors of the former offer the following categories to group their essays on the history of women's rhetorics: "excluded from the rhetorical tradition," "alongside the rhetorical tradition," "participating in the rhetorical tradition," "emerging into the rhetorical tradition," and "engaging the rhetorical tradition." In such an arrangement, "the rhetorical tradition," while hardly viewed as a staid monolith, figures centrally as a means to classify the many diverse strands of contemporary inquiry into rhetoric's past.

WORKS CITED

Bizzell, Patricia, and Bruce Herzberg, eds. *The Rhetorical Tradition: Readings from Classical Times to the Present*. 2nd ed. Boston: Bedford/St. Martin's, 2001. [1st ed., 1990].

Brummett, Barry, ed. *Reading Rhetorical Theory*. Fort Worth: Harcourt, 2000.

Charland, Maurice. "The Constitution of Rhetoric's Tradition." *Philosophy and Rhetoric* 36 (2003): 119–34.

Conley, Thomas. *Rhetoric in the European Tradition*. Chicago: U of Chicago P, 1990.

Duhamel, P. Albert. "The Function of Rhetoric as Effective Expression." *Journal of the History of Ideas* 10 (1949): 344–56.

Enos, Theresa, ed. *Encyclopedia of Rhetoric and Composition: Communication from Ancient Times to the Information Age*. New York: Garland, 1996.

Gray-Rosendale, Laura, and Sibylle Gruber, eds. *Alternative Rhetorics: Challenges to the Rhetorical Tradition*. Albany: State U of New York P, 2001.

Halloran, S. Michael. "Tradition and Theory in Rhetoric." *Quarterly Journal of Speech* 62 (1976): 234–41.

Kellner, Hans. "Afterword: Reading Rhetorical Redescriptions." In *Rethinking the History of Rhetoric*. Ed. Takis Poulakos. Boulder, CO: Westview, 1993. 241–56.

Kennedy, George A. *Classical Rhetoric in Its Christian and Secular Tradition from Ancient to Modern Times*. 2nd ed. Chapel Hill: U of North Carolina P, 1999. [1st ed., 1980].

Miller, Thomas P. "Reinventing Rhetorical Traditions." In *Learning from the Histories of Rhetoric: Essays in Honor of Winifred Bryan Horner*. Ed. Theresa Enos. Carbondale and Edwardsville: Southern Illinois UP, 1993. 26–41.

Royster, Jacqueline Jones. "Disciplinary Landscaping, or Contemporary Challenges in the History of Rhetoric." *Philosophy and Rhetoric* 36 (2003): 148–67.

Sloane, Thomas O., ed. *Encyclopedia of Rhetoric*. Oxford: Oxford UP, 2001.

Solmsen, Friedrich. "The Aristotelian Tradition in Ancient Rhetoric." Reprinted in *Aristotle: The Classical Heritage of Rhetoric*. Ed. Keith V. Erickson. Metuchen, NJ: Scarecrow, 1974.

Sutherland, Christine Mason, and Rebecca Sutcliffe, eds. *The Changing Tradition: Women in the History of Rhetoric*. Calgary: U of Calgary P, 1999.

PART ONE

Definitions:
Traditional and New

ONE

Revisionist Historiography and Rhetorical Tradition(s)

Richard Graff and Michael Leff

AT ONE TIME, not so long ago, people in our line of academic work used to talk about something called the "rhetorical tradition." It is unlikely that many of us could give a precise definition of the phrase, but we invoked it with unreflective confidence and assumed that our colleagues would understand what we meant. In fact, the term *rhetorical tradition* represented something more than an elegant synonym for "the history of rhetoric." It had a resonance that suggested not just what we studied but who we were in the academy. The history was our history.

Such confidence, however, is no longer possible in respect to either the meaning of the rhetorical tradition or the sentiment attached to it. Over the course of several decades, one prominent group of scholars has argued that the 'tradition' is excessively narrow and largely irrelevant to contemporary circumstances, and they have attempted to displace 'tradition' with the terms *theory* or *system*. Some of the same scholars also maintain that it is an error to think of *a* tradition and, under the banner of pluralism, insist on recognition of multiple traditions. In a more recent development, the influence of poststructuralism has led rhetoricians to note the biases and exclusions of "traditional" histories and to object to any single grand narrative for the history of rhetoric. And still others are skeptical about the desirability of the very concept of 'tradition.' Thus, Jane Sutton has written: "If we focus on the problem of representing rhetoric's history as a Tradition, we discover that unity—its theory—is created out of diversity of practice. . . . What can be seen in rhetoric's history, consequently, is only that which is framed as The Tradition," and Sutton adds, the result is an impoverished perspective that privileges "uniformity" and "consistency" and excludes "the rare, the exception, the unique" (Sutton, "Structuring" 157–58).

These revisionist complaints are not always well considered, and the older scholarship is hardly as monolithic or stultifying as it is sometimes represented. Nevertheless, the collective weight of the revisionist effort cannot be ignored. It does capture something important about the temper of our times, does reveal serious limitations in our conventional historical scholarship, and does make a strong case for complicating and expanding our efforts. Indeed, the calls issued only a relatively short time ago for new histories of rhetoric—or new rhetorical histories—have been answered and continue to be answered at a rather surprising clip. Such work demonstrates that, at minimum, we no longer can assume that the history of rhetoric consists in a stable, neutral record open to disinterested inquiry. It is itself a rhetorical achievement—a set of practices that respond to local interests and that come to attention through the intervention of a historian.

But while many of the new perspectives brought to the study of rhetoric's history/ies have much to commend them, they also involve some hazards, and probably the most noteworthy of these is the threat to obliterate any sense of tradition. The almost infinite sprawl of rhetorical practices encourages a splintering of interests, and without a tradition against which we can measure our innovations, we may lose the minimum level of coherence necessary to sustain an academic community. Consequently, we face a dilemma. While the received view of tradition is no longer acceptable, if we lack a usable sense of tradition, we risk dispersal, dismemberment, and the loss of any semblance of a collective identity.

In this chapter, we intend to tackle this problem directly and search for a source of tradition stable enough to provide an identity for a community of rhetorical scholars but flexible enough to allow for the diversity demanded by new approaches to our subject and its history. In fact, we believe that, when rightly understood, the concept of tradition can serve as a *via media* between the seamless uniformity demanded by theory (in the modern sense of the term) and the scatter of historically situated cases. For this purpose, we will begin with a review of revisionist efforts that originated from within the "modernist" perspective and note how this development tended to displace or distort tradition. Then, we will consider some of the more prominent postmodern efforts at revisionism, and by appropriating key points of this critique, we hope to demonstrate that in a conception of the rhetorical tradition as pedagogical (i.e., as a history of teaching speaking and writing), we can locate a mobile but coherent basis for intellectual and institutional community.

The First Wave of Revisionism:
Theory and System in the History of Rhetoric

In his three-volume study of rhetoric and poetic from antiquity through the renaissance, Charles Sears Baldwin established the standard pattern for twentieth-century studies of the history of rhetoric. Three main features marked this work: (1) Baldwin sharply divided rhetoric into two diametrically opposed conceptions. One of these was the sound art of Aristotle devoted to the content of what was said and designed to give effectiveness to truth. The other was the unsound art of sophistic devoted to style and designed to give effectiveness to the speaker. The history of rhetoric was a struggle between these forces. (2) The struggle served as the basis for a master narrative in which everything after Aristotle represented decline. On this view, the medieval history of rhetoric was one of constant diminution and regression, which culminated, by the thirteenth century, in a total loss of connection with the genuine classical art. To some extent, this situation was retrieved by the revival of classical learning in the Renaissance. (3) Historical research should concentrate on questions of influence, and Baldwin addressed this matter from a number of perspectives: how general conceptions of and attitudes toward rhetoric shifted from one author to the next; the influence of earlier works on the morphology and the preceptive content of later works; and the influence of rhetorical precepts on literary practice.

This pattern proved remarkably durable, but by midcentury some notable objections to it began to emerge. An early and influential critique appeared in P. Albert Duhamel's article, "The Function of Rhetoric as Effective Expression," published in the *Journal of the History of Ideas* in 1949. Like Richard McKeon before him, Duhamel decried narrowly technical studies of the history of rhetoric that focused on technical precept and influence: "There is a sufficiency of monographs," he wrote, "occupied with the determination of the influence of particular rhetoric books on selected authors, or histories supplying chronological lists of contents of successive manuals" (36). Instead, Duhamel proposed to step back from the detail and consider an "author's system taken as a whole." Viewed from this angle, every particular system of rhetoric arose from "the more basic elements of a rhetorician's philosophy," and thus rhetoric always proved "dependent upon the epistemology, psychology, and metaphysic of the system in which it occurs. The rhetorical is determined by the epistemological" (37). Furthermore, just as philosophical positions were various and irreducible to any common denominator, so also were rhetorics. Duhamel illustrated this point through a consideration of the variety of rhetorical systems indigenous just to the classical period, a period in which rhetorical systems emerged in accordance with Platonic, Aristotelian, Sophistic, and Stoic philosophies. "To say that there was a 'Classical

Rhetoric,'" he concluded, was "to compound a gratuitous tag. There were as many conceptions of rhetoric in the period usually called 'Classical' as there were philosophies, and rhetoric can be understood only within the commensurable terms of the philosophy" (48).

In one sense, Duhamel's argument elevated the status of rhetoric by setting the technical detail to the side and focusing on larger cultural and intellectual issues, and he also offered a much-needed counterstatement to the monolithic histories produced by writers who followed Baldwin's model. Nevertheless, on Duhamel's account, rhetoric was reconceived through its reduction to philosophical foundations. The older interest in preceptive lore helped maintain a connection between the history of rhetoric and the teaching of rhetoric, and it promoted concern about processes of transmission that linked this teaching within a tradition. If Baldwin and others rendered that tradition pedestrian through a commitment to simple dichotomies and compulsively detailed attention to influence, Duhamel threatened to obscure tradition by burying it beneath philosophical foundations. Rhetoric as a teaching practice commands little attention when we concentrate on the epistemological and metaphysical grounding of "rhetorical systems."

Almost fifteen years after the publication of Duhamel's essay, Otis Walter presented the first version of the philosophical approach to emerge from within the discipline then known as speech. Walter's paper, "On Views of Rhetoric: Whether Conservative or Progressive," began as a response to Wayne Thompson's effort to refurbish the traditional preceptive lore. Thompson (1963) had lamented the "dead hand of classical rhetoric" and the "traditionalism and inertia" that characterized contemporary rhetorical scholarship (1), and to solve this problem, he argued, among other things, that the classical principles ought to be tested and revised through the new methods of experimental social science. Walter agreed with Thompson's negative assessment of scholarship in the field but held that, in conceiving "the tradition of rhetoric" as "a body of hypotheses about persuasion," Thompson adhered to a position that was not just counterproductive but actually "part of the disease" (Walter 368). What was interesting about classical rhetoric, Walter asserted, was not the detail of the art—its "hypotheses about persuasion"—but its "different starting points, its myriad assumptions, its contrasting aims." These starting points represented the "foundations" of rhetoric, and significant historical scholarship depended upon the appreciation of their significance. Walter then proceeded to "look at" some of the starting points for a rhetorical system. These included the metaphysical (Protagoras and Plato), the social (Isocrates and Cicero), the epistemological (Descartes, Locke, Campbell), the educational-ethical (Quintilian), the theological (Augustine), the esthetic (Blair), the logical (Whately), and the psychological (Winans). "Great theories of rhetoric," Walter claimed, were revolutionary because they proceeded from new starting points. "Little theories," on the other hand, don't "revolutionize," they just "tinker" (373).

In addition to his negative judgment about the quality of existing scholarship, Walter also displayed a less obtrusive but perhaps more important
point of agreement with Thompson. Like Thompson, Walter located the
problem in terms of theory. Thompson sought to break from traditionalism by
revising and securing the theoretical ground for classical precepts through
abstract method; Walter attempted a theoretical cure by reducing the preceptive superstructure to philosophical foundations. From this perspective, the
history of rhetoric is decisively a "theoretical" question, and the concept of tradition gets shunted to the side. In his only explicit reference to the term, Walter treats tradition as something entirely static—as the ensemble of texts
devoted to rhetoric. Given the general direction of Walter's argument, we
might infer that tradition could also be regarded (more theoretically) in relationship to the ensemble of different rhetorical systems and the competing
starting points that they reflected. Walter, however, never expressed this view,
and the starting points that he enumerated were so many and so unsystemat-
ically arranged that the only theoretically significant feature of the tradition
would appear to be its constant revolutionary movement from one incommensurable foundation to another. Finally, we should note that Walter's attention was so thoroughly directed toward these foundations that the relationship
between rhetorical theory and any form of grounded practice was almost
totally occluded. Rhetorics were interesting as philosophical exercises in theory construction, and their preceptive content was no more than a superstructure. From this perspective, the process of handing down and modifying
teaching practices could not and should not warrant serious consideration. It
was simply not theoretically or philosophically important.

Both Duhamel and Walter refer to "systems of rhetoric," but neither
treats the concept in depth. Douglas Ehninger, however, uses "systems" as the
focal point in his revisionist approach to rhetorical historiography. For
Ehninger, a system is an organized, consistent, coherent way of talking about
practical discourse ("Systems" 15). As opposed to some random collection of
observations and precepts, a system is an "account of the communication
process that has a distinctive emphasis or focus" and is "ordered in a hierarchy
of terms" and "marked by a distinguishing method" (25). Moreover, for
Ehninger, a system could characterize a collective set of works of a "given
place or period" and not just an individual treatise (15).

In fact, Ehninger develops his notion of systems in relation to historical
periods, and in his best known formulation, he identifies three types: (1) classical rhetoric, which is essentially "grammatical" in orientation, (2) eighteenth-century rhetoric, which is essentially psychological, and (3) contemporary rhetoric (post 1930), which is essentially social.[1] Unlike Duhamel or
Walter, whose categories arise directly from philosophical criteria, Ehninger
turns first to rhetorical treatises and seeks to abstract from them a common
essence. This procedure leaves him in closer contact with the pedagogical and

practical aspects of rhetoric, but Ehninger still effects a very severe reduction, and his criteria of coherence, consistency, and methodological distinctiveness also indicate a strong affinity with "theory" in the modern sense of the term.

Ehninger's conception of rhetorical systems allows room for the operation of tradition, since each successive system invokes a starting point that does not simply overturn and obliterate its predecessor but also encompasses "that system to pass beyond it" (27). Nevertheless, to paraphrase Floyd Anderson, this is a conception of tradition with a decidedly Whigish attitude (Anderson). That is, Ehninger's version of rhetorical history sweeps relentlessly up and forward, and earlier phases in the development are no more than incomplete or primitive versions of the later phases, and as such, they do not retain genuine theoretical value.

Expanding on Anderson's point, Carole Blair has noted that Ehninger reverses the historical valences found in "influence" studies of the type practiced by Baldwin. While Baldwin establishes the earlier classical type as the proper norm for rhetoric, Ehninger fixes the norm at the other end of history in contemporary theory. In both instances, Blair argues, the historiography is badly flawed since it biases perception of the historical record and interferes with our ability to use history as a resource for rhetorical theory.

Blair's intervention in this debate comes at an interesting moment. Her essay "Contested Histories of Rhetoric: The Politics of Preservation, Progress, and Change" (1992) represents the last major entry in the wave of revisionism that proceeds from Duhamel through Ehninger, and it is also, within the field of speech communication, one of the earliest entries in the newer, poststructuralist approach to historiography. Rejecting both influence and systems studies, Blair advocates "critical history," and as she tries to work across the line between the older scholarship and her own neo-Foucaultian project, some new and rather complicated problems emerge.

Blair is clear and unequivocal about the purpose of the historical enterprise: "[T]he primary goal of historical study of rhetorical theory" is "the continued enrichment of our understanding of rhetoric." The most important reason to study "historical rhetorics" is to "provide material capable of appropriation and accommodation" or to prompt change and even "spur radical ways of retheorizing rhetoric" (404). In other words, we investigate the past for its relevance to our present situation. This orientation at least leans in a poststructuralist direction, especially since it is associated with a call for critical reflection about how the historian's interests are implicated in the construction of history. Nevertheless, because she unreflexively accepts the term *theory* as the object of historical inquiry, Blair retains some of the fundamental assumptions of the approaches she seeks to dislodge.

Blair's conception of theory is equivocal. At times, she suggests a view that has a self-reflective, grounded, and hermeneutic quality. For example, quoting from an earlier paper co-authored with Mary Kahl, Blair describes theory as an activity involving a conversation between past and present (403; Blair and Kahl), and toward the end of the essay, she explains that her version of critical history allows for a dialogic relationship between current theoretical interests and past texts (420, and see note 48). In these instances, we might regard theory as something that works through tradition—an activity that allows mediation between positioned subjects in the present and texts that are positioned in some past context.

At other times, however, Blair treats theory as an abstract and largely self-standing formation in much the same terms that Ehninger conceives it. For example, she complains about existing historiography because "[h]istorians ignore some rhetorical theories altogether, present some as more 'dominant' than others" (418). And she argues that instead of focusing on later appropriation of a work, we ought to concentrate on "its theoretical value or substance" (407) and that influence studies circumscribe "the unique substance of later theories" in comparison with antecedent models (409). Conceived in these terms theory is not an activity or a practice; rather it has an ontological status as something already fully existent prior to the historian's interpretation and whose substance can be discovered or ignored or categorized as one thing or another. This shift from a view of theory as grounded activity to theory as substantive object leaves Blair's project equivocal and somewhat confused. The reader is left to wonder whether she accepts the substantive view of theory in the older studies and critiques them for failing to realize their own ambitions or whether she is critiquing the very concept of theory in those studies. Ironically, as Blair wavers toward the older, more abstract view of theory, she produces a theoretically overdetermined critique of existing historiography and overlooks the potential of tradition as corrective to some of the problems that she identifies.

Blair's critique of influence studies rests upon an abstract and unqualified theoretical generalization about their nature. Such studies, she insists, embody a "politics of preservation," and more specifically, they "sacralize . . . ancient rhetorical theory by treating later rhetorics as monuments to classical rhetoric" (404). The privileging of classical antecedents, she claims, is not an incidental property of some influence studies but is an essential and innate feature of the whole enterprise. This point is a fundamental (one is tempted to say foundational) premise in Blair's argument, and its strength and persistence is indicated as much by its repetition as by the strength of its assertion: (1) "[The] tendency to eclipse the historical materials themselves is not an accident of application in influence studies; it is inherent in the model of influence itself" (406). (2) "'Influence' . . . is a marker for a preservative politics that *dictates* the maintenance or continuity of tradition. . . . This stance posits a privileged origin, a 'golden age' of rhetorical theorizing," and later works are dismissed "as monuments to classical rhetoric, not as contributors to rhetorical thought" (408; emphasis in the original). (3) "Influence studies . . . are inherently preservative."

Later rhetorics are "reduced to versions of, and thus monuments to, classical rhetoric. Any theoretical *difference* that they may have with ancient sources is sacrificed to the desire to maintain a linear, influential tradition" (409; emphasis in the original). (4) "[T]he influence study's message is that everything worthy in our understanding of rhetoric is always already present in prior doctrine. Valuable 'new' insight is unavailable for an historian can always find the 'real' source of insight in an earlier work. Or retheorizing will be condemned as a departure from 'the tradition'" (417).

Blair, then, associates rhetorical tradition with what she characterizes as the inherently preservationist bias of influence studies. From this perspective, tradition emerges as a staid monolith that at best obstructs theoretical understanding and at worst actively subverts it. But the cases that she cites support neither her sweeping claims about influence studies nor her representation of tradition as theoretically retrograde.

Consider, for example, Wilbur Samuel Howell. Howell is, just as Blair says, a major figure within the tradition of influence scholarship. But he hardly valorizes classical rhetoric or attempts to reduce other theoretical approaches to a classical model. In his magisterial *Eighteenth-Century British Logic and Rhetoric,* Howell argues that the rhetoric of the period was "derived either from Aristotle and Cicero or from attitudes associated with the rise of the new science" (696). He traces the second, or nonclassical, form of rhetoric from its origins in Bacon and Locke through the major rhetorical authors of the century—George Campbell, Adam Smith, John Witherspoon, and others. He does define this "new rhetoric" by way of contrast to classical rhetoric (a practice consistent with the emphasis on contrastive analysis that Blair builds into her critical historiography), but nowhere does Howell disguise the differences between the "new rhetoric" and the classical model. To the contrary, his attitude, like Ehninger's, is clearly progressive; Howell views the eighteenth-century deviations from classical dicta as an advance, and hence, his influence study reverses what Blair claims to be the inevitable result of influence studies—it distinguishes between old and new traditions in rhetorical theory in a way that privileges the new.[2]

A more subtle but perhaps more telling case has to do with Blair's interpretation of Murphy's *Rhetoric in the Middle Ages.* As evidence that the book sustains a preservationist conception of the history of rhetorical theory, Blair quotes this passage from its introduction: "This book, then, provides the first comparative study of the various forms in which medieval writers continued the preceptive tradition. Whether applied to preaching, verse-writing, letter-writing or other fields, it is clear that the basic preceptive assumption continues from Saint Augustine to the revival of classical learning in the Renaissance." Blair's commentary notwithstanding, Murphy does not assert a continuity of rhetorical theory; he argues for the continuity of a tradition, specifically the tradition of preceptive teaching, and on Murphy's account, that tradition is as much an engine of change as it is an element of stability.

We can most easily understand Murphy's position by comparing his history with the one offered in Baldwin's *Medieval Rhetoric and Poetic*. Baldwin truly is a preservationist and an apologist for what he interprets as *the* classical version of rhetoric theory. Thus, he establishes an Aristotelian norm at the outset of his book and proceeds to study the medieval period as one of progressive decline from that fixed and abiding standard. Murphy, by contrast, regards the changing configuration of rhetoric as a constructive adjustment to new circumstances. He characterizes medieval attitudes toward rhetoric as pragmatic, and he notes the creativity involved in shifting and reconfiguring elements of the preceptive lore from their original base in forensic oratory to new genres such as the sermon, poetic composition, and epistolography. Moreover, these alterations in classical rhetoric are enabled by tradition, since tradition preserves resources that prove useful to the practice of teaching even as the practice must adapt to changing cultural circumstances.

If, as Blair says, the most important goal of historical scholarship in rhetoric is to deepen our understanding of rhetoric itself, then Murphy's *Rhetoric in the Middle Ages* contributes to this goal through at least two lessons: first, tradition is not necessarily inert and reactionary; it can facilitate change by connecting the storehouse of "theoretical" resources to new tasks; second, the teaching of rhetoric offers an important site of practice where this mediation can occur over time. In these respects, Murphy's conception of tradition seems to complement Blair's project, and her failure to identify these points of affinity suggests a bias that she inherits from the earlier school of revisionism and its modernist attitudes toward rhetorical theory as a static body of substantive principles rather than as a dynamic and evolving activity.

The Second Wave of Revisionism:
Critical Historiography and Rhetorical Histories

Blair's essay, addressed primarily to rhetoricians working within the field of speech communication, registered discomfort that was being felt across disciplinary lines. Indeed, in the years immediately preceding its appearance, a number of scholars affiliated with the field of rhetoric and composition had advanced arguments consistent with Blair's concerning the shortcomings of received histories and the need for new histories written from a more self-conscious and critical perspective. Initiated at conference panels and in discussion groups devoted to the issue of historiography in rhetorical studies and developed subsequently in several publications,[3] the discussion sketched the contours of a self-consciously revisionist practice of historical inquiry. The debate provided impetus and opened intellectual space for what is now a substantial and ever-growing number of new studies treating aspects of rhetoric's past. We do not have space in this chapter to review all of the different perspectives featured even in the early stages of the discussion but can identify some of the basic tenets as well as characteristic assumptions and motives animating the broader revisionist project within the field of composition-rhetoric.

Essays published in a 1987 special issue of *Pre/Text* presented a prolegomenon to future studies of rhetoric's history. Contributors to the issue (James Berlin, Susan Jarratt, John Schilb, Victor Vitanza) offered critique of the then-available histories as a necessary first step. The critiques focus on the received, standard, or traditional accounts that by and large fall under the category of influence studies identified by Blair (indeed, the critiques prefigure Blair's and share some of its defects). The "official" histories are found wanting for four, sometimes overlapping, reasons: (1) The authors are unreflexive in their methods and fail to recognize crucial intellectual assumptions and biases. Consequently, the histories are presented as objective accounts of fact, potentially falsifiable, but only according to the same standards of historical inquiry left unremarked by the authors themselves. The histories unfold in confident ignorance (or, worse, denial) of their own rhetoricity. (2) The received histories are exclusionary. The scope of these histories is largely restricted to works closely tied to the Western tradition of teaching and theorizing the art of effective speech and writing—to works that draw on classical Greek and Latin sources or, most narrowly, to works calling themselves "rhetorics" (see Jarratt, "Sophistic" 11). By treating only a limited set of canonical texts, the histories valorize certain authors from the (usually classical) past while failing to consider individuals or groups outside the white, male, European demographic. This bias renders incomplete even those histories with the greatest chronological sweep; they are partial in both senses of the word. (3) The standard historical accounts display a general and frequently self-proclaimed commitment to continuity. The history of rhetoric is rendered as a story of connected episodes, tracing back to a common starting point or origin in classical (often Aristotelian) ideas and texts. Whether told as a tale of continuous decline from a classical golden age, of cyclic fragmentation and reintegration (as Vickers), or cast as a narrative featuring intermittent bursts of progress (as Howell), there is an obvious intolerance of discontinuities in the plot. No space is left for unique or eccentric works. True exceptions or alternatives to classical-traditional theory or practice are, again, left out of account. (4) Another shortcoming identified in contributions to the *Pre/Text* special issue and extended in subsequent publications concerned the tendency of traditional histories to remain at the level of intellectual history. A narrow focus on the study of ideas contained in texts and on the connections between texts produced in different eras comes with a concomitant failure to engage the social, political, and economic contexts of the texts' production and reception. As James Berlin put it, "The material conditions of the creator [of the text] count for nothing at all. Rhetorical history is the story of disembodied ideas freely floating in an intellectual ether" (Berlin, "Revisionary" 139; cf. Schilb, "Differences" 31).

Accompanying the critiques were calls for the production of new histories that would correct or overcome the deficiencies of the standard histories.
While varying in particulars and relative emphasis, the proposals address
themselves consistently to themes of multiplicity and inclusivity, and all urge
historians of rhetoric to interrogate presuppositions concerning methods of
research and objects of inquiry. Drawing insights from a wide range of poststructuralist and postmodern theorists—from Hayden White and Dominic
LaCapra to Michel Foucault's concept of 'genealogy' and neo-Marxian conceptions of historical reflection as dialectical engagement with the past—the
revisionist position opposes itself to any grand narrative about the history of
rhetoric constructed from a supposedly fixed and neutral perspective. It privileges the local instead of the universal and directs attention to sociopolitical
contexts and how they influence both the theory and practice of rhetoric. The
new historiography is to be, above all, *critical;* it searches for biases and exclusions, for disguised tactics of repression and marginalization, and it applies
that critical sensibility to the act of writing history itself. Thus, historians
ought to become self-conscious of their own placement within a historical situation and mindful of their assumptions and motives. The choice of research
methods, periods, and objects of study are indeed choices and the products of
argument. In sum, the practice of history writing is itself recognized as a
rhetorical act (e.g., Schilb, "History"; Berlin, "Revisionary"). Moreover, the
resulting historical accounts should confront contingency and change, eschew
the need for continuity and the imperative to tell a seamless and unified story.
The neat emplotment of one's historical narrative should be accompanied by
the historian's acknowledgment of its basically provisional character.

    Two sorts of studies were among the first to exemplify the critical per-
spective and new historiographical principles, each of which involves a reconsideration of tradition as a concept and its role in rhetorical inquiry. In one
sort, a specific binary opposition provides the structural base for revising or
challenging the prevailing understanding of some aspect of the history of
rhetoric. Here, the effort entails rearranging the valences attached to authors,
interpretations, and concepts that fall more or less within the ambit of the
"received" tradition. Thus, a marginalized sophistic conception of rhetoric is
revived to decenter the dominant Platonic/Aristotelian version of the art;[4] a
foundationalist/philosophical model of epistemology is shown to control
existing interpretations of Aristotelian rhetoric and then is corrected by reading *The Rhetoric* through a productionist epistemology (Atwill, "Instituting";
Atwill, *Rhetoric*); the patriarchal or gendered characterization of core concepts
within canonical texts is exposed for what it is and then reinterpreted through
a feminist lens (Enders); a classical text is read against the sociopolitical background of its period and shown to inscribe the biases of an elitist ideology at
odds with contemporary cultural values and educational aims (Berlin, "Aristotle's *Rhetoric*"; Neel). In all these cases, the tradition changes dramatically as

its elements are aligned in new ways, and perhaps more important, what once appeared as a single, coherent development now becomes conflicted and complex. In these new versions, rhetoric is itself divided between Aristotelian and sophistic values, between foundational and productionist orientations, between rational, orderly surfaces and troubled depths that reproduce systems of cultural repression.

Another broad category of revisionist work involves bringing attention to what is left out of the available histories or "traditional" accounts. It too can be characterized in binary terms, as it sets up an opposition between inside and outside (as contrasted with opposition involving the hierarchical placement of what is already inside). Instead of the rereading of canonical texts, this is often work of search and recovery, accompanied by a "first" reading, of what has been lost in the historical record. And instead of exposing conflicts internal to "the" tradition, the tendency here is to speak in terms of multiple, competing traditions. The effort to write women into the history of rhetoric is probably the best known of the efforts in this direction,[5] but there are other projects of roughly the same type: there is a call to attend to the voices of the marginalized and the oppressed that the canon implicitly silences, a demand to consider rhetorics developed in non-Western cultures, an injunction to emphasize the importance of practice over theory and to expand the domain of practice relevant to rhetorical inquiry. In this work, the scope of the history of rhetoric is thus enlarged and conceived as strands that cannot fit comfortably into a single structure—a woman's tradition as opposed to a male tradition, a subaltern tradition as opposed to an elite tradition, Chinese or Indian traditions as opposed to a Western tradition, a tradition of emergent literate practices as opposed to the tradition conveyed in the standard collections of technical treatises or systematic "theories," and so on.

We have characterized these two prominent strands of research in the history of rhetoric in fairly strict binary terms in order to identify some of the ways the idea of rhetorical tradition has been (re)configured under the pressure of a growing critical sensibility. To be sure, the two categories—"rereading" and "recovery"—are not as pure as our account suggests. Moreover, it should be clear that the simplification overlooks considerable variety in the methods of inquiry involved in each type of study, from very traditional forms of archival research and textual analysis, to more inventive historical reconstruction and theory-driven interpretation or critique. However, such diversity should not obscure certain commonalities in contemporary attitudes toward tradition associated with the more recent efforts to revise, challenge, or enrich our understanding of rhetoric's history. Clearly and most fundamentally, the proponents of critical historiography in its various guises adopt an unsentimental attitude toward tradition; this attitude is reflected in a keen perception of gaps and omissions perpetuated in the process of canon formation and a healthy skepticism toward received interpretations of those items that have long held a place in that canon. In this respect, the newer efforts subsume and go far beyond the older, modernist revisionist proposals, which by and large merely reorganized the canonical sources through identification of philosophical foundations or theoretical "starting points" and did not in any explicit way make tradition itself the subject of critique or object of suspicion.

The unsentimental attitude toward the rhetorical tradition was expressed most forcefully by Thomas Miller, who observed in 1993 that "[t]he rhetorical tradition is a fiction that has just about outlasted its usefulness" (26). On its surface, Miller's statement aptly encapsulates several of the basic convictions of the new historiography: that "the" rhetorical tradition, the one casually assumed in most of the standard histories, is not an objective entity, but a rhetorical production; that it is a story that should command no special deference, but rather must compete with any other narrative that could challenge it; and finally, that while it may have once served a purpose, the contemporary field of historical research in rhetoric no longer requires—or soon will no longer require—this (or any other) univocal rendering of rhetoric's past.

Miller goes on to argue that historians of rhetoric should shift the focus from the tradition of rhetoric to what he terms the "rhetoric of traditions." Lamenting the lack of true social histories of rhetorical praxis, he urges rhetoricians to "mov[e] beyond rereading the canonical texts of elite traditions to develop richly detailed descriptions of the shared experiences of local communities" (29). Communities develop forms of rhetorical practice that can be appreciated only when accompanied by thick description of the social contexts in which they arose and to which they responded. Suitably contextualized, the diverse forms of socially situated rhetorical practice can be characterized as traditions in their own right.

Miller's proposal echoes the critical-revisionist calls for a more serious engagement with rhetorical practice(s) than that found in standard influence studies. His call for social histories of rhetoric and thick description of local contexts represents an extension of a crucial insight left undeveloped in the "systems" approach of Ehninger, who observed that "[s]ystems of rhetoric arise out of a felt need and are shaped in part by the intellectual and social environment in which the need exists" but who failed to deliver a satisfactory account of any such environment (see Berlin, "Revisionary" 135–36). But more than this, Miller's proposal sets itself firmly against the reductionist tendencies of the older influence and systems approaches. There is no set limit to the number of local cases (or "traditions") that could command the historian's interest, and there is no compulsion to circumscribe what "counts" as rhetoric. This is so because the social history of rhetoric would not aim to abstract from the situated case some central or essential qualities that could be laid out for comparison across cases. The focus shifts from defining a rhetoric or a system of rhetoric to the interpretation of the cultural exigencies that enable or encourage multiple modes of rhetorical response.

It is in these respects that we can best understand Miller's assertion that the rhetorical tradition is a "fiction that has just about outlasted its usefulness." Clearly, by "the rhetorical tradition" Miller means to denote the group of texts that have achieved canonical status by their regular appearance in the standard histories, textbooks, and anthologies. So conceived, the tradition offers little to the social historian of rhetoric. It provides a rather slim body of evidence for any specific period being investigated—and for some periods, practically none at all. Moreover, the texts it does provide will by and large express only culturally dominant voices, being the technical discourses of an educated elite or in some cases the practical discourses of political leaders. For any period, a much larger mass of evidence will need to be located and sifted; it will need to represent a much greater range of rhetorical practice and a much more diverse set of perspectives and interests. To recover rhetorical traditions, then, historians must get beyond or overcome "the tradition."

Miller's proposal is here taken as representative of the "second wave" of serious reflection on historiography to emerge out of the field of rhetoric-composition and it presents an especially forceful statement on the question of tradition. In it, we can identify two by now familiar but seemingly incompatible ways of speaking of tradition. In one, tradition is "The Tradition" conceived as the ideas about rhetoric contained in a fixed canon of texts; from this perspective, the tradition is a blind that should be put to one side so that we can see the past more clearly. The other way of evoking tradition presumes the existence of multiple traditions, each of which has an integrity of its own and does not depend upon some larger historical metanarrative as guarantor of its significance or interest. These traditions arise out of specific historical-cultural circumstances and cannot be understood apart from their local contexts.

These are not the only ways to view tradition, however, and we would like to conclude by giving the issue further consideration. The contemporary study of rhetoric, in its various disciplinary guises, stands at an important crossroads and may soon face increasing institutional pressure to consolidate its intellectual resources. Reconsideration of the idea of tradition is not merely a defensive gesture, however, as it may provide grounds for genuine scholarly community (one of the aims of this volume as a whole). But is it possible to imagine a tradition that is both broad enough to resonate across disciplinary lines and flexible enough to allow for the diversity demanded by new approaches to our subject and its history?

RHETORICAL PEDAGOGY AS THE TRADITION OF RHETORIC

As we have indicated, each succeeding wave of self-reflection on the writing of rhetoric's past has in some way or another placed our sense of tradition at hazard—and this is not an insignificant problem, for without a tradition, as we have said earlier, we have only a history. If this history does not constitute an inheritance for us, we are in danger of distancing ourselves so far from our subject that we may lose our motive for studying it or of splintering our interests to the point that we lose the capacity to sustain an interdisciplinary scholarly community.

As the etymology of tradition (i.e., to hand over) suggests, tradition need not be reduced to a set of abstract principles or a fixed canon of texts. Rather, as Miller and others have suggested, tradition can be conceived as practices transmitted through time. Thus, we might discover a sense of tradition consistent with contemporary interests by viewing our subject, or some important part of it, as practices that have occurred within a community. To do this, of course, we need to identify some community that has a history relevant to us, and for that purpose, we suggest looking at the teaching of rhetoric. That is, we propose to conceive the rhetorical tradition in the modest key of the history of teaching writing and speaking. Whatever else we are or do, we all teach rhetoric, so the practices of past teachers clearly constitute something we can claim as our history.

We recognize that this orientation toward pedagogy will require adjustments in our thinking and that the kind and degree of accommodation will vary largely according to the disciplinary perspective of individual scholars. As we pointed out with reference to the "first wave" of revisionist historiography, the discipline of speech communication has tended to favor approaches that organize the history of rhetoric in terms of philosophical foundations or theoretical "starting points." Consequently, the pedagogical elements of historical texts have often been deemed inconsequential or simply ignored. A similarly dismissive attitude is manifest to greater or lesser extent in most of the standard synoptic treatments of rhetoric's history from antiquity to the present. For example, James Berlin rightly observed the tendency of such histories (he cites George Kennedy and Thomas Conley) to leave the rhetorical tradition in the hands of philosophers for the late modern and contemporary periods ("Postmodernism" 179–80).

In this respect, the field of rhetoric-composition contrasts sharply with that of speech communication. There, by virtue of its professed mission and institutional placement in the contemporary academy, pedagogy has been a central point of contact for the greater part of its scholarly activities. It is not surprising, then, to find multiple recent studies on the history of writing instruction but not a single comparable study written by a speech communication scholar.[6] But while pedagogy has long been taken more seriously by scholars in composition, the history of this pedagogy has most often been viewed through the lens of contemporary educational practice. Indeed, the studies that have appeared have focused heavily on the modern, institutionalized forms of college writing instruction in English-speaking countries.

The more expansive history of writing instruction is bound tightly to the tradition of rhetoric as we conceive it. In the West, the teaching of both writing and speaking has occurred continuously, but it also displays great variety both within a given period and at different historical moments. There are irregularities in this history, including the kinds of disparities brought out in recent work on the history of writing instruction: uneven access to such education, including, often, plain exclusion; and significant variability in the aims of such instruction (for example, in what *is meant* by "effective writing and speaking," and what purposes or interests does education in it serve?). All this is to say that teaching practices are intimately connected with sociopolitical conditions and educational institutions, and thus a study of them—as the second wave of historiographical reflection reminds us—demands sensitivity to local conditions.

In part, the study of this tradition must depend upon the same texts that constituted the source for the older conception of tradition—the various treatises and handbooks on rhetorical art. But if we are to approach these texts in order to understand how they were used for teaching, we have much new work to do. As Marjorie Woods has observed, the neglect of such works can be attributed to the two sources mentioned already: a long-standing indifference to pedagogy in the older historical scholarship and the tendency of more recent scholars to observe a rather strict divide between premodern and modern rhetorical instruction. (Woods' further point, that both "traditionalists" and "revisionists" have neglected and/or misrepresented rhetorical instruction in the Middle Ages, is still pertinent today.) The appreciation of such works will undoubtedly increase once they are understood as crucial elements of the tradition. But when approached from the perspective of pedagogical history, these books must be interpreted not just as the outward sign of some philosophical position or as a self-standing theory but as evidence of what teachers actually did in their classrooms.

The handbooks and technical treatises are only one sort of evidence relevant to the study of the tradition. To get a sense of pedagogy-as-practice, other sources need to be consulted. The history of rhetoric thus becomes an extremely spacious field of inquiry. Depending on the period, there is place for archival research into institutional records, paleographical or archaeological investigation. As Robert Gaines observes, the "representations of pedagogy" are many, conceivably embracing "all evidence of the goals, practices, activities, outcomes, texts, and material circumstances of rhetorical education at all levels, by all sorts of educators, in all relevant discourse venues" (Gaines, this volume).

So conceived, the tradition of teaching would seem to resist monolithic closure. What we will find in this tradition is a history that reflects our current disciplinary scene, where diversity and dispute are the norm. We have no reason to believe that past teachers of rhetoric were less given to squabbles than we are, and we have every reason to believe that teaching practices change and adapt to meet the pressure of existing circumstances. The teaching of rhetoric is a point of continuity in Western history, but teaching practices themselves vary and change. Thus, the teaching of rhetoric as a practice offers a stable referent for a historical tradition, but it does not lock us into grand narratives or perspectives that move us outside a local context.

Finally, we need to qualify our commitment to the pedagogical tradition. We are not claiming that it is the only tradition that can or should engage our attention. For example we might want to think of rhetorical practice or of some genre of such practice as forming a tradition; or we might want to redefine tradition in theoretical terms; or again we might consider countertraditions that fall outside officially sanctioned practices and institutions. At this point in our own history, we should be willing to acknowledge not only that tradition embraces opposed and changing elements but that no one tradition will serve our purposes. Consequently, our proposal is not intended to displace or discourage alternative possibilities. But we do believe that our historiography ought to recognize some tradition or traditions and that the most direct and advantageous option is the one that arises from our common work as teachers of rhetoric.

NOTES

1. These three types are discussed in his essay "On Systems of Rhetoric." In another well-known essay, Ehninger includes Renaissance rhetoric, oriented towards an aesthetics of expression, as a fourth system ("On Rhetoric").

2. Howell's valorization of Enlightenment (as opposed to classical) rhetoric should be clear to readers of any of his major writings. He is perhaps most explicit about this point at the end of his 1967 essay "John Locke and the New Rhetoric," where he concludes: "And if my discourse has led you to suppose that twentieth-century rhetoric should see itself as the offspring of the scientific energies released into the lifeblood of European culture by the speculations of Bacon, Descartes, and Locke, then I have done what I hoped to do on this occasion, and what I have striven to do throughout my recent writings on rhetoric" (333). In the Locke essay, Howell argues that two of the salutary developments in the Enlightenment were the rejection of classical influences concerning the use of commonplaces and the restriction of the domain of rhetoric to persuasion.

3. Early reports from several key participants appeared in special issues of *Pre/Text* (vol. 8.1–2, 1987) and *Rhetoric Review* (vol. 7, 1988, recording the CCCC's "Octalog"entitled "The Politics of Historiography"); see also Schilb, "History." The discussion was expanded and further advanced in collections edited by Victor Vitanza *(Writing Histories of Rhetoric)* and Theresa Enos *(Learning from the Histories of Rhetoric)*. Another collection, edited by Takis Poulakos, confronted the same themes and also included contributions from several authors from outside rhetoric-composi-

28   RICHARD GRAFF AND MICHAEL LEFF

tion (Poulakos, *Rethinking the History of Rhetoric*). For further reflection on the early revisionist proposals, see Brooks and [Octalog II].

4. Susan Jarratt's work on the sophists was pivotal in the field of composition studies (Jarratt, *Rereading;* see also, e.g., Jarratt, "Toward"; Sutton, "Marginalization"), but the rereading of the Sophists in both composition and speech communication continues unabated. Hans Kellner's comments on the lure of the Sophists are still relevant: "The decorum of revisionist rhetorical historiography involves reevaulating the Sophists, those archetypes of the 'usual suspects' who are periodically rounded up to make things happen" (243).

5. Some of the important studies in this area are Ede, Glenn, and Lunsford; Glenn; Lunsford; Sutherland and Sutcliffe; and Wertheimer.

6. There have been several volumes on the history of writing instruction, many considering it in relation to the development of English studies in American and British colleges and universities (e.g., Berlin, *Writing Instruction;* Berlin, *Rhetoric;* Johnson; see also Miller, *Formation*). For a wider historical perspective on the history of writing instruction, see Murphy, *Short History*.

WORKS CITED

Anderson, Floyd D. "On Systems of Rhetoric: A Response to 'Whig' Misreading." *Pennsylvania Speech Communication Annual* 38 (1982): 15–19.

Atwill, Janet M. "Instituting the Art of Rhetoric: Theory, Practice, and Productive Knowledge in Interpretations." In *Rethinking the History of Rhetoric*. Ed. Takis Poulakos. Boulder, CO: Westview, 1993. 91–118.

———. *Rhetoric Reclaimed: Aristotle and the Liberal Arts Tradition*. Ithaca: Cornell UP, 1998.

Baldwin, C. S. *Medieval Rhetoric and Poetic*. New York: Macmillan, 1928.

Berlin, James A. *Writing Instruction in Nineteenth-Century American Colleges*. Carbondale: Southern Illinois UP, 1984.

———. *Rhetoric and Reality: Writing Instruction in American Colleges 1900–1985*. Carbondale: Southern Illinois UP, 1987.

———. "Postmodernism, Politics, and the Histories of Rhetoric." *Pre/Text* 11 (1990): 169–87.

———. "Aristotle's *Rhetoric* in Context: Interpreting Historically." In *A Rhetoric of Doing*. Ed. Stephen P. Witte, Neil Nakadate, and Roger D. Cherry. Carbondale: Southern Illinois UP, 1992. 55–64.

———. "Revisionary History: The Dialectical Method." In *Rethinking the History of Rhetoric*. Ed. Takis Poulakos. Boulder, CO: Westview, 1993. 135–52.

Blair, Carole. "Contested Histories of Rhetoric: The Politics of Preservation, Progress, and Change." *Quarterly Journal of Speech* 78 (1992): 403–28.

Blair, Carole, and Mary L. Kahl. "Introduction: Revising the History of Rhetorical Theory." *Western Journal of Speech Communication* 54 (1990): 148–59.

Brooks, Kevin. "Reviewing and Redescribing 'The Politics of Historiography': Octalog I, 1988." *Rhetoric Review* 16 (1997): 6–21.

Duhamel, P. Albert. "The Function of Rhetoric as Effective Expression." *Journal of the History of Ideas* 10 (1949): 344–56.

Ede, Lisa, Cheryl Glenn, and Andrea Lunsford. "Border Crossings: Intersections of Rhetoric and Feminism." *Rhetorica* 13 (1995): 412–41.

Ehninger, Douglas. "On Rhetoric and Rhetorics." *Western Speech Journal* 31 (1967): 242–49.

——. "On Systems of Rhetoric." *Philosophy and Rhetoric* 1 (1968): 131–44.

Enders, Jody. "Delivering Delivery: Theatricality and the Emasculation of Eloquence." *Rhetorica* 15 (1997): 253–78.

Glenn, Cheryl. *Rhetoric Retold: Regendering the Tradition from Antiquity through the Renaissance.* Carbondale: Southern Illinois UP, 1997.

Howell, Wilbur Samuel. "John Locke and the New Rhetoric." *Quarterly Journal of Speech* 53 (1967): 321–33.

——. *Eighteenth-Century British Logic and Rhetoric.* Princeton: Princeton UP, 1971.

Jarratt, Susan. "Toward a Sophistic Historiography." *Pre/Text* 8.1–2 (1987): 9–27.

——. *Rereading the Sophists: Classical Rhetoric Refigured.* Carbondale: Southern Illinois UP, 1991.

Johnson, Nan. *Nineteenth-Century Rhetoric in North America.* Carbondale: Southern Illinois UP, 1991.

Kellner, Hans. "Afterword: Reading Rhetorical Redescriptions." In *Rethinking the History of Rhetoric.* Ed. Takis Poulakos. Boulder, CO: Westview, 1993. 241–56.

Lunsford, Andrea, ed. *Reclaiming Rhetorica: Women in the Rhetorical Tradition.* Pittsburgh: U of Pittsburgh P, 1995.

Miller, Thomas P. "Reinventing Rhetorical Traditions." In *Learning from the Histories of Rhetoric.* Ed. Theresa Enos. Carbondale: Southern Illinois UP, 1993. 26–41.

——. *The Formation of College English: Rhetoric and Belles Lettres in the British Cultural Provinces.* Pittsburgh: U of Pittsburgh P, 1997.

Murphy, James J. *Rhetoric in the Middle Ages.* Berkeley: U of California P, 1974.

——, ed. *A Short History of Writing Instruction.* 2nd ed. Mahwah, NJ: Lawrence Erlbaum, 2001.

Neel, Jasper. *Aristotle's Voice: Rhetoric, Theory and Writing in America.* Carbondale: Southern Illinois UP, 1994.

[Octalog I]. "The Politics of Historiography." *Rhetoric Review* 7 (1988): 5–49

[Octalog II]. "The (Continuing) Politics of Historiography." *Rhetoric Review* 16 (1997): 22–44.

Poulakos, Takis, ed. *Rethinking the History of Rhetoric: Multidisciplinary Essays on the Rhetorical Tradition.* Boulder, CO: Westview, 1993.

Schilb, John. "The History of Rhetoric and the Rhetoric of History." *Pre/Text* 7 (1986): 11–34.

——. "Differences, Displacements, and Disruptions: Toward Revisionary Histories of Rhetoric." *Pre/Text* 8.1–2 (1987): 29–45.

Sutherland, Christine Mason, and Rebecca Sutcliffe, eds. *The Changing Tradition: Women in the History of Rhetoric*. Calgary: U of Calgary P, 1999.

Sutton, Jane. "The Marginalization of Sophistical Rhetoric and the Loss of History." In *Rethinking the History of Rhetoric*. Ed. Takis Poulakos. Boulder, CO: Westview, 1993. 75–90.

———. "Structuring the Narrative for the Canon of Rhetoric: The Principles of Traditional Historiography (an Essay) with the Dead's *Différend* (a Collage)." In *Writing Histories of Rhetoric*. Ed. Victor Vitanza. Carbondale: Southern Illinois UP, 1994. 156–79.

Thompson, Wayne. "A Conservative View of Progressive Rhetoric." *Quarterly Journal of Speech* 49 (1963): 1–7.

Vitanza, Victor, ed. *Writing Histories of Rhetoric*. Carbondale: Southern Illinois UP, 1994.

Walter, Otis. "On Views of Rhetoric: Whether Conservative or Progressive." *Quarterly Journal of Speech* 49 (1963): 367–82.

Wertheimer, Molly Meijer, ed. *Listening to Their Voices: The Rhetorical Activities of Historical Women*. Columbia: U of South Carolina P, 1997.

Woods, Marjorie Curry. "Among Men—Not Boys: Histories of Rhetoric and the Exclusion of Pedagogy." *Rhetoric Society Quarterly* 22 (1992): 18–26.

TWO

The Rhetorical Tradition

Alan G. Gross

TO DEFINE THE rhetorical tradition, I shall follow Aristotle's advice; I shall begin my inquiry with assertions so commonplace that they have found their way into a book meant for students, a popular collection of excerpts on rhetorical theory, Bizzell and Herzberg's *The Rhetorical Tradition*. Let us look at the first paragraph of its general introduction:

> Rhetoric has a number of overlapping meanings: the practice of oratory; the study of the strategies of effective oratory; the use of language, written and spoken, to inform or persuade; the study of the persuasive effects of language; the study of the relation between language and knowledge; the classification and use of tropes and figures; and, of course, the use of empty promises and half-truths as a form of propaganda. Nor does this list exhaust the definitions that might be given. Rhetoric is a complex discipline with a long history: It is less helpful to try to define it once and for all than to look at the many definitions it has accumulated over the years and to attempt to understand how each arose and how each still inhabits and shapes the field. (1)

It is no criticism of the authors to say that they reproduce rather than resolve the confusions that generally characterize attempts to define the rhetorical tradition. Their central claim, that rhetoric is "a *complex discipline* with *a long history*," is especially open to serious question. The authors have not enumerated the components of a complex entity, but of an ill-formed one; their list seems to exclude no form of language study. An analogous problem of coherence faces us when we look at the thinkers the authors choose to

31

excerpt. What field of study is it that can comfortably accommodate Cicero, Nietzsche, and Bakhtin? There is the problem of balance as well: in what discipline would Francis Bacon and Thomas Sheridan be given equal treatment, as measured by the number of pages devoted to each? In their definition, the authors also make the dubious assertion that rhetorical theory has a long history. This assertion assumes a continuity that their selections do not exemplify. There are between Aristotle and Cicero and between Quintilian and Augustine gaps of nearly three centuries; between Boethius and Erasmus, the gap is a thousand years. Two centuries separate Thomas Wilson and George Campbell; one separates Richard Whately and Kenneth Burke. A history with such lacunae seems no history at all.

This lack of continuous intellectual progress is not, essentially, an artifact of anthology making; rather, it is an essential characteristic of the intellectual strand of the rhetorical tradition that the anthology makers attempt, unsuccessfully, to finesse. When we consider the pedagogical strand of the tradition, there is, of course, genuine continuity. Not so, the intellectual strand: a discipline is characterized by intellectual continuity and coherence, effects that cannot be achieved by the elevation of mediocrities to canonical status or by the specious transgression of disciplinary boundaries, the methods of Bizzell and Herzberg. The popularity of their work—it is now in a second edition more incoherent, possibly, than the first—is a symptom of a profession in disciplinary trouble. While the authors of a book for students cannot be expected to address these problems, the profession to which they belong needs to address them; we need to find an alternative approach to defining the rhetorical tradition and those who contributed to it. We need to do that or to drop the notion altogether as a bulwark against those who would deny us disciplinary status.

One might object that the task has already been accomplished, three times over: in Kennedy's *Classical Rhetoric and Its Christian and Secular Tradition* (1980), again in Vickers's *In Defense of Rhetoric* (1988), and yet again in Conley's *Rhetoric in the European Tradition* (1990). Do they succeed where Bizzell and Herzberg fail? No, they merely reproduce the confusions inherent in Bizzell and Herzberg. Kennedy proposes a tradition with three strands: the technical, narrowly focused on handbooks as forensic "how-to" manuals; the Sophistic, broadly focused on the character of the speaker as a spokesman for civic virtue; and the philosophical, broadly focused on rhetoric as an art of deliberation, an art in relationship to other arts and to knowledge. These strands unquestionably exist, but a history organized according to them permits Kennedy to avoid rather than address the problems of intellectual continuity and coherence. Instead, he creates the impression of continuity by expanding the rhetorical tradition to include secular literature and preaching, the Bible, and pedagogy, a strategy that also successfully masks the problem of coherence. This is essentially Conley's strategy as well. Vickers does not create a specious continuity by illegitimate conflation. He is unstinting in his praise for the classical period and very vocal in his distress over medieval fragmentation. While he justly praises the Renaissance rediscovery of classical rhetoric, he candidly admits that "all Renaissance rhetoric-books were of course eclectic [and] derivative" (269). Although he is pleased that rhetoric has revived in his time, he is severe concerning its use as an empty honorific and finds much to criticize in the ransacking of its tradition by theorists, such as Roman Jakobson and Paul de Man, who, he claims, do not understand it. Still, he does not address the problem of coherence; rather, he presents classical rhetoric as a coherent system, one that can be unproblematically developed.

I would like to suggest an alternate reconstruction of the intellectual strand of the tradition, one that accepts historical discontinuity and centers on the problem of coherence. This reconstruction sees the tradition as a succession of theorists, each of whom makes a contribution, one that is, at the same time, unique and dependent on past theorists; in other words, its focus is theory and theoretical refinement. This has two advantages. First, it brings into the forefront the problematic nature of the classical heritage, the fact that it creates at least as many problems as it solves. The second advantage is political. By providing rhetoric with an intellectual core, my reconstruction provides interested scholars with a legitimation they might not otherwise have. In a time when academic prestige is so implacably a matter of intellectual status relative to other disciplines, my reconstruction is not only defensible but prudential, a necessary condition of disciplinary flourishing.

As a discipline, rhetoric is clearly not flourishing in all places where it might be expected to; indeed, one disciplinary area in which it is usually housed is in retreat. At the National Communication Association Conference in New York, I was having lunch with two senior faculty housed in public universities. After the menu had been deciphered, the conversation turned to the continuing political difficulties in which departments of communication found themselves. At Iowa State, an independent program in communication was long gone; at the University of Washington, a battle royal had just occurred, endangering the department's integrity.[1] At Ohio State communication had recently gone under.

In reaction to this decline, professors of communication have spoken out concerning their status in the academy. A 1993 issue of *Journal of Communication* articulates concerns for the whole of communication that parallel those faced by rhetoricians working in departments of speech communication. The problem the symposiasts addressed was that "[c]ommunication lacks disciplinary status because it has no core of knowledge. Thus institutional and scholarly legitimacy remains a chimera for the field" (Shepherd 83). About the lack of legitimacy there is general agreement; there is also general agreement that overall coherence is an unlikely goal, given the fact of "different fields, brought together by institutional forces rather than considered choice" (O'Keefe 76).

But such forces are general in the university. What, after all, do literary biographers and postmodern theorists have in common, except for their membership in departments of English? What do analytical and existential philosophers have in common? Yet both find themselves in departments of philosophy. Conflicts that debilitate the search for coherence need not exist, however, *within* fields; in each, theoretical coherence is surely a possibility; *within* rhetorical theory and criticism, for example. This is true within both departments of speech communication and of English, where the rhetorical tradition survives in units devoted to rhetoric and composition. Realizing coherence is a job the rhetorical tradition can accomplish, if it is conceived as an intellectual enterprise.

An intellectual identity is a necessary condition for academic status, not, of course, a sufficient one. A sufficient condition is a body of work that commands general respect. This is *not* the equivalent of high productivity, which can take place in the absence of intellectual distinction. Clifford Geertz and his students created a body of work; Ludwig Wittgenstein and his students; Stanley Fish and his students; Robert Merton and his students. Such bodies of work as those of Geertz, Wittgenstein, Fish, and Merton and their students, have a commanding presence; they demand respect; in each case, considerable intellectual activity has been focused for long periods on central disciplinary problems. In a society essentially meritocratic, in academic society in other words, only the presence of such bodies of work will give rhetorical scholars, whether housed in departments of speech communication or English, the status they deserve.

AN INTELLECTUAL RECONSTRUCTION

My reconstruction views the tradition as united around the answers to a core of questions, the nature of which may be clarified by employing the notion of "essentially contested concepts," derived from the philosopher, W. B. Gallie.[2] Such concepts are and tend to remain at the center of disciplines, especially in the humanities. They are derived "from an original exemplar whose authority is acknowledged by all the contestant users of the concept" (168). For philosophy, Plato and Aristotle may count as these exemplars; they may count as exemplars for rhetoric as well. Fields centering around essentially contested concepts—fields such as philosophy and rhetoric—are also alike in that they are sustained intellectually by means of contests among adherents of particular interpretations of their exemplars' life and work (168). According to Whitehead, "the safest general characterization of the European philosophical tradition is that it consists of a series of footnotes to Plato" (Whitehead 607). Rhetoric may be similarly so viewed: philosophy and rhetoric are fields of study comprised of essentially contested concepts that originate in classical and preclassical times.[3]

Indeed, to some extent, the rhetorical and the philosophical traditions overlap. Since rhetoric is aimed at altering audience attitudes and actions by discovering and deploying all available means of persuasion, two philosophical questions naturally arise: the metaphysical question of whether rhetoric is merely persuasive, or is a mode of truth, and the epistemological question of whether it is an art or merely a knack. These questions are broached first in the *Gorgias,* an early dialogue in which Plato argues that rhetoric is "a spurious counterfeit of a branch of the art of government" (44), one that "has no rational account to give of the nature of the various things which it offers" (46). It is the second charge that is particularly devastating to the disciplinary status of rhetoric. And it is this charge that Aristotle will address in the *Rhetoric.*

Aristotle's conclusions are familiar. The art of rhetoric consists of the search for all the means of persuasion appropriate to particular audiences. These are divided into the three *pisteis* or proofs: those arising from logic or reasoning, those arising from the character of the speaker, and those arising from the emotions. In orations, the *pisteis* are enabled by the canon of memory and expressed through the invention of arguments, through style, and through arrangement and communicated by means of the canon of delivery. The classical genres—forensic, deliberative, epideictic—are realizations of the *pisteis* under particular sociopolitical and ideological constraints, in these cases the need to prosecute defendants, to deliberate in public forums, and to perform on ceremonial occasions. Audiences are the master constraint on the use of the *pisteis* and deployment of the canons. But while the audience for a particular rhetorical performance is of course real, the tradition acknowledges no real audiences. It is rather the orator's idea of audience that controls.[4] Given this view, a particular rhetorical performance must be judged against normative criteria derived from "ideal" rhetorical performances, never in terms of effect (see also Leff, "Textual Criticism"; "Words").

This conceptual system generates the set of questions whose answers form the rhetorical tradition as I conceive it. How are the *pisteis* related? In what sense are *pathos* and *ethos* proofs? In what sense are the canons persuasive, especially the canons of style and arrangement? What is the relationship between the concept of 'genre' and the social, political, and ideological forces that are its formative base? What is a rhetorical audience, and how does it constrain the speaker's use of the *pisteis* and the canons? Is rhetoric a technique or a mode of truth? And if the latter, is it a vehicle only, or does it have a creative function? The idea that tradition consists of a set of answers to such questions is central also to Gadamer's universal hermeneutics, a system founded on Plato's notions of dialogue and dialectic as the core of intellectual activity.

I have not tried to define the intellectual rhetorical tradition exhaustively or to exhaust the scholarly quandaries it can generate; each reader can think of extensions, emendations, and points of contestation. My point is simply this: to agree that there is a such a tradition and that it generates scholarly quandaries turns such texts as *The Rhetorical Tradition* from scrapbooks of selections into exemplary disciplinary documents. The rhetorical tradition is now legitimately unified: its unity consists in attempts over two and a half millennia to grapple with one or another scholarly quandary that its conceptual system generates. Some thinkers, such as Aristotle, Campbell, Burke, and Perelman, address these questions directly; others, such as Nietzsche, Locke, and Derrida, address issues that bear directly on the answers to these questions. This latter group forms an open set of thinkers who are not rhetoricians but whose fields of study—philosophy of language and cognitive psychology might be examples—legitimately influence rhetorical theory and can help form and re-form the rhetorical tradition.

PROGRESS WITHIN THE RHETORICAL TRADITION

The existence of a rhetorical tradition is vital because it permits us to give substance to the idea of intellectual progress in rhetorical theory and criticism. We may take the work of Mohrmann and Leff as our example that such progress has already occurred, that it only needs to be properly labeled to be recognized. In "Lincoln at the Cooper Union: A Rationale for Neo-Classical Criticism," these two critics "treat Lincoln's speech within the framework of the classical conception of oratorical genres" (459). They find that "this is a campaign speech, an oratorical form well-known to American audiences and easily distinguished from other types of public address. Nevertheless, this type does not fall within the tripartite Aristotelian division" (464). Mohrmann and Leff have made three discoveries. They have discovered, first, that Aristotle's notion of genre stands the test of time as a transcultural rhetorical category. Second, they have discovered that the membership of this set of genres is variable, that is, it depends on factors that differ from society to society. And third and finally, they have discovered a new genre.

Leff and Mohrmann's discoveries represent an intellectual progress very different from that in the sciences. These discoveries do not nullify those of the past, as is the case with science; rather, they affirm the continuing value of the tradition, and simultaneously, the continuing need to interpret that tradition by means of further theoretical and critical efforts. For example, though Plato and Aristotle remain worth reading, inevitably, continuing theoretical efforts change the past, that is, our view of it, and with it, our view of Plato and Aristotle. After Leff and Mohrmann, the classical tradition must be regarded as having been slightly and subtly transformed in the manner suggested by T. S. Eliot when he speaks about aesthetic change, saying that the existing monuments form an ideal order among themselves, which is modified by the introduction of the new work of art among them. The existing order is complete before the new work arrives; for order to persist after the supervention of novelty, the *whole* existing order must be, if ever so slightly, altered, and so the relations, proportions, values of each work of art toward the whole are readjusted; and this is the conformity of the older and the new. (5; his emphasis)

Although Eliot's seems to be a good first approximation of the idea of progress as it applies to rhetorical theories or treatises on the art, I do not want to imply that our relation to the rhetorical past is one simply of indebtedness. I want to acknowledge instead the sort of complexity in the tradition that art historian Michael Baxandall sees in the visual arts when the successor artist is viewed, not as the patient, but as the agent. In that case, the predicate "to be influenced by" takes on a rich array of meanings. It can mean

draw on, resort to, avail oneself of, appropriate from, have recourse to, adapt, misunderstand, refer to, pick up, take on, engage with, react to, quote, differentiate oneself from, assimilate oneself to, assimilate, align oneself with, copy, address, paraphrase, absorb, make a variation on, revive, continue, remodel, ape, emulate, travesty, parody, extract from, distort, attend to, resist, simplify, reconstitute, elaborate on, develop, face up to, master, subvert, perpetuate, reduce, promote, respond to, transform, tackle . . . everyone will be able to think of others. (Baxandall 58–59)

I want to accept Baxandall's invitation and add to his list: "incorporate, improve while depending upon." To me these predicates encapsulate the notion of intellectual progress within the rhetorical tradition, a progress I will illustrate in some detail by recounting the rhetorical history of the concept Chaim Perelman calls "presence."

ARISTOTELIAN BEGINNINGS

This story of presence is not designed to be complete; completeness is not necessary to show that intellectual progress has taken place. My story begins with Aristotle's division of metaphors into those that function by "bringing-before-the-eyes," and those that function without employing this quality (*Rhetoric* 3.11.1). For Aristotle, to bring before the eyes is to invest an inanimate object with *energeia*, the ability to actualize itself through motion. Aristotle compares saying that a man is "four-square" with saying that he has "his prime of life in full bloom." In the first case, the poet Simonides brings nothing before the eyes; in the second case, the orator Isocrates "makes [this characteristic of the man] move and live, and *energeia* is motion." While in the first case, the reference is probably to the Pythagoreans for whom the square of a number was equated with perfection (Cope, III, 125–26), in the second, a man's stage of life is being compared to a flower at maximum growth. For Aristotle, growth is a form of motion; in Aristotle's terms, a flower that is at full growth has fully realized its potential, is completely actualized.[5]

Aristotle regards bringing-before-the eyes as a feature of style. While style is one of the canons, and therefore, presumably one of the means of persuasion on which the orator relies, Aristotle does not address the question of how bringing-before-the-eyes might persuade.

CAMPBELL IMPROVES ON ARISTOTLE

For George Campbell, bringing-before-the-eyes is also a feature of style, one he translates as vivacity. The link with book 3 of the *Rhetoric* is firm, though indirect. Campbell mentions Aristotle in connection with vivacity (289); moreover, his language is Aristotelian. Concerning the stylistic substitution of the term *snatch'd* for *ta'en*, Campbell asserts "that it is principally in those parts of speech which regard *life* and *action* that this species of *energy* takes place" (288; my emphasis).

Campbell represents an advance on Aristotle concerning the sources and scope of vivacity. First, he analyzes the sources: "the choice of words, their number, and their arrangement" (285).[6] To exemplify stylistic arrangement, Campbell quotes scripture: "Among many nations there was no king like Solomon, who was beloved of his God, and God made him king over all Israel; nevertheless even him did outlandish women cause to sin." Of the passage, Campbell says: "My remark concerns only the last clause of the sentence. It is manifest that the emphasis here ought to rest on the *him*, who, from what immediately precedes, might have been thought proof against all the arts, even of female seduction" (363; his emphasis).

Vivacity also depends on brevity of expression. Typical of Campbell's examples is a quotation from *Eccesiasticus* 19.11: "A fool travaileth with a word, as a woman in labour of a child." Campbell admits that this "degree of conciseness is scarcely attainable, unless the style be figurative"; nevertheless, "it is also true, that the vivacity of expression is not to be attributed solely to the figure, but partly to the brevity occasioned by the figure" (337). To prove his point, he quotes a sentence by Swift that owes its effect solely to brevity: "I am too proud to be vain" (337).

The choice of words is the most important source of stylistic vivacity. For the purpose of analysis, Campbell divides words into "proper terms" and "rhetorical tropes." Proper terms exhibit vivacity in being "as particular and determinate in their signification as will suit the nature and the scope of the discourse" (286). Concerning this distinction, Campbell again cites scripture. After the Israelites, the Egyptians attempt to cross the Red Sea and are drowned: "They *sank* as *lead* in the mighty waters." "Make but a small alteration in the expression," Campbell asserts, "and say, 'They *fell* as *metal* in the mighty waters,' and the difference in effect will be quite astonishing" (286; his emphasis).

For Campbell, rhetorical tropes create vivacity in four ways: (1) by substituting the less for the more general, (2) by fixing attention on the most interesting particular of the subject, (3) by expressing things intelligible as things sensible, and finally, (4) by expressing things lifeless as things animate. As an example of the first, Campbell instances the substitution of Solomon for a wise man, or of Judas for a traitor. As an example of the second, he points to the substitution of "hands" for "sailors," or "sail" for "ship." As an example of the third, he quotes *Deuteronomy* 23.25: "The *sword* without, and terror within." Of this quotation, he says, "the term sword, which represents a particular and perceivable image to the fancy, must be more picturesque than the word *war*, which conveys an idea that is vague and only conceivable, not being otherwise sensible but by its consequences" (306; his emphasis). Campbell exemplifies his final category, expressing things lifeless as things sensible, with a quotation from the *Tatler:* "Every hedge was *conscious* of more than what the representations of enamoured swains admit of" (307; his emphasis).

But Campbell does more than merely elaborate a stylistic category that Aristotle already noted; he also extends vivacity to include matters of invention as well as style, the circumstances that create "vivacity of ideas" in narration (73). Campbell names seven circumstances whose management contributes to vivacity: the probability and importance of the event, its plausibility, its proximity in place and time, the closeness of the audience to the persons mentioned, and the magnitude of audience interest in its consequences. These circumstances can operate in concert, as his example from Cicero's last oration against Verres shows (90–93):

> Does freedom, that precious thing, mean nothing? Nor the proud privileges of a citizen of Rome? Nor the laws of Porcius, the laws of Sempronius? Nor the tribunes' power, whose loss our people felt so deeply till now at last it has been restored to them? Have all these things come in the end to mean so little that in a Roman province, in a town whose people have special privileges, a Roman citizen could be bound and flogged in the marketplace by a man who owed his rods and axes [signs of Imperial power] to the favour of the Roman people? (647)[7]

This passage illustrates four of the seven circumstances conducive to the vivacity of ideas in narration. The event, the flogging of a Roman citizen, is important as it undermines the very meaning of being such a citizen; the

connection is local since to be in a province controlled by Rome is the political equivalent to being in Rome itself. The relation to the audience is personal, since in his action Verres has abused the power that Roman citizens
have bestowed upon him. Proximity of time is suggested by the phrase, "now
at last *(tandem)*": Verres has abused a power that has been so recently and so
thankfully restored to the people.[8]

In an isolated passage in book 3 of *The Rhetoric,* Aristotle links style
firmly to emotional 'proofs': "emotion is expressed if the style, in the case of
insolence, is that of an angry man; in the case of impious and shameful things,
if it is that of one who is indignant and reluctant even to say the words"
(3.7.3). He grounds this view in audience psychology: "The proper *lexis* also
makes the matter credible: the mind [of the listener] draws a false inference of
the truth of what the speaker says because they [in the audience] feel the same
about such things, so they think the facts to be so, even if they are not as the
speaker represents them; and the hearer suffers along with the pathetic
speaker, even if what he says amounts to nothing" (3.7.4–5).

Campbell's analysis parallels that of Aristotle, but it is far more explicit
and emphatic in linking the stylistic features with the analysis of the emotions, and in connecting both with the analysis of persuasion in book 1.
Campbell starts with an emotional theory of persuasion about whose positive
value he harbors few Aristotelian doubts.

> What will persuade to a certain conduct . . . is in reality an artful mixture of
> that which proposes to convince the judgement, and that which interests the
> passions, its distinguished excellency [resulting] from these two, the argu-
> mentative and the pathetic incorporated together. These acting with united
> force, and if I may so express myself, in concert, constitute that passionate
> eviction, that *vehemence* of contention, which is admirably fitted for persua-
> sion, and hath always been regarded as the supreme qualification in an ora-
> tor. (4; his emphasis)

This vehemence is linked especially to certain of the emotions, those, like
hope and anger, that are most capable of "elevat[ing] the soul, and
stimulat[ing] to action" (5).[9]

Vehement emotions "must be awakened by communicating lively ideas of
the object" (81). The orator may do this, not only by indicating the circumstances of events but also by expressing those circumstances in words whose
vivacity creates in auditors a resemblance between their own impressions and
the reality to which the speaker refers:

> we have seen in what manner passion to an absent object may be excited by
> eloquence, which, by enlivening and invigorating the ideas of the imagina-
> tion, makes them resemble the impressions of sense and traces of memory;

and in this respect hath an effect on the mind similar to that produced by a telescope on the sight: things remote are brought near, things obscure rendered conspicuous. (94)

Of vivacity in general we may say what Campbell says of a particular stylistic feature, the arrangement of words in a sentence: "In such cases the end of speaking is not to make us *believe*, but to make us *feel*. It is the heart and not the head which ought to be addressed" (364; his emphasis).

TWO BELGIANS IMPROVE ON A SCOT

While Campbell provides an opportunity for linking "vivacity of ideas" with "vivacity of style," he does not explicitly link the two. This is the work of Chaim Perelman and Lucie Olbrechts-Tyteca who unite these two aspects of persuasion, and much else, under the concept of 'presence.' Into this concept, the two Belgians explicitly incorporate Campbell's circumstances (118) and implicitly, his idea of stylistic vivacity (144–45, 160, 334–35). To these, they add arrangement: "[T]he order of the arguments will . . . be dictated in [some] measure by the desire . . . to confer presence on certain elements" (492).

What, precisely, is presence? While Perelman and Olbrechts-Tyteca insist that it has a supreme persuasive force, it is by no means clear how presence actually functions as an element in argumentation. Initially, the Belgians say, its effect is merely psychological. This means that those aspects of invention that constitute the resources for presence must *exclude* the *pisteis* or Aristotelian proofs. But, they also say, these techniques can have a rhetorical role, that is, they can play a part in increasing or decreasing adherence to beliefs. In this role, they function in a manner analogous to the *pisteis:* when this happens, presence, which is "at first a psychological phenomenon, becomes an essential element in argumentation" (117).

How can such an important transformation—from the psychological to the argumentative—take place? To see how presence might be transformed in this way, we need to distinguish between its isolated instances, such as the use of metaphor with *energeia,* and presence as an overall effect of interaction. To say that the metaphor *The arrow is eager to fly* makes its impending flight present to listeners is to speak of presence in its narrow sense. But in its patterned and synergistic guises, presence does more than merely fix the attention. It is a strategy whose central purpose Louise Karon captures when she says that through presence, *"we establish the real"* (169). It is its role in the creation of rhetorical reality that invests presence with its persuasive force, a force analogous to the force of the *pisteis.* In Cicero, for example, style and circumstance combine to make present the magnitude of Verres's crimes. In this case, we may legitimately say that style and circumstance have an argumentative force.

Rhetorical critics have shown that presence exists in a wide variety of texts. In his study of presence in Al Gore's rhetoric, John Murphy deals with the interaction of analogies in environmental polemic; in their study of presence in the debate over nuclear weapons, Charles Kauffman and Donn Parson address patterns of metaphor in a debate over nuclear defense. In my study of presence in avian taxonomy, I discuss patterns of style and arrangement in texts from biology. These analyses conform to Karon's interpretation of presence as "created chiefly through techniques of style, delivery, and disposition [arrangement]" (64)[10] and to her more encompassing notion that in concert these techniques transform the psychological into the argumentative.

In *Rhetoric of Science*, I also make the point that presence can also be nonverbal: it can be created by the use of tables, figures, photographs, white space, and type size, a set of techniques Perelman and Olbrechts-Tyteca do not mention. Kauffman and Parson also refine the Belgians' concept; they reiterate and expand the important point that even the absence of presence can have a persuasive effect. Metaphors with and without *energeia*, they argue, can be used systematically, on the one hand, to invoke, and on the other, to dampen, public anxieties. For example, using metaphors with *energeia*, President Reagan speaks of "antique" Titan missiles that leave the United States "naked" to attack; he depicts the Soviet Union as an "Evil Empire" led by "monsters." Using metaphors without *energeia*, General Gordon Fornell creates a dampening *antipresence:* "The current Soviet ICBM force of 1,398 missiles, of which over 800 are SS-17, SS-18, and SS-19 ICBMs, represents a dangerous countermilitary asymmetry which must be corrected in the near term" (99–100). The systematic use of such colorless metaphors dampens what might otherwise be legitimate anxieties concerning nuclear arms procurement.

CONCLUSION

On the one hand, seeing the purely intellectual strand of the rhetorical tradition as historical creates a story with unexplainable gaps and without coherence. On the other hand, seeing that aspect of the tradition as generated by a set of problems, initiated by an exemplar, and subsequently addressed, directly and indirectly, by various thinkers, creates the intellectual core of an authentic discipline with a solid past of problem solving and a solid future of questions to answer. Common intellectual efforts are enabled, and steady intellectual progress is realizable. The evolution of the concept of presence is an example of this progress.

While this reconstruction is legitimate and necessary, it is hardly sufficient. Surely the pedagogical tradition, so ably discussed by Richard Graff and Michael Leff in this volume, deserves equal attention. It is a tradition that, unlike the one I discuss, has a continuous history. But whereas the tradition I reconstruct concerns *episteme,* the tradition they reconstruct concerns *phronesis.* In my view, no discipline of rhetoric can be complete that does not include at its foundations *both episteme* and *phronesis.* We need all of the intellectual insight and all of the practical wisdom we can get.

NOTES

1. As I learned afterward, the speech communication department eventually lost its identity in a merger with the School of Communications.

2. Gallie limited his definition to those concepts, such as 'art,' 'democracy,' and 'Christianity,' that were essentially appraisive, but there is no need so to limit so fruitful an idea. As he himself says, "[I]t is in those fields of human endeavour in which achievements are prized chiefly as renewals or advances of commonly accepted traditions of thought and work that our concepts are likely to prove essentially contested" (190).

3. Richard Rorty regards this standard view of philosophy as a mistake, which Heidegger tries to transcend and Dewey succeeds in transcending. Even if Rorty's view is true and can be generalized to cover rhetoric, it does not undermine my claim, which depends either on taking a position within the tradition or on acknowledging a tradition, if only to discard it.

4. In any particular instance, genre will be included in the idea of audience. There have been occasional attempts to give rhetorical criticism an empirical dimension by considering its effect on actual audiences. And of course there is a widespread enterprise devoted to measuring the effects of advertising and political speech on actual audiences.

5. The link between bringing before the eyes will perhaps be clearer to the contemporary reader in connection with such metaphors, also cited by Aristotle, in which Homer says of an arrow that it is "eager to fly," that its "point sped eagerly through the breast."

6. The sound of words is a fourth source. But as Campbell admits, "hardly any compositions in prose, unless those whose end is to persuade, and which aim at a certain vehemence in style and sentiment, give access to exemplify this resemblance" (332).

7. The English is a pale reflection of the Latin where word order is also a part of the meaning: "O nomen dulce liberatis! O ius eximium nostrae civitatis! O lex Porcia legesque Semproniae! O graviter desiderata et aliquando reddita plebi Romanae tribunicia potestas! Hucine tandem haec omnia reciderunt, ut civis Romanus in provincia populi Romani in oppido foederatorum, ab eo qui beneficio populi Romani fasces et secures haberet deligatus in foro virgis caedentur?"

8. This passage can also be used to illustrate the strict division between stylistic vivacity and vivacity of ideas. In analyzing this passage stylistically, Campbell might well have emphasized the brevity of the Latin over English (399–400) or its superior freedom in matters of the arrangement of words (369–70). He might also have praised

Cicero's brilliant periods in this passage, as he praised Latin in general: "It is remarkable, that any inscription in which it is intended to convey something striking or emphatical, we can scarcely endure a modern language. . . . [This] proceeds from the general conviction there is of its superiority in point of vivacity. . . . [In English, t]he luggage of particles, such as pronouns, prepositions, and auxiliary verbs, from which it is impossible for us entirely to disencumber ourselves, clogs the expression, and enervates the sentiment" (401).

  9. Campbell mentions "hope, patriotism, ambition, emulation, anger." Such emotions contrast with "sorrow, fear, shame, humility," emotions that are "naturally inert and torpid" (5).

  10. Perelman does not deal with delivery, nor will I. There is no implication, however, that this would not be a fruitful area of inquiry.

WORKS CITED

Aristotle. *On Rhetoric: A Theory of Civic Discourse.* Trans. George A. Kennedy. New York: Oxford UP, 1991.

Baxandall, Michael. *Patterns of Intention: On the Historical Explanation of Pictures.* New Haven: Yale UP, 1985.

Bizzell, Patricia, and Bruce Herzberg, eds. *The Rhetorical Tradition: Readings from Classical Times to the Present.* Boston: Bedford Books, 1990.

Campbell, George. *The Philosophy of Rhetoric.* Ed. Lloyd F. Bitzer. Carbondale: Southern Illinois UP, 1963.

Cicero. *The Verrine Orations II.* Trans. L. H. G. Greenwood. Cambridge, MA: Harvard UP, 1987.

Conley, Thomas M. *Rhetoric in the European Tradition.* New York: Longman, 1990.

Cope, Edward Meredith. *The Rhetoric of Aristotle with a Commentary.* Ed. John Edwin Sandys. [Reprint] Salem, NH: Ayer, 1988.

Eliot, T. S. *Selected Essays.* New York: Harcourt, Brace, 1950.

Furley, David J., and Alexander Nehamas, eds. *Aristotle's Rhetoric: Philosophical Essays.* Princeton: Princeton UP, 1994.

Gadamer, Hans-Georg. *Truth and Method.* 2nd ed. Trans. Joel Weinsheimer and Donald G. Marshall. New York: Crossroad, 1989.

Gallie, W. B. *Philosophy and the Historical Understanding.* 2nd ed. New York: Schocken Books, 1968.

Gross, Alan G. *The Rhetoric of Science.* Cambridge, MA: Harvard UP, 1996.

Karon, Louise. "Presence in the New Rhetoric." In *The New Rhetoric of Chaim Perelman: Statement and Response.* Ed. Ray D. Dearin. Lanham, MD: UP of America, 1988 [1976]. 163–78.

Kauffman, Charles, and Donn W. Parson. "Metaphor and Presence in Argument." In *Argument Theory and the Rhetoric of Assent.* Ed. David Cratis Williams and Michael David Hazen. Tuscaloosa: U of Alabama P, 1990. 91–102.

Kennedy, George A. *Classical Rhetoric and Its Christian and Secular Tradition from Ancient to Modern Times*. Chapel Hill: U of North Carolina P, 1980.

Lakoff, George. "The Contemporary Theory of Metaphor." In *Metaphor and Thought*, 2nd ed. Ed. Andrew Ortony. Cambridge: Cambridge UP, 1993. 202–51.

Leff, Michael. "Textual Criticism: The Legacy of G. P. Mohrmann." *Quarterly Journal of Speech* 72 (1986): 377–89.

———. "Things Made by Words: Reflections on Textual Criticism." *Quarterly Journal of Speech* 78 (1992): 223–31.

Leff, Michael C., and Gerald P. Mohrmann. "Lincoln at Cooper Union: A Rhetorical Analysis of the Text." *Quarterly Journal of Speech* 60 (1974): 346–58.

Lincoln, Abraham. *Abraham Lincoln: His Speeches and Writings*. Ed. Roy Basler. New York: Da Capo, 1946.

Mohrmann, G. P., and Michael C. Leff. "Lincoln at the Cooper Union: A Rationale for Neo-Classical Criticism." *Quarterly Journal of Speech* 60 (1974): 459–67.

Murphy, John M. "Presence, Analogy, and Earth in the Balance." *Argumentation and Advocacy* 31 (1994): 1–16.

O'Keefe, Barbara. "Against Theory." *Journal of Communication* 43 (1993): 75–82.

Ortony, Andrew, ed. *Metaphor and Thought*. 2nd ed. Cambridge: Cambridge UP, 1993.

Perelman, Chaim, and Lucie Olbrechts-Tyteca. *The New Rhetoric: A Treatise on Argumentation*. Trans. John Wilkinson and Purcell Weaver. South Bend: U of Notre Dame P, 1969.

Plato. *Gorgias*. Trans. Walter Hamilton. London: Penguin, 1960.

Rorty, Richard. "Overcoming the Tradition: Heidegger and Dewey." In *Consequences of Pragmatism*. Minneapolis: U of Minnesota P, 1982. 37–59.

Shepherd, Gregory J. "Building a Discipline of Communication." *Journal of Communication* 43 (1993): 83–91.

Vickers, Brian. *In Defense of Rhetoric*. Oxford: Clarendon, 1988.

Whitehead, Alfred North. *Alfred North Whitehead: An Anthology*. Ed. F. S. C. Northrop and Mason W. Gross. New York: Macmillan, 1953.

THREE

The Ends of Rhetoric Revisited

Three Readings of Lincoln's Gettysburg Address

Leah Ceccarelli

IN AN EARLIER ESSAY, I argued that a useful way of thinking about the rhetorical tradition is to consider three different ends that guide rhetorical scholars (Ceccarelli, "Ends"). I called these implicit purposes the "aesthetic," the "epistemic," and the "political," and I described them in the context of ancient and contemporary rhetorical theory. A conception of rhetoric that seeks an aesthetic end is held by those who, like Gorgias, extol the power of eloquence to move the audience; their work builds an appreciation for the artistry of spoken or written discourse. Those who most value an epistemic end for rhetoric are, like Plato, driven to discover as much as possible about the nature of things; although contemporary rhetoricians are unlikely to see rhetoric as a way of helping the soul reach an ideal Truth, they nevertheless seek an epistemic end when their scholarship is designed to build knowledge about how persuasion works.[1] Finally, those who, like Isocrates, value the practical affairs of the polis over objective knowledge or linguistic artistry adopt a political end for rhetoric; they promote an active and engaged scholarship that seeks what is good for the social body.[2]

After outlining the existence of these three ends in the ancient tradition, that earlier essay reproduced metacritical statements from several contemporary scholars to show that each fit most closely with a particular purpose. What that essay did not do was reproduce or develop scholarship to exemplify

each of the three ends; as a result, the outlines of the three ends were established, but it was difficult to get a sense for what scholarship driven by each
end really entailed. This chapter extends the largely theoretical argument of
the earlier essay with a practical illustration. It performs three complementary
readings of an established touchstone in American public address—Abraham
Lincoln's Gettysburg Address. Adopting approaches to rhetorical criticism
that are driven by three different purposes, this chapter demonstrates how
unarticulated assumptions might guide rhetoricians to produce alternative
readings of an artifact. This illustration is meant to offer a useful frame for
appreciating, understanding, and organizing scholarship in the rhetorical tradition; it is also hoped that it will encourage improved communication
between scholars who approach their subject with different interests.

An Aesthetic Reading

Before undertaking an aesthetic reading of Lincoln's Gettysburg Address, I
should acknowledge that scholars who are far more accomplished than
myself have produced more worthy interpretations along these lines. But
since the goal of an aesthetic reading is not to add new knowledge to the academic record but to share an appreciation for the artistry of a text, I am not
uncomfortable about tracing parts of what others have revealed about this
American masterpiece.

Some scholars of Lincoln's work prefer an aesthetic reading of the Gettysburg Address because they think of it as a successful piece of literature,
though an unsuccessful oration (Barton 114; Highet 87; Einhorn). Others are
attracted to an aesthetic reading of this text because they are driven by the
conviction that this sort of interpretation is worthwhile, "that aesthetic experience is a component of rhetorical activity, that—in its simplest formulation—an attraction to beauty and a repulsion by ugliness influence the composition and reception of discourse" (Black, "Aesthetics" 1). Because Edwin
Black's "Gettysburg and Silence" is influenced by the latter impulse, it is an
excellent model for the aesthetic reading of this most "celebrated example of
eloquence" (21); my reading will rely heavily upon his, acting as a sketch that
traces the lines of Black's expert illustration while adding a flourish here or
there from other critics.

As Black puts it, "[t]he Gettysburg Address has been, from its genesis, an
aesthetic object" ("Gettysburg" 21). Recognizing the object as aesthetic, Black
develops a reading that has as its object an appreciation of the object's aesthetic qualities. It is not surprising that Black's essay uses analogies and
metaphors that compare Lincoln's oration to more typical artistic media, like
a musical performance (31) and a tapestry (31). Like Gorgias, Black recognizes and appreciates the almost magical power of speech, equating the Get-

tysburg Address with mysticism and describing it as a spell that holds its audience rapt (Gorgias 82 B11.10; Black, "Gettysburg" 29, 32, 33). Also like Gorgias, he expresses interest in how the form of a speech produces powerful visceral effects on its auditors (Gorgias 82 B 11.8–9, 14, 17–18; Black, "Gettysburg" 26–27). And like Gorgias, Black adopts an attitude of play that resonates with the aesthetic motto of art for art's sake; rather than describe his reading as a scholarly contribution along political or epistemic lines, Black indicates that he approaches this text for the same reason that a climber attacks a mountain (Gorgias 82 B 11.5, 21; Black, "Gettysburg" 22).

At only 272 words, the Gettysburg Address is perhaps better compared to a challenge that requires intricate moves than a feat of athleticism and stamina; it is more like a puzzle, a poem, or a painting than a mountain climb. Yet there is something about its structure that suggests the ascent and descent of a peak. Consider the way in which Black describes its arrangement: "In visual terms, the speech is shaped like an hour glass. Temporally, it is past, present, then future. Its visceral effects are contraction, strain, and then release. Respirationally, it is an exhalation, then a pause, then an inhalation" ("Gettysburg" 26).

Other accounts of the arrangement of this speech can be added to these. Geographically, the speech moves inward from this continent and nation to a great battlefield, then it tightens our focus further to a portion of that field, before finally moving out again to the world, this nation, and the earth. Metaphorically it moves from birth (the new nation is conceived in liberty and brought forth by our fathers) to death (this Civil War cemetery is recognized as a final resting place for those who here gave their lives) to resurrection (the dedication of the living leads to a new birth of freedom for this nation, a resurrection that ensures that it "shall not perish from this earth"). Mathematically the speech is divided into three sections comprising approximately 40 percent, 30 percent, and 30 percent of the total (Black, "Gettysburg" 26). The first section constitutes the setup in which the audience is located ever more precisely in time and space. This section ends with a statement of the obvious: the act of dedicating the cemetery, the act in which Lincoln and his audience are engaged, is "altogether fitting and proper." The next section of the address marks a turning point. After assuring his audience that they are appropriately fulfilling their duty, Lincoln uses the rhetorical device of correctio to announce that their actions are not sufficient, that the seemingly appropriate ceremony they are in the midst of performing is inadequate (Leff and Goodwin 64). "But, in larger sense, we can not dedicate—we can not consecrate—we can not hallow—this ground." This section of the speech sets up a number of antitheses, between the audience and the "brave men" who struggled here, between forgetfulness and memory, and between words ("what we say here") and deeds ("what they did here"). The tension of these antitheses constitutes the strain between contraction and release, the pause between exhalation and inhalation. The final section of the speech focuses on the future action of the audience, with anaphora and epistrophe serving as the figures of choice for motivating the auditors, leading to a tricolon crescendo in which "government of the people, by the people, for the people, shall not perish from the earth." In short, "[w]e are coiled by the Address, and then sprung. The structure of the Gettysburg Address is an organization of the auditor's energy" (Black, "Gettysburg" 27).

Black's coil metaphor is apt. Garry Wills describes the style of Lincoln's speech in similar language. "His speech is economical, taut, interconnected, like the machinery he tested and developed for battle. Words were weapons, for him, even though he meant them to be weapons of peace in the midst of war" (174). A close look at Lincoln's use of words can help us to appreciate the subtle and powerful design of this address. The speech is composed mostly of short words; as William Barton points out, only eighteen words in the address are three or more syllables long, and a majority of the words Lincoln uses are of Anglo-Saxon not Latin origin (145). Yet the speech is not written in a simple style. It begins with a formal, biblical phrase ("Four score and seven years ago") and ends with another ("shall not perish from the earth"), traversing several lengthy complex and right-branching sentences along the way. The combination of simple words with formal sentence structure makes the speech's style paradoxically both plain and grand at the same time.

Wills notes the way in which the intricate design of the speech contributes to the feeling that it was decorous, even though it was written economically and with relatively simple language. He points to the interlocking phrases that connect most sentences to their predecessors. Rather than use referential words such as *former* and *latter* or pronouns such as *it* and *they*, Lincoln repeats words such as *nation, conceived and dedicated, field,* and *consecrate* in successive sentences, creating a "hook-and-eye" structure that binds the work together (172–73). In doing so, Wills maintains, Lincoln "wove a spell" out of words that has yet to be broken (175).

Another example of this kind of weaving of words can be seen in the way Lincoln used the term *dedicate* in this speech. It appears six times, in three pairs, with different meanings attending each pair (Black, "Gettysburg" 30; Leff and Goodwin 64). The first pair denotes dedication as a setting aside, a designation of something as special: the fathers dedicated the new nation to a proposition, and a great civil war tests whether any nation so dedicated can long endure. The second pair denotes the consecration of holy ground: we have come to dedicate a portion of that field as a cemetery, but in a larger sense, we cannot dedicate this ground. The final pair denotes the commitment of a person to a particular course of action: it is for the living to be dedicated to the unfinished work of the dead, dedicated to the great task remaining before us. This subtle morphing of a term from one meaning to another prepares the audience to think of their role as more than the standard ceremonial one and connects the actions of our fathers to our own: in order to preserve the proposition to which our fathers dedicated the nation, we must dedicate this cemetery by dedicating ourselves to the cause.

Other observations can be made about the intricate design of this speech, such as the way in which the thirteen uses of the word *that* help to integrate the speech even while working a disintegrative role by serving different functions at different points (Booth 41–44), or the way in which the speech achieves a sense of decorum through pairs ("so conceived and so dedicated," "fitting and proper," "little note nor long remember") and triplets ("we can not dedicate, we can not consecrate, we can not hallow"). But rather than overanalyze this remarkable work of art, I will leave my aesthetic reading with a metaphor that Black introduces. "The Address is prismatic. Its aspects reflect back and forth on one another in such radiant multiplicity that, diamond-like, its fires are somehow both protean and integral" ("Gettysburg" 22). Recognizing and appreciating the beauty of those fires is the aim of an aesthetic reading.

AN EPISTEMIC READING

There are doubtless many ways in which I could produce a reading of Lincoln's address that would expand our knowledge of how rhetoric works and thus make a contribution to the scholarly record. I choose here to develop a reading that builds upon an approach to scholarship I have described elsewhere that connects textual features to their purported effects through the close reading of documents that record the reception of particular audiences (Ceccarelli, "Polysemy" 410; Ceccarelli, *Shaping Science* 171–77).

Scholars examining Lincoln's speech have naturally turned their appreciation for its aesthetic qualities into a positive judgment of its effects on its auditors. For example, Black argues that the "structure of the Gettysburg Address imposes a corresponding form on the experience of its auditor," taking the audience through a building of reverence, a short soothing reassurance that the "energy of reverence will be discharged in an appropriate ceremony," a sudden denial and "repudiation that dislocates the reverence," and then a controlled release of tension through "the prescription for the continuing task of self-dedication by which the audience can be constructively absorbed and into which its reverence can be invested" ("Gettysburg" 26–27). What is not clear in his assessment of this effect is the identity of the auditor experiencing these emotions.

Throughout his essay, Black shifts between conjectures about how an audience in 1863 would have experienced the text and claims about the experience of today's readers. Sometimes he notes the way in which Lincoln's contemporaries would be sensitive to resonances in the text that a modern audience might miss (28, 29, 32), or he notes the way in which previous speeches heard by the immediate audience on that day might have influenced their interpretation of Lincoln's speech (27–28, 35); other times he draws the modern reader into the audience by discussing how "we" are affected by the design of the speech (24, 27). But most of the time, Black talks about auditors in a vague sense that does not distinguish between Lincoln's contemporaries and today's readers.

Harold Zyskind's "Rhetorical Analysis of the Gettysburg Address" is more consistent in focusing on an image of Lincoln's contemporary audience when he discusses the effect of the text. He recognizes the speech as a work of rhetoric, "designed primarily to create a certain effect on, or to persuade, a particular audience" (202). In describing the speech this way, he differentiates the rhetorical analyst from those who see the speech as a way of talking about "the facts of Lincoln's life" and from those who uncover "the historical or psychological causes which motivated Lincoln to write the Address"; Zyskind says that in contrast to these approaches, the rhetorical analyst would seek to discover the text's "meaning and power" as "an artistic creation designed for some end" (203).

Taking on the role of a rhetorical analyst, Zyskind reaches a conclusion about the effect of the speech on its auditors that is similar to the conclusion drawn by Black. According to Zyskind, Lincoln's speech was designed to serve not merely the epideictic function of celebrating the memory of the fallen soldiers but the deliberative function of persuading audience members to devote themselves to actions necessary for the Union's survival (206–07). Zyskind traces the temporal sequence of the speech and the listener's roles at each stage of the sequence (206–09); he describes "the diverse feelings and sympathies which Lincoln awakens" in his audience (210–11); and he comments on the appropriateness of Lincoln's stylistic choices (211–12); then he concludes that Lincoln's emotional and intuitive appeals were successful in "stirring his audience thus to action on behalf of the Union" (212).

However, when it comes to discussing evidence that Lincoln's contemporaries were thus stirred, Zyskind equivocates. The kind of research required to study the audience is too difficult to conduct, he says, and is not the real interest of the rhetorical analyst (209–10). Instead of finding evidence that would support his claims about the way this piece of rhetoric works, he retreats to the implied audience. But at the same time, he engages in a sleight of hand that in many parts of the paper makes it appear as if he is talking about the influence of particular appeals on Lincoln's historically situated audience.

It is my contention that we can test the hypothesis shared by Black and Zyskind that this speech was well designed to achieve a transformative power on its audience if we conduct a close reading of the traces of reception left in intertextual material produced by Lincoln's contemporaries (i.e., those who heard him deliver the speech at Gettysburg and those who read it in the papers at the time). Material such as editorials, diaries, and letters that refer to the primary text, if closely scrutinized, could confirm or refute the critics' conjectures about the way the text worked on its situated audience. No one has yet examined the reception texts to determine if Lincoln's speech was experienced by audience members in the way that critics suggest.[3] Instead, most have either assumed that the speech was universally effective because it was so perfectly designed to utilize the available means of persuasion (e.g. Cooper xxxi–xxxv), or they have assumed the opposite, that because many of Lincoln's contemporaries judged the speech negatively or responded to the speech with indifference, the majority of the audience must have misinterpreted or ignored the speech (e.g., Einhorn 93, 105). Neither assumption is accurate; Lincoln's speech was neither universally effective on its situated audience, nor was it universally ineffective as an oration seeking a particular effect on a specific group of people. What is more important, we can come to understand the way in which it achieved its influence by examining closely the words of those who experienced the text at the time.

A close reading of reception texts partially confirms the hypothesis of people such as Black and Zyskind that the design of Lincoln's speech created a corresponding form on its audience, transforming an epideictic reverence to a deliberative self-dedication. A great many of those who heard the speech at Gettysburg or who read the transcript distributed in the papers recognized and responded to the deliberative nature of the address. For example, an editorial in the *Boston Daily Evening Transcript* focuses on a single sentence of the speech that it says "should shine in golden letters throughout the land as an exhortation to wake up apathetic and indolent patriotism. 'It is for us, the living, rather to be dedicated here to the unfinished work that they have thus so far nobly carried on'" ("True Word"). According to this editor, the ideas of duty introduced by Lincoln "are the noble ideas the times demand as the inspiration not only of public opinion, but of public action also."

> This affirmation embodies the practical lesson to be taught by the ceremonies at Gettysburg. Those ceremonies will be but a poor and empty honor to the heroic dead, if the living leave their dust, after uttering or listening to words of eulogy, to its silent rest, without imitating the example set in their lives. From these "sepulchres in the garden," loyalty must go with a sterner determination to the rescue and save the Republic, else its honor paid to the dead will be hardly more than a sentimental mockery.

Other newspaper reports of the events at Gettysburg show evidence that their authors too were inspired by Lincoln's call to action. Some of them paraphrased the speech in a way that emphasized the thesis sentence dedicating the audience to action ("Celebration," "Gettysburg National"). Some barely mentioned Lincoln's address, but showed by their commentary on the event that they were likely influenced by it in just the way that Zyskind and Black predicted; they proclaim that the dedication event will "deepen the resolution of the living to conquer at all hazards," ("From Gettysburg") and they exhort readers to "see the future in the present" ("Gettysburgh Celebration").

Of course a look at the historical record also shows that the claims of Zyskind and Black must be put into perspective; not everyone was so obviously or immediately influenced by the deliberative function of the final two sentences of the Gettysburg Address. Some ignored the speech altogether or printed the address but made no comments that could be interpreted as evidence that they were influenced by it.[4] Significantly, at least one editor of a newspaper critical to the administration interpreted the speech as participating in the deliberative genre, but this editor was not persuaded by Lincoln's speech. Instead, this member of the opposition party was offended by the shift of generic expectations; he complained that Lincoln's use of the political genre in a funeral sermon "is an innovation upon established conventionalities, which, a year or two ago, would have been regarded with scorn by all who thought custom should, to a greater or less extent, be consulted in determining social and public proprieties."

> And the custom which forbids its introduction is founded on the propriety which grows out of the fitness of things, and is not therefore merely arbitrary, or confined to special localities, but has suggested to all nations the exclusion of political partisanship in funeral discourses. Common sense, then, should have taught Mr. Lincoln that its intrusion upon such an occasion was an offensive exhibition of boorishness and vulgarity. ("President at Gettysburg")

After hearing this vehement critique, and getting over the shock of realizing that some people at the time thought the Gettysburg Address was indecorous, it is really not all that surprising to find that those who were hostile to Lincoln were not immediately persuaded by his speech. But what is interesting about this piece of reception evidence is that a close look at *what* this editor attacks demonstrates that Zyskind and Black are right about one thing; a significant effect of the speech may very well be attributed to the transformative effect of its last part, that is, to its participation in the deliberative genre. This editorialist in the *Chicago Times* recognized the power behind Lincoln's speech design, even if he disliked it and sought to counter its effect by judging the move negatively for his readers. If we look at reception evidence to determine not only how audiences *judged* the speech (as appropriate, honest-hearted, and impressive, or as mawkish, offensive, and vulgar) but instead examine the reception texts to uncover how audiences *interpreted* it, we find that Zyskind's discussion of genre shift and Black's discussion of coil and release develop a fairly accurate understanding of the relationship between the speech's form and its function.

Lest we conclude from this limited evidence that the speech was universally experienced by its audience as a more or less successful attempt to transform reverence into deliberative action, we should note that the other line that
was most quoted by newspapers and by members of the immediate audience
was from the first part of the speech, before Lincoln undertakes the shift that
transforms the address from an epideictic to a deliberative effort. "The world
will little note nor long remember what we said here, but it can never forget
what they did here"—this passage was the focus of several commentaries at
the time that seemed to recognize only the way in which the speech did honor
to the dead, not how it rededicated the living to the unfinished work they left
behind.[5] So Zyskind's claim about the rhetorical structure and function of the
speech might be qualified in the following way: for those in his audience who
were prepared to hear it, Lincoln's structural shift from epideictic to deliberative address built upon their emotional need to transform the heroism of the
dead into their own dedication to future action. Black's claim that the structure of the speech imposes a corresponding form on the experience of the
auditor might be qualified to acknowledge that some auditors got stuck in the
first part of the speech, arresting its forward movement; in their sorrow for the
dead, they connected most closely with the denial and repudiation stage of the
speech and were thus unable to move past their grief to the slow release of tension that marks the final two sentences of the address.

A careful reading of the reception evidence, that is, the traces of how people interpreted and judged the text at the time, helps us to better understand
how textual design and textual function correspond to each other. One could
even say it helps us build new knowledge about the way in which a speech that
is designed to soothe, deny, and then transform its listeners might be experienced positively and negatively by audience members with different precon-
ceptions about the speaker, and only partially experienced by other audience
members who are unready to see beyond the soothing reassurances of its
opening section.

A POLITICAL READING

The final reading I will produce in this chapter explores the way in which Lincoln's address embodies a political philosophy, a concept of 'civic virtue' that
both preserves tradition and makes an innovation upon it, leading those who
would recognize and accept it to embrace a new understanding of their relationship to history, the nation, and their fellow citizens. As with the aesthetic
reading, my intent is not to add new knowledge to the scholarly record, so I
am not adverse to relating what others have so effectively demonstrated elsewhere. Unlike the aesthetic reading though, my purpose is not to help readers
better appreciate the text but to persuade them to commit themselves to a

political vision and its corresponding action. That action should involve not merely private acceptance but also public advocacy that shares with others the lessons that a political reading of the Gettysburg Address can offer.

This reading begins with Lincoln's allusion to the Declaration of Independence made in the opening line of his speech. "Four score and seven years ago our fathers brought forth on this continent, a new nation, conceived in Liberty, and dedicated to the proposition that all men are created equal." In locating the birth of the nation in 1776, the signing of the Declaration of Independence, Lincoln sought to shape public memory. As Glen Thurow points out, Lincoln "could have chosen another date, back to, say, the New England Puritans, or to the Articles of Confederation, or to the Constitution" (71). The fact that he chose to mark the birth of the nation as the year in which our fathers signed the document committing them to fight for an independent political body was significant since Lincoln calls for a similar wartime commitment from his audience.

More significant was Lincoln's decision to imagine the nation as "conceived in Liberty" and established upon the "proposition" that all men are created equal. Those who have read the Declaration know that it does not consider the equality of man to be a proposition, but a self-evident truth, an axiom that one need not prove (Brann 25; Thurow 58). By reenvisioning this concept of the 'equality of men' as a proposition, Lincoln changes our understanding of these words and our relationship to them. Our fathers who signed the Declaration, many of them slaveholders, could hardly have included black men in the phrase "all men are created equal" if that phrase were a "self-evident truth" for them. But if that phrase were instead a proposition out of which the nation was conceived and to which the nation was dedicated (that is, set apart for and/or committed to), then it could be considered an ideal, not a reality, an objective that one seeks to achieve through a lifetime of struggle. Such dreams are not true or false; they are realized or unrealized.[6] In his second sentence, Lincoln explains that the "great civil war" was a test, not of the truth of a proposition, but of "whether that nation, or any nation so conceived and so dedicated, can long endure." One does not test a proposition that is an objective or a plan; one chooses it and enacts it, but in doing so, one might test one's own limits. In this case, the test of limits is whether a nation, in trying to enact the ideal of equality, can survive.

When Lincoln says that the soldiers who died at Gettysburg "gave their lives that that nation might live," he implies that they shared the hope of the fathers, giving their lives to the struggle to achieve the ideal of equality for all men. When Lincoln calls for the dedication of the living to "a new birth of freedom" for this nation so that "government of the people, by the people, for the people, shall not perish from the earth," he likewise commits the audience to the struggle for that ideal.

As Wills puts it, by offering a new way of thinking about our nation and its mission, "Lincoln had revolutionized the Revolution, giving people a new past to live with that would change their future indefinitely" (38). Because Lincoln reinterpreted the past, rather than rejecting it or accepting it on its own terms, he was able to "change tradition without destroying it" (Leff 212). But we should not forget that the tradition was altered by Lincoln's reinterpretation of the Declaration of Independence, and that change was a positive one. He made equality the central proposition of our nation, a nation whose constitution does not even use the term. While there were some at the time who would resist this conception and some today who would contest it, it has been overwhelmingly accepted as our preferred self-image (Wills 38–39, 146).

Recognizing the way in which Lincoln rhetorically constructed this nation through the Gettysburg Address is important not because it reaffirms our commitment to the proposition of equality; recognizing Lincoln's construction of our nation as bound to this ideal may or may not inspire us to embrace that ideal. Instead, this reading is important because it reminds us that our history is alive, that we are not constrained to a conception of ourselves that is tied to a hidebound past, that we can and do reinvent ourselves and our history to meet our changing visions of who we are and how we relate to each other. However, recognition is not enough. Sharing this understanding with each other is a good first step, but if we do not also share it with a larger public, through our teaching or by writing for audiences outside the academy, it will remain an empty knowledge that lies stagnant in the academy rather than infusing our civic culture.

CONCLUSION

In real life, the three ends of rhetoric are not as artificially divided as I have made them out to be in this chapter. Real critics meld aesthetic, epistemic, and political observations in their readings of particular texts. It is a rare critic who focuses on the aesthetic workings of an influential public oration without recognizing its political import, and critics who offer aesthetic or political readings without adding *something* new to the scholarly record are unlikely to see their work published. But in researching this chapter, when I attempted to determine which goal dominated for each Lincoln scholar, I found the work fairly easy to categorize. This suggests that the three ends are a useful way to group critical approaches even if they are rarely found in pure form.

In providing exemplars of aesthetic, epistemic, and political readings of a single speech, it has not been my intent to offer rigid models that can be used to limit what is said in these three types of criticism. The readings here are specific to the text and the inflection of each perspective that I chose. In particular, my aesthetic reading describes in detail the artistic complexity of Lincoln's address, my epistemic reading offers new evidence of how the rhetoric of Lincoln's speech worked on his audience, and my political reading describes the constitutive rhetorical force of Lincoln's address and asks readers to recognize, accept, and promote an awareness of this function outside the academy. Rather than constrain what might be described as aesthetic, epistemic, and political readings, I hope that these exemplars are taken as suggestive possibilities of what can be offered by rhetoricians interested in different things.

More generally, I hope that I have made the argument of my earlier paper more clear through this three-part case study. In recognizing that different purposes guide rhetoricians, from ancient to contemporary times, and acknowledging that a plurality of goals is legitimate and healthy for a group of scholars, I think we can learn to better appreciate, understand, and interact with each other, no matter what interests drive our research.

NOTES

1. I am not using the term *epistemic* in the classical sense, as a particular form of exact knowledge, but in the broader contemporary sense, as knowledge developed through research.

2. The purpose of this chapter is not to reargue the earlier essay. Since its publication, there have been works by scholars of classical rhetoric that are in line with my categorization (e.g., regarding Isocrates, see Poulakos) and others that might dispute it (e.g., regarding Gorgias, see McComiskey). Since the characterizations are meant to be heuristic, not definitive, further development of my case for these depictions is outside the scope of this chapter.

3. There have been several studies that have recorded some aspects of the reception of Lincoln's audience (Reid; Wiley; Barton 113–23, 161–210). Unfortunately, scholars who discuss the reception of historical audiences almost always fail to conduct close readings of this material in conjunction with a close reading of the primary text; instead, they catalog judgments of the text but do little to explain how audiences arrived at those judgments. Because they do not note which parts of the address made it into the descriptions that preceded that audience's positive or negative judgments, it is difficult to use the information provided in these catalogs of assessments to determine whether or not Lincoln's speech was experienced in the ways that critics of the speech have suggested.

4. According to Ronald F. Reid, 70 of the 158 weeklies and 2 of the 96 dailies he examined ignored the Gettysburg dedication ceremony. Of the 61 editorials he read about Gettysburg oratory, 40 were devoted primarily to Everett; in addition, most evaluative commentary in new reports about the event was about Everett's speech.

5. See for example, *Harper's Weekly*, April 23, 1864, quoted in Barton 121; *Ohio State Journal*, November 23, 1863, quoted in Wiley 7; and the comments of Governor William Dennison, quoted in Barton 165.

6. My reading of the word *proposition* draws on its meaning as a proposal or plan, not the senses more familiar in mathematics (a theorem to be demonstrated or proved) or in rhetoric (a statement to be upheld) (Guralnik 1140). It thus differs from the readings offered for this passage by some other critics (e.g., Brann 25; Thurow 58).

WORKS CITED

Barton, William E. *Lincoln at Gettysburg.* New York: Peter Smith, 1950.
Black, Edwin. "Gettysburg and Silence." *Quarterly Journal of Speech* 80 (1994): 21–36.
———. "The Aesthetics of Rhetoric, American Style." In *Rhetoric and Political Culture in Nineteenth Century America.* Ed. Thomas Benson. East Lansing: Michigan State UP, 1997.
Booth, Stephen. *Precious Nonsense: The Gettysburg Address, Ben Johson's Epitaphs on His Children, and Twelfth Night.* Berkeley: U of California P, 1998.
Brann, Eva. "A Reading of the Gettysburg Address." In *Abraham Lincoln, The Gettysburg Address and American Constitutionalism.* Ed. Leo Paul S. de Alvarez. Irving, TX: U of Dallas P, 1976. 15–53.
Ceccarelli, Leah. "The Ends of Rhetoric: Aesthetic, Political, and Epistemic." In *Making and Unmaking the Prospects for Rhetoric: Selected Papers from the 1996 Rhetoric Society of America Conference.* Ed. Theresa Enos. Mahwah, NJ: Lawrence Erlbaum Associates, 1997. 65–73.
———. "Polysemy: Multiple Meanings in Rhetorical Criticism." *Quarterly Journal of Speech* 84 (1998): 395–415.
———. *Shaping Science with Rhetoric: The Cases of Dobzhansky, Schrödinger, and Wilson.* Chicago: U of Chicago P, 2001.
"The Celebration at Gettysburg." *Philadelphia Public Ledger and Daily Transcript* 23 November 1863: 2.
Cooper, Lane. *The Rhetoric of Aristotle.* New York: Appleton-Century-Crofts, 1932.
Einhorn, Lois J. *Abraham Lincoln the Orator.* Westport, CT: Greenwood, 1992.
"From Gettysburg, PA." *Chicago Tribune* 21 November 1863: 1.
"The Gettysburgh Celebration." *New York Times* 21 November 1863: 1.
"Gettysburg National Cemetery." *The Missouri Republican* 21 November 1863: 3.
Gorgias. "Encomium of Helen." *The Older Sophists: A Complete Translation by Several Hands of the Fragments in Die Fragmente Der Vorsokratiker edited by Diels-Kranz,* ed. Rosamond Kent Sprague. Columbia: U of Southern Carolina P, 1972.
Guralnik, David B., ed. *Webster's New World Dictionary of the American Language.* New York: Prentice Hall, 1986.
Highet, Gilbert. *A Clerk of Oxenford: Essays on Literature and Life.* New York: Oxford UP, 1954.
Leff, Michael. "Hermeneutical Rhetoric." In *Rhetoric and Hermeneutics in Our Time: A Reader.* Ed. Walter Jost and Michael J. Hyde. New Haven: Yale UP, 1997. 196–214

Leff, Michael, and Jean Goodwin. "Dialogic Figures and Dialectical Argument in Lincoln's Rhetoric." *Rhetoric and Public Affairs* 3 (2000): 59–69.

McComiskey, Bruce. *Gorgias and the New Sophistic Rhetoric.* Carbondale: Southern Illinois UP, 2002.

Poulakos, Takis. *Speaking for the Polis: Isocrates' Rhetorical Education.* Columbia: U of South Carolina P, 1997.

"The President at Gettysburg." *Chicago Times* 23 November 1863, reprinted in *Abraham Lincoln: A Press Portrait.* Ed. Herbert Mitgang. New York: Fordham UP, 2000. 360.

Reid, Ronald F. "Newspaper Response to the Gettysburg Addresses." *Quarterly Journal of Speech* 53 (1967): 50–60.

Thurow, Glen E. "The Gettysburg Address and the Declaration of Independence." In *Abraham Lincoln: The Gettysburg Address and American Constitutionalism.* Ed. Leo Paul S. de Alvarez. Irving, TX: U of Dallas P, 1976. 55–75.

"The True Word." *Boston Daily Evening Transcript* 21 November 1863: 2.

Wiley, Earl W. "Buckeye Criticism of the Gettysburg Address." *Communication Monographs* 23 (1956): 1–8.

Wills, Garry. *Lincoln at Gettysburg: The Words That Remade America.* New York: Simon and Schuster, 1992.

Zyskind, Harold. "A Rhetorical Analysis of the Gettysburg Address." *Journal of General Education* 4 (1950): 202–12.

FOUR

De-Canonizing Ancient Rhetoric

Robert N. Gaines

MY SUBJECT IS THE canon of ancient rhetoric, sometimes known as the classical tradition of rhetoric or even more simply as classical rhetoric. The sense of the term *canon* that occupies me in this regard is hardly ambiguous to anyone in the rhetorical discipline, but it bears specification—at least in a preliminary way—if only because it is often unquestioned on account of its familiarity. Accordingly, let me quote a brief account of 'canon' by Frank Kermode:

> [P]eople who use the word "canon" usually have in mind quite practical issues. They may, for example, be stating that there is for students of literature a list of books or authors certified by tradition or by an institution as worthy of intensive study and required reading for all who may aspire to professional standing within the institution. Or they may be disputing the constitution of the canon, or even the right of the institution to certify it. (78)

Consistent with this account, I understand the canon of ancient rhetoric as a list of major books pertinent to rhetorical theory by certain authors from the ancient times. Further, within the rhetorical discipline, a mastery of this list is frequently expected of students and generally presupposed of professionals. And finally, the list is the subject of controversy, not least on account of its constitution and authority.

My purpose in addressing this subject is to extend the controversy that surrounds it. However before I attend explicitly to this purpose, I think it is important—even necessary—to point out that the current dispute over the ancient rhetorical canon is not an issue that arose or even could have arisen until relatively recently. In ancient times the words *kanôn* in Greek and *canon* in Latin were never used with reference to a list of rhetoric books such as we understand as constituting the ancient canon. Rather, in connection with ancient rhetoric we find only rhetorical performers described as canons. For example, Dionysius of Halicarnassus describes Thucydides as a *kanôn* or model of the elaborate style (*de Demosthene* 1), and he assigns similar places to Lysias and Isocrates in regard to the plain and middle styles respectively (*de Demosthene* 2; cf. Cole 33). Such imitative or exemplary canons are separated by form and function from the ancient rhetorical canon we contemplate today. For, they neither furnish a list of theoretical rhetorics nor construct a field of inquiry authorized for disciplinary study.

In form at least, we find a precursor of our disciplinary concept in the Christian doctrine of an ecclesiastical canon. Beginning in the fourth century CE, there are uses of the Greek 'kanôn' and Latin 'canon,' which refer to the list of books accepted by the church as genuine and inspired.[1] Here, surely, we have a limited catalogue of books imbued with institutional authority. But just as surely, the function of the ecclesiastical canon may be distinguished from the function of our disciplinary canon. The former is normative—it specifies a group of texts that in some way or other must be obeyed. The latter is constitutive—it establishes an institutional sphere of authorized instruction and investigation.[2]

Of course, it hardly takes an active imagination to conceive of our disciplinary use of canon as a kind of literary extension of the ecclesiastical sense. That it occurred, I think, is doubtless. When it occurred is by no means clear; nonetheless, the evidence available on English usage suggests that the extension dates only from the twentieth century. Although we find secular uses of canon-cognates in reference to authors as early as 1595,[3] *OED* provides no evidence for use of 'canon' in reference to a list of secular authors or texts until 1885,[4] and even that sense applies only to the authentic texts of a single author. Perhaps most significant, up to the present day our disciplinary understanding of canon—that is, a list of major theoretical authors and works imbued with disciplinary authority—has not been recognized or documented in the *OED*.

From the foregoing, my conclusion is that specific disciplinary conceptualizations of a "canon" of ancient rhetoric almost certainly represent twentieth-century innovation. Moreover, as a corollary, I further conclude that the current controversy over the canon of ancient rhetoric is a contemporary dispute waged by contemporary scholars. In light of these preliminary findings, my position in this chapter may be summarized as follows. The dispute over the ancient rhetorical canon is essentially a tug-of-war between contemporary scholarly factions whose chief interests are not the comprehension of rhetoric in ancient times but rather the exploitation or imposition of disciplinary authority. Such appropriations of the canon are problematic, because they render the canon unrepresentative and inconsistent in its conceptualization of ancient rhetoric. To redress this problem, we cannot simply construct a new canon, because that will lead to further disputes over disciplinary authority. Rather, we must reconstitute "ancient rhetoric" as a corpus, one that contains all known texts, artifacts, and discourse venues that represent the theory, pedagogy, practice, criticism, and cultural apprehension of rhetoric in ancient times. Let me now turn to the argument on behalf of this position.

I begin with an essay entitled "A Small History of Rhetoric" by Terry Eagleton in 1981. Within this essay Eagleton proposed a brief account of ancient rhetoric (101–04) and suggested that during ancient times rhetoric offered the possibility of "political literary criticism" with "a 'portable' analytic method independent of any particular object" (101–02). Regarding ancient rhetoric, Eagleton had recourse to a set of authors he knew readers would recognize as authoritative: Corax, Plato, Cicero, Quintilian (101–04). And in positing rhetoric as an unlimited mode of political criticism, he offered the first glimpse of his critique of the literary canon as a set of privileged objects that strengthen as well as reinforce the assumptions of the dominant power system (cf. Eagleton, *Literary Theory*, 195–96). In view of these two discursive activities, I believe Eagleton's essay offers a near epitome for the future dispute over the canon of ancient rhetoric. On the one hand, he embraces the ancient rhetorical canon as an instrument of convenience to secure disciplinary credibility for his survey of critical theory in rhetoric. On the other hand, he denounces existing literary canons as perpetuators of dominant—and elitist—ideologies. In fact, Eagleton's two postures toward the canon, embracement and denunciation, would come to characterize the discussion of ancient rhetoric among all its parties for the next two decades.

Embracement of an ancient rhetorical canon was not unheard of prior to 1981. Rather it was a common if only partly conscious practice among historians of rhetoric as early as the 1920s. For example, Baldwin's *Ancient Rhetoric and Poetic* limits the discussion of rhetoric to five canonical authors: Aristotle, Cicero, Quintilian, Dionysius of Halicarnassus, and Pseudo-Longinus (5, 103). Right or wrong, Baldwin conceived of the works of these authors as "representative" of ancient rhetoric. And the tendency to focus on a few major authors and works remains a staple in the history of rhetoric, particularly within accounts that fashion themselves as introductory (e.g., Vickers 13–52; Bizzell and Herzberg 19–363; and Murphy and Katula).

More conscious embracement may be noted in scholarship that applies the canon as a convenient delimiter for the scope of responsible inquiry. For instance, when Kathy Eden wanted to discuss hermeneutics and the ancient rhetorical tradition, her investigation was simplified considerably by defining her subject with reference to the canon, in this case, works of Isocrates, Plato, Aristotle, Cicero, Quintilian, and Demetrius. Likewise, when Knoblauch and Brannon wanted to debunk ancient rhetoric as a possible basis for contemporary composition theory, they happily embraced the canon in order to limit the range of an "authoritative" critique to just five works: Aristotle's *Rhetoric*, Cicero's *De inventione* and *De oratore, Rhetorica ad Herennium,* and Quintilian's *Institutio oratoria* (22–50). Some radical embracements of the canon collapse ancient rhetoric into a single representative, this as a strategy for infusing new stances with classical authority. For example, in defense of classical rhetoric as a basis for contemporary composition theory, Lundsford and Ede condense the canon into a single author, Aristotle, whose *Rhetoric*—after a bit of reinterpretation—turns out to be thoroughly modern in its conception and motivation (40–44). Likewise, Welch, who repudiates Aristotelian rhetoric as the prime representative of the ancient canon, rehistoricizes "classical rhetoric," installing a regendered, reraced, sophistic construction of Isocratean rhetoric precisely in its place (6–7).

Denunciation of the ancient rhetoric canon has taken a variety of forms, all of which share postmodern motivations for opposition and each of which may be characterized as the conscious promotion of a particular ideology. Marxist denunciations of the canon attempt to subvert the ideological assumptions that ancient rhetoric was a unified, linear, intellectual development. Thus, Berlin insists that our conception of ancient rhetoric must be historicized within the economic, social, political, and cultural conditions of its production; the result, he argues, is that we are confronted with multiple ancient rhetorics, which represent differing discourse practices and political orders (116–17). Feminist denunciations of the canon have sought both to promote resistant interpretations of canonical history and to redress the omission of women and their concerns from the canon in one way or other (cf. Bizzell). A good example of a resistant reading is provided by Jarratt, who argues that the sophists—who were formerly marginalized and excluded from the canon—should be central to the narrative of ancient rhetoric. Feminist arguments to redress omissions have generally proposed inclusion of women and their interests in the canon. Here instances include Glenn's refiguring of Aspasia and Swearingen's reconstitution of Diotima as figures pertinent to ancient rhetoric. In a similar connection we may recognize Woods' insistence that rhetorical pedagogy—long dismissed as historically unimportant—must be added to the ancient rhetorical canon. Postmodernist denunciations of the canon conceive it as a manifestation—even an instrument—of oppression; accordingly they address themselves to exposing issues of gender, race, and class frequently hidden or marginalized in institutional conceptions of ancient rhetoric. An example is Imber's recovery of the "voice" of a Roman matron, Pudentilla, from the *Apology* of Apuleius; here we learn that Pudentilla argued, wrote letters, and acted to secure her fortune and marry when she wished—all in opposition to the dominant cultural ideology. Finally, there has recently arisen a postcolonial denunciation of the rhetorical canon, including ancient rhetoric. The basis of the critique is that the canon privileges "imperial voices," ignores "racially and culturally marginalized voices," and generally

fails to account for "rhetorical strategies through which neocolonialism establishes its hegemony" (Shome 43–44, 51). Consistent with this critique, the
postcolonial denunciation aims at introduction of marginalized voices into the
canon and the repositioning of canonical texts in relation to the "Other"
(Hasian 24–25). For instance, Pfau has recently constructed Gorgias'
"Encomium to Helen" as a "barbarian" discourse that cloaks an elitist theory
of political persuasion in allegorical terms for reception by a radical democratic audience.

My complaint about the scholarly postures that embrace and denounce
the canon of ancient rhetoric is simple: neither posture has the design or
capacity to tell us much about rhetoric in ancient times. The scholarship of
embracement either recapitulates the canon without widening or deepening
its intellectual significance, or it exploits the canon to lend disciplinary
authority to an interpretation or radical reduction of its contents. Similarly,
the scholarship of denunciation, which imposes canonical authority on
rhetorical authors and works to achieve ideological objectives, actually weak-
ens the canon by proliferating the positions of intellectual privilege that constitute one or many conceptions of rhetoric in ancient times. The result is an
ideological hodgepodge incapable of representing, much less defining ancient
rhetoric with any consistency or coherence.

Now the standard thing to say at this juncture is that the canon of ancient
rhetoric must be revised according to some new set of principles. However, I
shall say no such thing. The reason is that I do not believe any new canon can
resolve the problems that created our current predicament. I am led to this
belief from having been persuaded that any selection of ancient rhetorical
authors or works for any purpose will necessarily be shot through with ideology. Accordingly, any conceptualization of a limited canon of ancient rhetoric
will necessarily privilege some authors and works and therefore invite the sort
of controversy over disciplinary authority that affects and undermines the current canon.

My proposal to resolve the current dispute over ancient rhetoric is to conceive it as a corpus. In particular, I believe that we should understand ancient
rhetoric to be that body of information that contains all known texts, artifacts,
and discourse venues that represent the theory, pedagogy, practice, criticism,
and cultural apprehension of rhetoric in the ancient European discourse community. Let me specify this conception at least a little. By texts I mean anything written using any medium that has survived complete or in fragments
or otherwise for which we have evidence in another text or artifact, including—among other possibilities—original and copied writing on papyrus,
wood, wax, or animal skin or writing on or in pottery, masonry, stone, or
metal.[5] By artifacts I mean man-made objects of aesthetic, practical, religious,
or other cultural significance.[6] And by discourse venues I mean places culturally associated with purposive communication, including rostra, legislative

assembly areas, courts, theaters, temples, salons, schools, libraries, festivals, and other public and private locations—permanent and occasional—associated with speaking, writing, and reading.[7]

By representations of rhetorical theory I mean all discussions of rhetoric, its principles and precepts, as well as its practical, political, and cultural functions and consequences, including, for example, technical treatises, handbooks, epitomes, compendia, textbooks, commentaries, specimen and model speeches, letters, and literary works by rhetoricians, philosophers, and other writers.[8] By representations of pedagogy I mean all evidence of the goals, practices, activities, outcomes, texts, and material circumstances of rhetorical education at all levels, by all sorts of educators, in all relevant discourse venues. Included here, among other things, would be technical treatises, textbooks, epitomes, letters, evidence of progymnasmatic exercises, declamations, and other student performances, indications of rhetorical pedagogy in rhetorical, philosophical, and other literary works of mature authors, depictions of educational scenes or circumstances in artifacts, and existing or reconstructable sites of instruction.[9] By representations of rhetorical practice I mean all evidence of every form of public and private communication designed to achieve practical effects in every discourse venue, including forensic, deliberative, ceremonial, demonstrative, philosophical, and religious discourses, biographies, essays, letters, conversations, and other symbolic practices of cultural significance.[10] By representations of criticism I mean all indications of an evaluative impulse directed toward rhetorical practice. This would include, for example, critical treatises, technical treatises, speeches, essays, letters, conversations, manifestations of audience response in artifacts, and depictions of spectator attendance and conduct at rhetorical performances.[11] By representations of cultural apprehension I mean the whole range of responses to rhetorical theory, rhetorical pedagogy, rhetorical practice, and rhetorical criticism in the discourse community. Among other things this would include constructions of rhetorical theory, pedagogy, practice, criticism, and their practitioners in literature and artifacts, public or private development of discourse venues, and even legislation regarding rhetorical practice and pedagogy.[12]

Now, there are three properties of the corpus conception of ancient rhetoric that I would like to make clear. First, in associating the conception with the ancient European discourse community I do not mean to privilege European culture or disprivilege any other culture. In fact, I heartily acknowledge the possible existence of rhetorical corpora in association with other discourse communities before and contemporary with what I have been calling "ancient times" in Europe (see, e.g., Fox and Lu). However, because culture significantly affects discourse theory, pedagogy, practice, criticism, and community apprehension in a variety of ways, I believe it is best to observe a distinction among discourse communities when defining and constructing the rhetorical corpora relevant to their unique histories. And if it is necessary to distinguish among ancient rhetorical corpora terminologically, then I am perfectly satisfied with the term *ancient European rhetoric*.

Second, in proposing a corpus conception of ancient rhetoric it is my intention to open up inquiry into the subject matter. In my view the proposed corpus conception clearly "authorizes" a wide range of intellectual activities that have recently been positioned in opposition to the canon conception of ancient rhetoric. For example, the recovery of women's contributions to rhetoric and the reconstitution of voices of marginalized genders, races, classes, and cultures are facilitated by inclusion in the corpus of *all evidence* related to theory, pedagogy, practice, criticism, and cultural apprehension of rhetoric. Much the same may be said for traditional forms of historical, theoretical, and critical inquiry, since the corpus conception enables and encourages deeper consideration of a wider range of sources.

Third, the proposed corpus conception hardly precludes the identification and application of subcorpora for particular disciplinary purposes, that is, instruction, theory development, cultural critique, or historiography. I raise this issue, because for some time, limited lists of "major works" have guided much of the teaching and research related to ancient rhetoric. The importance accorded "major works" is certainly explicable in light of two disciplinary realities: rhetorical instruction is generally carried out in finite institutional courses of study, and rhetorical investigation is generally approved for its treatment of "significant" subject matters. But in my view, the adoption of a corpus conception of ancient rhetoric will neither challenge nor disrupt curricular and heuristic uses of selective lists of disciplinary materials. Consistent with the corpus conception, professors and scholars will still identify lists of objects that require or deserve disciplinary attention, and the only essential difference between these lists and the limited "canons" they replace will be the need for an argument by the list maker on behalf of list contents. For example, a teacher or scholar might argue that individual works by Plato, Aristotle, Hermagoras, Cicero, Philodemus, Quintilian, and Sextus Empiricus deserve disciplinary attention, because they disclose the relationship between rhetoric and philosophy in ancient times. Equally, an argument might be made that individual works by Aristophanes, Plato, Quintilian, Petronius, Juvenal, Appian, Apuleius, and Philostratus deserve disciplinary attention because they represent diverse modes of participation by women in ancient rhetoric. As these examples disclose, justified selections of objects from the corpus of ancient rhetoric will serve just as well as "canons" to authorize the intellectual focus of disciplinary instruction and investigation. Moreover, the mechanism by which authority will be distributed in relation to the corpus conception (namely, disciplinary argument) will open the field of inquiry to include a multiplicity of object lists and methodological orientations, all with disciplinary authority for use in teaching and research on ancient rhetoric. Thus, the corpus conception of ancient rhetoric will not frustrate but rather sustain and widen the intellectual activities formerly "authorized" by the notion of a "canon."

In all, a corpus conception enlarges the scope of ancient rhetoric, democratizes its evidence, and supports a plurality of methods and ideological stances in its intellectual pursuit. For these reasons, I believe it offers a sound basis for the future investigation of ancient rhetoric.

NOTES

1. Early uses of '*kanôn*' and '*canon*' in the ecclesiastical sense are identified by Kennedy (107, Euseb. *Hist. eccl.* 6.25.3, c. 313/314 CE [on this date see Burgess]) and Schoeck (99, August. *Ep.* 93.36, 408 CE). Even earlier than the fourth century CE, various critics drew up lists of good authors in various literary genres (cf. Kennedy 106–07). We know, for example, that Aristophanes of Byzantium and Aristarchus of Samothrace conceived lists of poets (Quint. 10.1.54). Likewise, there is evidence for separate lists of orators by Caecilius of Caleacte (Suid. *kappa* 1165) and Dionysius of Halicarnassus (D. H. *Orat. Vett.* 4). Our best source for this practice is Quintilian, who commends an extensive list of "most eminent" *(eminentissimi)* authors to the attention of his students (10.1.45) and arranges the list to include poetry, history, oratory, and philosophy (10.1.46–131). With regard to these early list makers, however, there is no evidence that any of them ever used a form of '*kanôn*' or '*canon*' to refer to a group of secular authors (or works).

2. For the distinction of canons into exemplary, normative, and constitutive types, I generally follow Halbertal (3).

3. Covell (36), "to canonize your own writers," that is, poets (see *OED*, s.v. canonize, v., def. 5).

4. *Encyclopedia Britannica*, 9th. ed., 19 (1885): 211: "The dialogues forming part of the 'Platonic canon'" (see *OED*, s.v. canon, n.1, def. 4). Long before this comment, in 1768, David Ruhnken used the word 'canon' with reference to author lists created by ancient critics (see this chapter, note 1); here is a typical example of this usage (388): "Scriptores, quos Critici in talem canonem retulissent, proprie dicebantur in ordinem venire, *in ordine redigi, in numerum redigi, recipi:* contra, quos repudiassent, *numero eximi,* Quinctilian. I. 4. p. 18" ("Authors, whom the Critics had assigned to such a canon, were properly said *to be included in the order, to be brought under the order, to be brought under the category, to be accepted:* on the other hand, authors whom they had rejected were said *to be omitted from the category.* Quint. 1.4.3"). As Kennedy suggests (107), Ruhnken's sense of 'canon' was applied by some classical philologists of the nineteenth century (consider, e.g., Steffen and Brozka). But all these uses of 'canon' arose in academic Latin, and we do not find parallels in English. In fact, from the evidence currently available, it appears that Ruhnken's terminological innovation had no impact on English usage.

5. Examples of texts would include the following: *P. Herc.* 1007 (papyrus, c. 50 BCE), Phld. *Rh.* 4; B.M. Add. MS. 33293 (ink on painted wood, c. 3rd cent. CE) lines

from Hom. *Il.* marked for instruction in pronunciation; B.M. Add. MS. 34186(1) (wooden tablet leaf filled with wax, c. 2nd cent. CE) writing exercise of two Greek maxims; *P. Oxy.* 1353 (letter copied in parchment codex, 4th cent. CE) 1 Pet.; B.M. ostrakon no. 18711 (inscribed potsherd) lines from E. *Ph.* apparently for instructional use; Si ti<bi> Cicero do<let>, vapulabis ("If Cicero causes you pain, you will be thrashed"; school graffito on masonry, villa of Albucius Celsus, Pompeii, before 80 CE [see Bonner 119, Corte 85]; Diog. Oen. (monumental inscription in stone, Oenoanda, c. 2nd cent. CE [see Smith]) protreptic summary of Epicurean philosophy; BMCRE 3, Nr. 827 (bronze coin, c. 104–11 CE) depiction of Imperial address by Trajan with text S<ENATUS> P<OPULUS>Q<UE> R<OMANUS> OPTIMO PRINCIPI (refers to title of "Best Ruler" conferred on Trajan by the senate).

6. Examples of artifacts would be London E 697, inv. no. 1856.5–12.15 (vase, c. 410–400 BCE), Peithô (Persuasion as goddess) with Aphrodite, Eros, Paidia, Eunomia, Eudaimonia, and Kleopatra; Hermes Logios, Museo Nazionale Romana, Palazzo Altemps (marble sculpture, copy of bronze original from the school Myron, c. 450 BCE), Hermes (god of rhetoric) standing in an oratorical pose.

7. Obvious instances of discourse venues are the Athenian Pnyx, Areopagus, and Painted Stoa as well as the Roman rostra, forum, basilicas, Comitium, Curia, and temple of Jupiter Capitolinus. Temples were sometimes used as schools (Philostr. *VS* 618–19), but improvised, open-air locations (Hor. *Ep.* 1.20.17–18, on which see Bonner, 116–17), public arcades (Naples 9066 [painted plasterwork, mid-first century CE] school session in a portico of the forum at Pompeii), and indoor schools were also typical (Sen. *Con.* 9.pr.3–4). Declamatory exhibitions—including competitions—were often held in theatres (Philostr. *VS* 579; Eun. *VS* 489), while practice and advanced training frequently took place in private homes (Cic. *Fam.* 9.16.7; Sen. *Con.* 1.pr. 11; 1.pr.12). Private homes also served as sites of for preliminary instruction in discourse (Cic. *Brut.* 207), supplementary study (e.g., in a personal library, Philostr. *VS* 604), and even spontaneous displays of eloquence (Juv. 6.434–56).

8. Among textual representations, Berkowitz and Squitier (436) recognize at least 219 works by 63 Greek authors relevant to rhetorical theory (i.e., rhetorica) within the Thesaurus Linguae Graecae (TLG) data bank of ancient Greek texts (TLG authors from 5th cent. CE forward or of unknown date have been excluded). Similarly, the Latin canon of the Packard Humanities Institute CD ROM Version 5.3 includes at least 18 works by 10 authors that are germane to rhetorical theory. Berkowitz and Squitier do not include monumental inscriptions or fragments of anonymous, untitled works; accordingly, they omit some texts of a theoretical nature related to rhetoric (e.g., Diog. Oen. Fr. 112 [Smith 294–95], an account of occupational stresses on the speaker, and *P. Hamb.* 131, a fragment of a rhetorical treatise from 3rd cent. BCE). The Latin canon also omits epigraphical and fragmentary texts unassociated with particular authors. Perhaps less understandable is that it overlooks all but one of the ancient Latin texts collected in Halm. The objectives of both indices prohibit their systematic identification of letters and literary works that treat rhetorical theory by the way (e.g., the Latin canon specially identifies Fro. *Ant. [De eloquentia]*, but it does not call similar

attention to Cic. *Att.* 4.16 (where Cicero comments on the theoretical structure of *de Orat.*); likewise, Berkowitz and Squitier classify Arist. *Rh.* among rhetorical works, yet they omit from the classification Pl. *Phdr.* Currently there is no systematic means of access to artifacts and venues pertinent to ancient rhetorical theory. Still, even from the few well-known artifactual representations of speaking (e.g., Hermes Logios [this chapter, note 6] and Naples 5591 [bronze statue, c. 50 CE], L. Mammio Maximo standing in an oratorical pose), relations to the theory of rhetorical delivery seem obvious (cf. Brilliant 29–30, 68–69). Likewise, with reference to speech venues, one need only visit an ancient site of assembly—such as the Athenian Pnyx or Roman forum—to realize that successful speeches in public settings often required both a strong voice and a conception of style suitable to sustain such a voice (cf. Johnstone).

9. Representation of pedagogy might include, e.g., Cic. *Inv.* and Anon. *Rhet. Her.* (educational treatises); Ruf. Rh. and Julius Severianus, *Praecepta artis rhetoricae* (abbreviated textbooks); Isoc. *Ep.* 6 and Cic. *Att.* 6.1 (letters); *P. Oxy.* 3235 and Sen. *Con.* 1.1.1–3 (school declamations); Pl. *Phdr.* 267d–68a and Cic. *de Orat.* 1.137–47 (indications of rhetorical pedagogy); Berlin, Antikensammlung, F2285 (cup, c. 500–450), man reading papyrus roll, youth writing in wax tablet (educational scene), and Naples 9066 (this chapter, note 7, educational site).

10. With reference to texts, Berkowitz and Squitier recognize at least 1186 works by 163 Greek authors relevant to rhetorical practice as follows (TLG authors from 5th cent. CE forward and of unknown date have been excluded): encomiastica—102 works by 25 authors (430–31); epistolographa—241 works by 92 authors (431–32); homiletica—556 works by 20 authors (434), oratio—287 works by 26 authors (435). The Latin canon of the Packard Humanities Institute provides access to about 309 works by 81 ancient Latin authors pertinent to rhetorical practice in the following categories: oratio—272 works by 67 authors; epistulae—36 works by 13 authors; panegyrici—1 work by 1 author. Both indices underrepresent individual rhetorical texts. Neither abstracts individual letters for all authors (e.g., Berkowitz and Squitier credit Synezius with one epistolary work, but that work contains 156 individual letters; similarly, the Latin canon assigns Cicero six epistolary works, when the number of his extant letters exceeds 400). Again, neither index attempts to abstract all evidence of orations, letters, and other rhetorical discourses from literary works (e.g., Berkowitz and Squitier do not account for Hortensia's oration to the triumvirs preserved in Appian [*BC* 4.32–34], neither does the Latin canon refer to Julius Caesar's speech on the Catilinarian conspiracy as reported by Sallust [*Cat.* 51.1–43]). Finally, the Latin canon omits all but one Latin speech from Mynors and completely excludes the Latin letters published by Cugusi. Aids for finding artifacts and venues concerned with rhetorical practice do not currently exist; nonetheless, typical instances might include BMCRE 3, Nrs. 1309–1311 (coin, c. 121–22 CE), depiction of Hadrian's eulogy of Plotina at the temple of Divus Julius in Rome (see Brilliant 134–35), and Eun. *VS* 488–89, a description of circumstances in which Prohaeresius delivered a declamation in an Athenian theater.

11. Some instances representing criticism are as follows: [Longinus] *Subl.*, Cic. *Opt. Gen.* (critical treatises), Arist. *Rh.* 3.17.10 on Isoc., Cic. *de Orat.*2.220–28 on Cras-

sus (technical treatises), Isoc. *Hel.* 14–15 on Gorg. (speech), S. E. *M* 2.4 on Hyp., Plu. *Cic.* (essays), D. H. *Pomp.,* Cic. *Att.* 1.13 (letters), Isoc. *Panath.* 201–65 (conversations), BMCRE 3, Nrs. 1309–11 (this chapter, note 10), audience with right arms raised toward Hadrian during his eulogy of Plotina (manifestation of audience response in an artifact), and Eun. *VS* 489–90 on audience reception of Prohaeresius as well as Cic. *Brut.* 289–90 on favorable audience response in the forum (depictions of spectator attendance and conduct at rhetorical performances).

12. Among representations of cultural apprehension of rhetoric might be noted the following: Ar. *Nu.* (comedic critique of rhetorical theory, education, and practice), Cic. *Cael.* 41 (oratorical comment on the state of rhetorical education), Petron. *Sat.* 1–5 (novelistic satire of rhetorical education), Juv. 7.139–214 (poetic satire on rhetors and teachers of rhetoric), Tac. *Dial.* (dialogic critique of rhetorical education and practice), Lucianus *Rh. Pr.* (literary satire on rhetorical education and practice), Suet. *Rhet.* 25.1.5–10; 25.1.12–2.1 (state opposition to rhetorical instruction in official edicts), Suet. *Ves.* 18 (state support of rhetorical instruction by Vespasian), Naples Inv. 5467 (sculpture [bronze bust], copy of Greek original by Polyeucton, c. 280 BCE, honorary portrait of Demosthenes found in Roman mansion at Herculaneum), Philostr. *VS* 589, Dio Cass. 73.17 (historical evidence for the Athenaeum at Rome, a venue for oratorical presentation, established c. 135 CE, by Hadrian).

WORKS CITED

Baldwin, Charles Sears. *Ancient Rhetoric and Poetic, Interpreted from Representative Works.* New York: Macmillan, 1924.

Berkowitz, Luci, and Karl A. Squitier. *Thesaurus Linguae Graecae: Canon of Greek Authors and Works.* 3d ed. New York: Oxford UP, 1990.

Berlin, James. "Revisionary Histories of Rhetoric: Politics, Power, and Plurality." *Writing Histories of Rhetoric.* Ed. Victor Vitanza. Carbondale: Southern Illinois UP, 1994. 112–27.

Bizzell, Patricia. "Opportunities for Feminist Research in the History of Rhetoric." *Rhetoric Review* 11.1 (1992): 50–58.

Bizzell, Patricia, and Bruce Herzberg. *The Rhetorical Tradition: Readings from Classical Times to the Present.* Boston: St. Martin's, 1990.

Bonner, Stanley F. *Education in Ancient Rome: From the Elder Cato to the Younger Pliny.* Berkeley: U of California P, 1977.

Brilliant, Richard. *Gesture and Rank in Roman Art. The Uses of Gestures to Denote Status in Roman Sculpture and Coinage.* Memoirs of the Connecticut Academy of Arts and Sciences, 14. New Haven: Connecticut Academy of Arts and Sciences, 1963.

British Museum. *British Museum Catalogue: Coins of the Roman Empire in the British Museum.* Vol. 3. Nerva to Hadrian. London: Trustees of the British Museum, 1936.

Brozka, Julius. *De canone decem oratorum Atticorum quaestiones.* Vratislaviae: Apud G. Koebnerum, 1883.

Burgess, Richard W. "The Dates and Editions of Eusebius' *Chronici Canones* and *Historia Ecclesiastica*." *The Journal of Theological Studies* 48 (1997): 471–504.

Cole, Thomas. "Canonicity and Multivalence: The Case of Cicero." In *The Rhetoric Canon*. Ed. Brenda Deen Schildgen. Detroit: Wayne State UP, 1997. 33–45.

Corte, Matteo della. *Case ed abitanti di Pompei*. Pompei-Scavi: Presso l'autore, 1954.

C[ovell?], W[illiam]. *Polimanteia, or, the Meanes lawfull and vnlawfull, to judge of the fall of a common-wealth, against the friuolous and foolish conjectures of this age. Whereunto is added, A letter from England to her three daughters, Cambridge, Oxford, Innes of Court, and to all the rest of her inhabitants: perswading them to a constant vnitie of what religion soever they are, for the defence of our dread soveraigne, etc. Elizabethan England in Gentle and Simple Life. Being I. England's Address to her three Daughters, the Universities of Cambridge and Oxford, and Lincoln's Inn: from Polimanteia, 1595. II. A Quest of Enquirie by Women to know whether the tripe-woman was trimmed, 1595*. Ed. Alexander B. Grosart. Manchester: Printed for the Subscribers [by C.E. Simms], 1881.

Cugusi, Paulus. *Epistolographi Latini minores*. 2 vols. in 3. Corpus scriptorum Latinorum Paravianum. Paravia: Io. Bapt. Paraviae, 1970–79.

Eagleton, Terry. "A Small History of Rhetoric." In *Walter Benjamin or Towards a Revolutionary Criticism*. London: Verso Editions and NLB, 1981. 101–13.

———. *Literary Theory: An Introduction*. Minneapolis: U of Minnesota P, 1983.

Eden, Kathy. "Hermeneutics and the Ancient Rhetorical Tradition." *Rhetorica* 5 (1987): 59–86.

Encyclopedia Britannica. 9th ed. 1875–89.

Fox, Michael V. "Ancient Egyptian Rhetoric." *Rhetorica* 1 (1983): 9–22.

Glenn, Cheryl. "Sex, Lies, and Manuscript: Refiguring Aspasia in the History of Rhetoric." *College Composition and Communication* 45 (1994): 180–99.

Halbertal, Moshe. "Authority, Controversy and Tradition." In *People of the Book: Canon, Meaning and Authority*. Cambridge: Harvard UP, 1997.

Halm, Carolus. *Rhetores Latini minores*. Lipsiae: Teubner, 1863.

Hasian, Marouf, Jr. "Rhetorical Studies and the Future of Postcolonial Theories and Practices." *Rhetoric Review* 20.1 (2001): 22–28.

Imber, Margaret. "Pudentilla's Anger: The Indirect Discourse of a Roman Matron." In *Rhetoric, the Polis, and the Global Village. Selected Papers from the 1998 Thirtieth Anniversary Rhetoric Society of America Conference*. Ed. C. Jan Swearingen. Mahwah, NJ: Erlbaum, 1999. 93–102

Jarratt, Susan C. *Rereading the Sophists: Classical Rhetoric Refigured*. Carbondale: Southern Illinois UP, 1991.

Johnstone, Christopher Lyle. "Communicating in Classical Contexts: The Centrality of Delivery." *Quarterly Journal of Speech* 87 (2001): 121–43.

Kennedy, George A. "The Origin of the Concept of a Canon and Its Application to the Greek and Latin Classics." In *Canon vs. Culture: Reflections on the Current Debate*. Ed. Jan Gorak. Wellesley Studies in Critical Theory, Literary History, and Culture. New York: Garland, 2001. 105–16.

Kermode, Frank. 1986. "The Argument about Canons." In *The Bible and the Narrative Tradition*. Ed. Frank McConnell. Oxford: Oxford UP. 78–96.

Knoblauch, C. H., and Lil Brannon. *Rhetorical Traditions and the Teaching of Writing.* Upper Montclair, NJ: Boynton/Cook, 1984.

Lu, Xing. *Rhetoric in Ancient China, Fifth to Third Century, B.C.E.: A Comparison with Classical Greek Rhetoric.* Columbia: U of South Carolina P, 1998.

Lunsford, Andrea A., and Lisa S. Ede. "On Distinctions between Classical and Modern Rhetoric." In *Essays on Classical Rhetoric and Modern Discourse*. Ed. Robert J. Connors, Lisa S. Ede, and Andrea A. Lunsford. Carbondale: Southern Illinois UP, 1984. 37–49.

Murphy, James Jerome, and Richard A. Katula. *A Synoptic History of Classical Rhetoric.* 2nd ed. Davis, CA: Hermagoras, 1995.

Mynors, R. A. B. *XII panegyrici Latini.* Scriptorum classicorum bibliotheca Oxoniensis. Oxford: Clarendon, 1964.

Oxford English Dictionary. 2nd ed. Oxford: Oxford UP, 1989.

Packard Humanities Institute, comp. *Latin Canon.* CD ROM. Ver. 5.3. Los Altos, CA: Packard Humanities Institute, 1991.

Pfau, Michael William. "Encomium on Helen as Advertisement: Political Life according to Gorgias the Barbarian." *Advances in the History of Rhetoric* 3 (1999): 11–22.

Ruhnken, David. "Historia critica oratorum Graecorum" (1768). In *Davidis Ruhnkenii opuscula, varii argumenti, oratoria, historica, critica.* Editio altera, cum aliis partibus, tum epistolis auctior. 2 vols. Lugduni Batavorum, apud S. et J. Luchtmans, Academiae typographos, 1823. 1: 310–92.

Schoeck, R. J. "Intertextuality and the Rhetoric Canon." In *Criticism, History, and Intertextuality.* Ed. Richard Fleming and Michael Payne. *Bucknell Review* 31.1 (1988): 98–112.

Shome, Raka. "Postcolonial Interventions in the Rhetorical Canon: An 'Other' View." *Communication Theory* 6 (1996): 40–49.

Smith, Martin Ferguson. *Diogenes of Oinoanda: The Epicurean Inscription.* La scuola di Epicuro, Supplemento 1. Naples: Bibliopolis, 1993.

Steffen, Georgius. *De canone qui dicitur Aristophanis et Aristarchi.* Lipsiae: Typis Reuschi, 1876.

Swearingen, C. Jan. "A Lover's Discourse: Diotima, Discourse, and Desire." In *Reclaiming Rhetorica.* Ed. Andrea Lunsford. Pittsburgh: U of Pittsburgh P, 1995. 26–76.

Vickers, Brian. *In Defence of Rhetoric.* Oxford: Clarendon, 1988.

Welch, Kathleen E. *Electric Rhetoric: Classical Rhetoric, Oralism, and a New Literacy.* Cambridge, MA: MIT P, 1999.

Woods, Marjorie Curry. "Among Men Not Boys: Histories of Rhetoric and the Exclusion of Pedagogy." *Rhetoric Society Quarterly* 22 (1992): 18–26.

FIVE

Rhetoric and Civic Virtue

Janet M. Atwill

Historical scholarship resembles nothing so much as the layering
of cities on an ancient site. Like the river confluences and defensible escarpments that have drawn successive waves of city-builders
to the same location, ideologically potent issues attract cohorts of
historians to the same topics. Historiography, in this view, is a
form of archaeology. Understanding the history of the history of
an event involves digging through the remains of previous historical accounts. . . . No scholar—at least no scholar today at the end
of three centuries of intense historical consciousness begins his or
her work fresh. Prior interpretations structure curiosity, point out
sources, and define what makes a plausible explanation.
          —Joyce Applebee, *Liberalism and*
          Republicanism in the Historical Imagination

WHILE THE IDEA OF civic rhetoric that we identify with classical traditions
may be one of our richest legacies, it may also be one of the most difficult to
appropriate. The province and pedagogy questions that arise when we critically examine civic rhetorical traditions are, to be sure, shaped by our various
disciplinary contexts. The texts of public discourse that have been studied in
speech communication departments have not always found as comfortable a
home in departments of English. Whatever our disciplinary setting, however,
we are confronted with similar questions—some reminiscent of ancient
debates concerning the ethics and province of rhetoric, others more specific to
our own polis. Would teaching rhetoric as a civic art mean focusing on the

invention of effective public discourse, or would it include the skills of deliberation necessary to the invention of a just public? What normative models of
gender, race, and class are embedded in conceptions of civic rhetoric? Would
a particular model of civic rhetoric necessarily bring with it a corresponding
model of political order?

My purpose is not so much to answer these questions as it is to probe
their terms and contexts. I shall do this by examining one dimension of the
civic rhetorical tradition—Greek notions of civic virtue. I explore civic virtue
because it is often invoked without being carefully defined to authorize conceptions of civic rhetoric. I suggest that models of virtue are, indeed, tied to
models of political order and that what we now call "civic virtue" was, in fifth-
and fourth-century Greek political and philosophical thought, part of a con-
stellation of contested notions of virtue, justice, and political order. In the
philosophical discourses of Plato and Aristotle, that contest is framed in terms
of two competing models of political order, known as *harmonia* and *isonomia*.
While philosophical treatises provide some of their most explicit descriptions,
the terms are not the exclusive property of philosophy, for *harmonia* and *isonomia* are commonplaces that appear in Greek literature from Solon to Thucydides and Isocrates. This chapter suggests that these ancient debates yield
three versions of virtue that are tied to *harmonia* and *isonomia*: virtue as social-
political order *(harmonia)*; virtue as political *technē (isonomia)*; and virtue as art
and honor, a kind of synthesis of *isonomia* and *harmonia*. I conclude with a
brief look at contemporary models of political order in two recent treatments
of civic virtue in rhetorical scholarship.

ANCIENT MODELS OF CIVIC VIRTUE

The challenges facing efforts to define *civic virtue* begin with the term itself.
The Latin root *civicus* generally means simply "belonging to citizens." Two of
the closest Greek equivalents for civic virtue are *political virtue (politikē aretē)*
and *political wisdom (sophia politikē),* both terms used by Protagoras and Aristotle. Strictly speaking, then, 'civic virtue' is something of an anachronism in
Greek philosophical and rhetorical treatises. Virtue is, however, tied to Greek
concepts of 'justice' and 'order'—political and otherwise. Gregory Vlastos
explains the conflation of the political and cosmological that was characteristic of Greek thought:

> Cosmic justice is a conception of nature at large as a harmonious association,
> whose members observe, or are compelled to observe, the law of the mea-
> sure. There may be death, destruction, strife, even encroachment (as in
> Anaximander). There is justice nonetheless, if encroachment is invariably
> repaired and things are reinstated within their proper limit. ("Equality" 156)[1]

By Vlastos' account, both natural and political orders consist in the equilibrium that results when a relation of restraint is established between its elements. But how are these elements and relationships defined? The two major answers to that question reside in *harmonia* and *isonomia*.[2] Vlastos explains that justice as *harmonia* views "harmony and nonencroachment as a relation between unequals" ("Equality" 156). In this model, elements are grouped and hierarchized so that equality might obtain, but it is equality *within* not *between* classes. With regard to Athenian political order, *harmonia* reflects the restricted democracy that preceded fifth-century reforms. In contrast, justice as *isonomia* defines relationships among elements of a whole in terms of equality: "Cosmic equality was conceived as the *guaranty* of cosmic justice: the order of nature is maintained *because* it is an order of equals" (Vlastos, "Equality" 156). The sense of equality in *isonomia* reflects the political order of Athenian democratic reforms at their most radical.

Both models are frequently described in terms of their "allocation" of shares in or claims to the state, both of which determine the extent of citizens' power. *Harmonia* invokes the laws of Solon, which gave citizens the right to participate in government based on their "ratable [or taxable] property" (Vlastos, "Solonian Justice" 80). Aristotle would later describe other versions of this state whereby citizens' shares are based on honor or merit: those with the most of either deserve the greatest share in the state. Justice as *isonomia* holds that all members of the state have an equal share or claim. This sense of justice is expressed in the democratic mechanism of the "lot" because the rotation of citizen service in the assembly made all citizens, at least with regard to this legislative function, equally responsible for the affairs of the state.

Aristotle refers to both models of justice throughout *Nicomachean Ethics* and *Politics*. In the passage below, "numerical equality" is equivalent to *isonomia* and equality "according to worth" to *harmonia:*

> (E)quality is of two kinds, numerical equality and equality according to worth—by numerically equal I mean that which is the same and equal in number or dimension, by equal according to worth that which is equal by proportion; for instance numerically 3 exceeds 2 and 2 exceeds 1 by an equal amount, but by proportion 4 exceeds 2 and 2 exceeds 1 equally, since 2 and 1 are equal parts of 4 and 2, both being halves. But although men agree that the absolutely just is what is according to worth, they disagree as was said before in that some think that if they are equal in something they are wholly equal [democrats], and others claim that if they are unequal in something they deserve an unequal share of all things [oligarchs]. (*Politics* 1301b30–35)[3]

Given the different values embedded in these versions of social order, it is hardly surprising that they would yield different concepts of virtue.

CIVIC VIRTUE AS SOCIAL FUNCTION

Civic virtue as social function is shaped by the oldest model of virtue in Greek culture, the heroic conception of *aretē*, the ideal of *kalos kagathos*, defined by noble birth and valor in battle. Homeric virtue, as Arthur Adkins explains, has less to do with conscience, moral reasoning, or private piety than it does with the social function and class position that are tied to nobility (36). Heroic *aretē* is one with the notion of the *aristos* as "the best in birth and rank" or the "noblest" (Liddell, Scott, and Jones 241). That it refers only to males goes without saying. As warrior, the *kalos kagathos* unites virtue and honor; as *aristos*, he unites virtue and class. The sense of the superlative in *aristos* grounds the identification of virtue with excellence.

The class character of this notion of virtue undergoes a number of changes in the sixth and fifth centuries BCE, as political reforms displaced requisites of birth with those of property. In *Politics*, Aristotle defines aristocracy as rule by the most virtuous: "aristocracy in the fullest sense seems to consist in the distribution of honors according to virtue" (1294a11–12). However, he acknowledges that, for a number of reasons, this aristocratic concept of virtue no longer accounts for "the best" citizens. In a discussion of types of constitutions, Aristotle defends the association of aristocracy with oligarchy. By custom, he observes, people "entitle those [constitutions] that incline towards oligarchy aristocracies, because education and good birth go more with the wealthier and also the wealthy are thought to have already the things to get which wrongdoers commit wrong" (1293b36–39).

In the political theories of both Plato and Aristotle, what remains of heroic virtue is its identification with class. As this logic goes, to the extent that there are class differences, there are corresponding differences in virtue. When differences in kind authorize the hierarchical ordering of parts, virtue and class reflect justice as *harmonia*. As Plato and Aristotle describe the respective virtues of different classes, however, virtue becomes identified not only with class function but also with the act of submitting to that function.

Plato's ideal republic is largely structured by this notion of class function. Socrates explains that "there is a specific virtue or excellence of everything for which a specific work or function is appointed" (*Republic* 353b). These "specific" virtues decide one's place in the state, and it belongs to the higher order art of statesmanship to determine the respective virtues of each group. This functionalism appears throughout Aristotle's *Politics*. Book 1 affirms that all parts of the state should partake of "*ēthikē aretē*," variously translated as "excellences of character" or "moral virtues" (1260a18, 21). This does not mean, however, that all elements are capable of achieving the same kind and level of virtue: "All should partake of them, but only in such manner and degree as is required by each for the fulfillment of his function" (1260a18–20). For example, "a slave is serviceable for the mere necessaries of life, so that clearly he needs only a small amount of virtue, in fact just enough to prevent him from failing in his tasks owing to intemperance and cowardice" (1260a34–37).

Aristotle tries to finesse these distinctions among parts of the state by pointing to one thing citizens do share, the security of their community:

> Now a citizen we pronounced to be one sort of partner in a community, as is a sailor. And although sailors differ from each other in function . . . the most exact definition of their excellence *(aretē)* will be special to each, yet there will also be a common definition of excellence that will apply alike to all of them; for security in navigation is the business of them all, since each of the sailors aims at that. Similarly therefore with the citizens, although they are dissimilar from one another, their business is the security of their community. (*Politics* 1276b21–31)

As the discussion progresses, however, it becomes clear that the common business of security is contingent on the virtue of citizens' fulfilling—and thus submitting to—their distinctive class functions.

Aristotle's concept of function and virtue is especially important in the context of debates concerning rhetoric and ethics since Aristotelian *phronēsis* is frequently accorded the task of defining rhetoric's ethical boundaries.[4] Aristotle would seem, however, to make it quite clear that *phronēsis* is not something shared by all parts of the state. Before offering the analogy of ship to state, Aristotle poses the question of whether or not the virtue of the *phronimos* (or *andros agathos*) is the same as that of the citizen *(politēs):* "[A]re we to hold that the goodness of a good man *(aretēn andros agathou)* is the same as that of a good citizen *(politou spoudaiou)?"* (*Politics* 1276b16–18). He draws on the functional model to affirm that they are not:

> (S)ince the state consists of unlike persons—just as an animal . . . consists of soul and body, and a soul of reason and appetite and a household of husband and wife and . . . master and slave, in the same manner a state consists of all of these persons and also of others of different classes in addition to these,— it necessarily follows that the goodness of all the citizens is not one and the same, just as among dancers the skill of a head dancer is not the same as that of a subordinate leader. It is clear then from these considerations that the goodness of a good citizen and that of a good man are not the same in general. (*Politics* 1277a6–15)

As Aristotle suggests in this passage, because the leader's function is distinct from that of the citizen, his virtue will also be distinctive:

> (P)ractical wisdom *(phronēsis)* alone of the virtues is a virtue peculiar to a ruler; for the other virtues seem to be necessary alike for both subjects and

rulers to possess, but wisdom *(phronēsis)* assuredly is not a subject's virtue, but only right opinion *(doxa alēthēs):* the subject corresponds to the man who makes flutes and the ruler to the fluteplayer who uses them. (*Politics* 1277b25–30).

Aristotle's treatment of *phronēsis* reaffirms his sense of the just state as one that is guided by *harmonia,* with practical wisdom the designated virtue of the "leader class."

Aristotle does describe a state in which virtue is more equally distributed. He admits that a state governed by a middle class may be characterized by virtue when citizens come together. What results, however, is a compromised sort of virtue that cannot be judged "by the standard of a virtue that is above the level of private citizens or of an education that needs natural gifts and means supplied by fortune, nor by the standard of the ideal constitution" (*Politics* 1295a25–30).[5] Since practical wisdom is not a citizen attribute that would ever be equally distributed throughout the polis, there are problems with invoking Aristotelian *phronēsis* as the authority for a democratic notion of civic rhetoric.

CIVIC VIRTUE AS POLITICAL TECHNĒ

Plato's *Protagoras* could just as easily have provided examples of justice as *harmonia* and virtue as social function, for the conflict between *isonomia* and *harmonia* is largely what is at issue throughout the dialogue. Plato's version of functional virtue foregrounds *technē*'s identification with expertise. According to this logic, classes have distinctive *technai,* which means they are in possession of distinctive forms of expertise; consequently, if politics is like any other art, it is restricted to a particular class. One of the most explicit descriptions of *isonomia* and *harmonia* in relation to expertise is found in Socrates' familiar discussion of virtue, art, and Protagoras's rhetorical instruction:

> Now I observe when we are collected for the Assembly, and the city has to deal with an affair of building, we send for builders to advise us on what is proposed to be built; and when it is a case of laying down a ship, we send for shipwrights; and so in all other matters which are considered learnable and teachable: but if anyone else, whom the people do not regard as a craftsman, attempts to advise them, no matter how handsome and wealthy and well-born he may be, not one of these things induces them to accept him; they merely laugh him to scorn and shout him down. (319b–c)

Socrates contrasts this reasoning with deliberation in the democratic polis, where "the man who rises to advise them on this way may equally well be a smith, a shoemaker, a merchant, a sea-captain, a rich man, a poor man, of good family or of none" (319d). Socrates' point, of course, is that it is democracy's folly not to view the ability to rule the affairs of state as a form of expertise.

Protagoras responds to Socrates' challenge with his version of *isonomia*, embedded in the Prometheus myth. The Sophist recounts that Zeus observed humankind coming together in cities, but "they did wrong to one another through the lack of *politikē technē*" (322b). Zeus responds by giving humankind the art of politics, which he identifies with respect and justice (*aidōs* and *dikē*). His emissary, Hermes, asks if he is "to deal them [*aidōs* and *dikē*] out as the arts have been dealt?"—according to the principle of compensation whereby "one man possessing medical art is able to treat many ordinary men, and so with the other craftsmen" (322c). Zeus responds that they must be distributed equally to all citizens: "[L]et all have their share; for cities cannot be formed if only a few have a share of these as of other arts" (322d). Thus Protagoras concludes that "virtue *(aretē)* is something in which no one may be a layman *(idiōteuein)* if a state is to exist at all" (327a).

Protagoras's depiction of social order, political art, and virtue may be viewed as richly complex or simply confused. Dependent as we are on Plato's presentation of Protagoras's position, that judgment may be difficult to make. At one point, Protagoras replaces *dikē* and *aidōs* with *dikē* and *sōphrosunē* ("justice" and "good sense"—or "moderation"), which are referred to in the singular as "this excellence *(aretē)*." Protagoras also invokes "justice" and the rest of *politikēs aretēs*, without clearly defining just what those virtues are. Despite these ambiguities, Protagoras's discussion of political art and the virtues of *dikē* and *aidōs* would seem to merit further scrutiny, especially given the problems that attend a democratic interpretation of Aristotelian *phronēsis*. Protagoras's conception of political order, however, is less ambiguous. His insistence that the art of politics be distributed to all exemplifies the key principle of *isonomia*. According to the anthropology that shapes his version of the Prometheus myth, diversity of function may create economic and social order; but only political art can create the social harmony that makes a political order viable.[6]

CIVIC VIRTUE AS HONOR AND ART

Isocrates' depiction of virtue and political order might be interpreted as a curious synthesis of *isonomia* and *harmonia*. He explicitly endorses one version of justice as *harmonia* by affirming a state in which one's share is relative to one's honor. At the same time, he offers in his rhetorical pedagogy a teachable (and, consequently, transferable) means of accruing honor. Thus, Isocrates might be said to have inverted Aristotle's formula that virtue merits honor; for Isocrates, honor seems to bring about virtue.

One of Isocrates' most explicit endorsements of *harmonia* is found in the *Areopagiticus*, where he contrasts it with *isonomia:*

> For those who directed the state in the time of Solon and Cleisthenes did not establish a polity . . . which trained the citizens in such fashion that they looked upon insolence as democracy, lawlessness as liberty, impudence of speech as equality, and license to do what they pleased as happiness *(eudaimonia),* but rather a polity which detested and punished such men and by so doing made all the citizens better and wiser. But what contributed most to their good government of the state was that of the two recognized kinds of equality—that which makes the same award to all alike and that which gives to each man his due—they did not fail to grasp which was the more serviceable; but, rejecting as unjust that which holds that the good and the bad are worthy of the same honors, and preferring rather that which rewards and punishes every man according to his deserts, they governed the city on this principle, not filling the offices by lot from all the citizens, but selecting the best and the ablest for each function of the state; for they believed that the rest of the people would reflect the character of those who were placed in charge of their affairs. (20–23)

The discussion continues with Isocrates' affirmation of the practice of "selecting the worthiest men" over election by lot (23).

While Isocrates praises the social-political structure of *harmonia,* his rhetorical pedagogy complicates it in other ways. For Isocrates, honor can be both earned and invented. A rhetorical education can make one strive for honor: "The stronger a man's desire to persuade his hearers, the more zealously will he strive to be honorable *(kalos kagathos)* and to have the esteem of his fellow citizens" (*Antidosis* 278). Moreover, rhetoric can create honor in words that may in varying degrees be confirmed in deeds. Isocrates writes in the *Antidosis:* "I wonder if you realize how many men have either come to grief or failed of honor *(atimous)* because of the misrepresentations of these orators. . . . Therefore, if you will only heed me and be sensible, . . . you will in some measure pay court to them in order that you may be held in honor both because of your own deeds and because of their words" (136–38).

The passages in which Isocrates describes the power of training in rhetoric to make up for deficits in nature are almost too numerous to mention. This Isocratean principle underscores the sense in which rhetoric as a teachable art is a kind of symbolic capital with the potential to increase one's share of honor. Thus, while Isocrates' politics appears to be grounded in *harmonia,* his rhetorical pedagogy suggests that those portions may be recalculated:

> I marvel at men who felicitate those who are eloquent by nature on being blessed with a noble gift, and yet rail at those who wish to become eloquent,

on the ground that they deem an immoral and debasing education. Pray, what that is noble by nature becomes shameful and base when one attains it by effort? We shall find that there is no such thing, but that, on the contrary, we praise, at least in other fields, those who by their own devoted toil are able to acquire some good thing more than we praise those who inherit it from their ancestors. And rightly so; for it is well that in all activities, and most of all in the art of speaking, credit is won, not by gifts of fortune, but by efforts of study. For men who have been gifted with eloquence by nature and by fortune, are governed in what they say by chance, and not by any standard of what is best, whereas those who have gained this power by the study of philosophy and by the exercise of reason never speak without weighing their words, and so are less often in error as to a course of action. (*Antidosis* 291–92)

Isocrates' timocracy in which honor can be earned (thus, to that extent, a meritocracy) is consistent with the principle of *harmonia* that accords relative, not absolute, shares in the state. At the same time, Isocrates' rhetorical pedagogy aims at enabling the recalculation of honor by which one's share is assessed. Recalculation is hardly equivalent to the equal distribution of *isonomia;* but where *harmonia* generally rationalizes social boundaries, Isocrates' pedagogy seems calculated to enable their transgression.

One cannot fairly address Greek 'civic virtue' without some discussion of Pericles' Funeral Oration. *Isonomia* and *harmonia* are both invoked in the speech, and the subject of honor is raised at two levels. The dead who are praised won honor through their demonstration of "manly courage" *(andros aretēn).*[7] In order to give them their due, Pericles makes a distinction between the *isonomia* of the democratic polis and the *harmonia* that justifies their special recognition. Pericles asserts that a democracy, where administration is "in the hands, not of the few but of the many," establishes "equality for the settlement of their [citizens'] private disputes" (II.xxxvii.1). In other words, though democracy ensures that citizens are equal before the law, it does not assume that they are equal in all things. "Public honors" may be conferred on a man "not because he belongs to a particular class, but because of personal merits" (II.xxxvii.1). Thus Pericles also affirms a timocracy, whereby shares in the state are won through honor; however, he distinguishes this version of *harmonia* from its aristocratic ancestor, which attributed honor on the basis of class.

At a second, subtler level Pericles, like Isocrates, ties honor to discourse. In this case, however, honor due is contingent on honor praised in speech.[8] In an epideictic commonplace, Pericles begins by denying honor's contingency and questioning speech's adequacy to do justice to the fallen men. Referring to the state's funeral ceremony, he says: "To me . . . it would have seemed sufficient, when men have proved themselves brave by valiant acts, by act only to make manifest the honors we render them" (II.xxxv.1). He suggests that it is unfair that "the valor of many men should be hazarded on one man to be believed or not according as he spoke well or ill" (II.xxxv.1). By the speech's conclusion, however, he suggests that only speech will ensure that "their glory survives" as they are "celebrated on every occasion which gives rise to word of eulogy or deed of emulation" (II.xliii.2). Pericles in no way proposes the rhetorical meritocracy later proposed by Isocrates; he does suggest, however, that honor has not been fully won until it has been recognized in discourse.

CIVIC VIRTUE AND CONTEMPORARY CONTEXTS

I hope I have shown, at the very least, that fifth- and fourth-century Greek sources present various configurations of the relationship between virtue and political order. Thus, however easily we invoke 'civic virtue' in contemporary discussions of civic rhetoric, it is a term that is far from univocal in the dominant surviving discourse of fifth- and fourth-century BCE Greece. By necessity, I have not raised the complicated debates about virtue, particularly in Aristotle, that we generally identify with ethics and philosophy. One implication of my argument thus far is that the disciplinary boundaries we draw among ethics, philosophy, and politics are neither as well defined nor as impermeable in fifth- and fourth-century Greek thought. Though discussions of virtue in antiquity do, indeed, take a number of forms, the relationship between virtue and political order is one part of that discussion that is frequently ignored.

Contemporary understanding of civic virtue has, however, been less influenced by the analysis of Greek models than by the terms of the ideological divisions that characterized eighteenth-century political debate.[9] If *isonomia* and *harmonia* are the models of political order that shaped ancient notions of civic virtue, their twentieth-century Western counterparts are liberalism and civic republicanism.[10] Both models take a variety of forms that reflect their complex and often ambiguous historical sources. For the purposes of this discussion, I provide the broadest possible definitions. Civic republicanism places virtue at the heart of social-political order, where it is identified with consensus concerning the "common good" in the context of civil society. While civic republicanism is generally identified with cultural and economic developments of eighteenth-century Europe, scholars also point to the influence of its precepts in the development of the United States's form of representative democracy and constitutional government.[11] By most accounts of civic republican virtue, the "common good" more accurately reflects the specific values of the propertied, educated classes, who have special responsibility for political rule in a republic. Liberalism, in contrast, privileges "freedom" over group consensus; and by some accounts, it is concerned with securing boundaries that protect competing visions of virtue—or "the good."[12] In other words, as John

R. Wallach puts it, "virtue, for liberals, is a function of liberty" (322). Liberalism is generally tied to sixteenth- and seventeenth-century European theories of a social order based on individual self-interest and an economic order based on free markets; thus competition—in the sense of competing interests—is at the heart of the liberal paradigm. And this paradigm has had a special hold on American culture and politics. As historian Joyce Appleby puts it, what "in Europe formed the program for a political party became in the United States a description of reality" (1).

A number of disciplines have critiqued the character of the political communities enfranchised by liberalism and civic republicanism. Feminist scholars, in particular, have argued that neither model fairly accounts for the injustices that result from the power differentials created by gender, race, and class. They suggest civic republicanism secures consensus either by suppressing dissent or by setting boundaries that create homogeneous deliberating bodies, whose shared interests and values make consensus a relatively easy task. Critics charge that this paradigm, in a manner of speaking, "blames the victim" because to invoke such specificities as gender, class, and race is to violate the civic republican principle that discourse must focus on only the "common good." As Nancy Fraser puts it, civic republicanism "limits deliberation to talk framed from the standpoint of a single, all-encompassing 'we,' thereby ruling claims of self-interest and group interest out of order" (130). In other words, civic republicanism effectively universalizes the values and interests of a particular class and denies the existence of conflicts of interest that create and reproduce injustices.

Liberalism, in contrast, has been criticized for providing no positive ethical base for political community and encouraging a brash rhetoric of "rights" over discourses of responsibility.[13] Critics argue that liberalism is no better than civic republicanism in accounting for the injustices of gender, class, and race as it similarly "disappears" injustices by claiming that democracy can prevail, as Fraser puts it, in the face of "socio-economic and socio-sexual structures that generate systemic inequalities" (65).[14] Fraser's critique, in particular, suggests the need for alternative models of justice and political community better able to deal with "systemic" inequities. Other scholars, such as Joan Williams, suggest that some synthesis or reconciliation is possible; thus Williams outlines what she calls a "neo-republicanism," characterized by "participation without exclusion, virtue without elitism" (321).

Liberalism and civic republicanism have shaped contemporary rhetorical scholarship in a number of ways. The freedom of speech secured by liberal theory has influenced concepts of civic rhetoric and theories of persuasion, while the privileging of deliberation about the common good that grounds civic republicanism has offered an ethical basis for rhetoric. The public sphere theory in Habermas's version of civic republicanism has exerted a special force on contemporary reconstructions of classical civic rhetoric. I point briefly to

two versions of civic rhetoric and virtue that illustrate their influence, Harvey
Yunis's *Taming Democracy* and Gerard Hauser's *Vernacular Voices*.[15]

Yunis draws on the classical rhetorical tradition to outline a political
rhetoric that enables a community to prosper, a rhetoric he suggests is
defined by Plato and practiced by Pericles and Demosthenes. The terms in
which he describes this rhetoric are clearly set by liberalism and civic republicanism; he argues, however, that this ideal rhetoric can accommodate both.
Yunis contends that the Athenian public was not so different from our own.
He draws on the liberal paradigm to describe that public as an "arena of managed conflict," where "democratic procedures guide an open competition in
which groups and individuals advance their interests while (ostensibly)
respecting the needs and rules of the community" (28). In this context, an
"ideal" political rhetoric can reclaim civic republican virtue to the extent that
it is capable of "instructing mature, autonomous citizens in the real choices,
problems, and best interests of the *polis;* establishing the authority of rationality in the public realm; or even summoning the *polis* into actuality as a
community" (28). This rhetoric mitigates liberal conflict since its mission is
to create "in the minds of the audience an enlightened self-understanding
that actually dispels conflict and realizes the politically harmonious community" (28). Thus, rhetoric protects the civic republican interest of defining the
common good; at the same time that liberal "individual self-interest is not
sacrificed" (29).[16]

If Yunis is read as accommodating both paradigms by subordinating
liberalism to republican virtue, Hauser might be read as challenging the
civic republican "public sphere" with the reformulated liberalism of his
"vernacular rhetorics." Hauser also invokes the classical tradition in his
articulation of a contemporary civic rhetoric, but to argue against, not for,
its adequacy as a model. Hauser insists that qualitative differences between
contemporary and Greco-Roman sites of public discourse challenge dominant conceptions of rhetoric, civic virtue, and the public sphere. Hauser
identifies Aristotelian *phronēsis* with rhetoric and civic virtue: "Aristotle's
argument on *phronēsis* firmly situated rhetoric within a politics based on
the ideal of civic virtue" (19). Hauser maintains, however, that this sense of
civic virtue is grounded in historically specific senses of the public and the
individual (not the least of which was the requirement that the "individual"
be male):

> Ancient rhetoric reflected the ideal of civic virtue permeating Greek and
> Roman political thought. This tradition emphasized the role of the individ-
> ual as a public person. A public performance whose virtuosity commanded
> respect was a personal accomplishment that signified *arete* for the Greeks
> and *virtu* for the Romans and would have included the oratorical accom-
> plishments of those in the public realm. (19)

Hauser's characterization of the relationship between virtue and public performance, which invokes Hannah Arendt, also resembles what I have called "civic virtue as honor and art"—to the extent that it stresses the recognition entailed in performance.[17] Hauser argues, however, this depiction is no longer useful because it was situated in a unique historical context, in which there was no "buffer between social and political life" (19).[18] Hauser explains that Athenian "ideals of civic virtue presuppose a public space that enables every citizen to speak and cast ballots in an official capacity" (40). Thus the "state" had no well-defined boundaries. Indeed, the context of citizen activity, at least in Athens, could not be defined in terms of Habermas's public sphere because "the ongoing negotiation of how Athenians would act and interact, or politics, fused discussions in the official assembly with those in the street" (19). Since "the political organized the social," according to Hauser, "Athenians had no need to conceptualize a public sphere as a discursive arena apart from that of the legislative assembly" (19). What they had, then, was a "public" without "civil society." Thus, Hauser follows Habermas in maintaining that civil society is a later European invention that irreversibly changed the character of contemporary "public(s)."

Hauser maintains that to hold to a "conception of rhetoric predicated on assumptions of civic virtues" is to reproduce assumptions concerning individuals and the "public" that are "inconsistent with the realities of contemporary public life" (20). Though contemporary civil society foregrounds the inadequacy of classical rhetoric and civic virtue, Hauser argues that our concept of "civil society" is just as inadequate to account for the "discursive arenas" that serve as contemporary public spheres, arenas which are "situated in the larger and not always coterminous arena of *civil society*" (20). Hauser accounts for these arenas in a rearticulated liberalism that conceptualizes "the public as a plurality of publics grounded on their capacity for rhetorical engagement" (14). In describing these publics as "*emergences* manifested through vernacular rhetoric," Hauser underscores that what is at issue is not the civic republican value of determining the "common good" that unites these publics, but rather the liberal value of legitimizing their distinctive characters (14).

CONCLUSION

The issues raised in this chapter are, of course, far more complicated than my summaries have suggested. Many senses of virtue persist in fifth- and fourth-century Greek thought; moreover, I have deliberately avoided addressing the public/private binary. While this opposition has shaped our conceptions of ancient democracy as well as the liberal/civic republican opposition, it raises issues that quickly proliferate beyond the boundaries of a single chapter.[19] Because I have suggested 'civic virtue' has been oversimplified, I am especially wary of proffering overly simple conclusions. I conclude with what might more accurately be characterized as reflections concerning civic virtue and our own attempts to define and teach civic rhetoric.

Like the work of Yunis and Hauser, my discussion of civic virtue is shaped by scholarly conventions with political stakes. A tradition of scholarship in classics and political philosophy has challenged the relatively benign story of Greek democracy found in many humanistic treatises by critiquing the social, political, and economic orders of fifth- and fourth-century BCE Athens. Even Vlastos points to a third model of justice that preceded *harmonia* and *isonomia,* arguing that *isonomia* as equality before the law displaced an older sense of equality as *isomoiria,* "equality of portion." He maintains that prior to democratic reforms appeals for justice from Attica's peasantry focused on economic, political equality—the redistribution of land, not the attainment of the franchise ("Isonomia" 352–53). In this context, the ascent of democratic law was an ambiguous victory, for it formalized—indeed, legalized—the separation of justice before the law from the just distribution of resources. Other discussions, such as *Class Ideology and Ancient Political Theory* by Ellen Meiksins Wood and Neal Wood, situate themselves more explicitly as left political critique. Similarly, many analyses of liberalism and civic republicanism, such as that of Nancy Fraser, are influenced by left theory that aims in part to expose the ways the scholarly discourses of philosophy and history have obscured the roles of class, race, and gender. The somewhat uncomfortable conclusion is that scholarship that foregrounds ideological critique is itself a historical and ideological product.

That scholarly interpretations are shaped by ideology is hardly a new observation; indeed, in English studies it may be less a hypothesis than an article of faith. However, this observation has proven to be particularly vexing for our efforts to define and teach civic rhetoric. The problem of what in the vernacular is simply "political bias" in civic rhetoric would seem to find two expressions. Version one is based on the assumption that a "democratic society" is an unassailable good. There are, however, various models of democratic society; and, as in the cases of Yunis and Hauser, these models have conflicting premises. In this context, the "problem" of civic rhetoric is less an issue of bias than it is a contest between competing theories of rhetoric and democratic order. Moreover, it would appear that according to this version of civic rhetoric, theoretical problems must be resolved before going on to create arts of public discourse. The second version sacrifices theoretical (and, perhaps, ethical) coherence in the interest of constructing effective arts of political discourse. Since this version stipulates that a civic art is instrumental, "bias" is an issue only for those who believe there is a neutral reference point from which it can be judged. Indeed, from this perspective civic rhetoric consists of the very arguments that version one views as symptoms of bias. When this second version of political rhetoric is done well, however, it is more likely to appear in the curriculum of professional political consulting than in a usable *technē* of popular political knowledge. Put another way, version one leads to theoretical coherence and disciplinary research; version two leads to art and professional school.

I end by suggesting that we rethink the role of theory as we consider what it means to be "stewards" of rhetoric as a civic art. Plato as philosopher and Aristotle in his philosopher's mantle offer perfectly coherent treatments of social order and virtue that should lead to equally coherent and virtuous states. However, both admit that these states are utopian ideals that could be created only by the rule of a wise philosopher. Isocrates' account of social order and Protagoras's account of virtue are, in contrast, far less coherent, but their "virtue" may be their orientation toward rhetorical practice rather than theoretical consistency. Aristotle offers us a rich and curious exemplar in the *Rhetoric*—a "theory" of rhetoric in the sense of an "account" of practice.[20] In other words, his discourse taxonomy and account of *peitho* provide the principles for organizing the "usable" topics of political argument in his polis, but what is at stake is an account of practice, not a theory of the state—or of the "public sphere." To question the role of theory is not to question its importance, for theory can help us see both the complexities of practice and its potential for reinvention. But I would suggest that one of the richest legacies of classical rhetorical traditions may be the relative "poverty" of its theories—its resistance to setting fixed boundaries to the always evolving and incalculable complexity of rhetorical practice.

NOTES

1. For more discussion of political and cosmological order, see Cynthia Farrar, *The Origins of Democratic Thinking: The Invention of Politics in Classical Athens*.

2. For another account of *harmonia* and *isonomia*, see Ellen Meiksins Wood and Neal Wood, *Class Ideology and Ancient Political Theory*.

3. For more critiques of *isonomia*, see Aristotle's *Politics* 1317b5; 1318a5–6.

4. I restrict this evaluation of *phronēsis* to Aristotle's version. For an account of Isocratean *phronēsis*, for example, see Takis Poulakos, *Speaking for the Polis: Isocrates' Rhetorical Education*, especially chapter 4.

5. Aristotle also qualifies his endorsement of *harmonia* in *Politics* 1302a3–16.

6. For an excellent discussion of these anthropological accounts, see Thomas Cole, *Democritus and the Sources of Greek Anthropology*.

7. Quotations from the oration are taken from the Loeb *Thucydides*.

8. See Nicole Loraux, *The Invention of Athens*.

9. Notable representatives include J. G. A. Pocock's historical accounts of the eighteenth century and Jürgen Habermas's philosophy of the public sphere. See Pocock, *The Machiavellian Moment*, and Habermas, *The Structural Transformation of the Public Sphere*. Alasdair C. MacIntyre's *After Virtue* is another important text from philosophy.

10. In fact, it is possible to find points of similarity between civic republicanism and *harmonia*, on the one hand, and liberalism and *isonomia*, on the other, but that is not my purpose here.

11. Representative democracy follows civic republicanism to the extent that representatives, though elected, constitute an elite class. For an excellent discussion of James Madison's efforts to ameliorate American liberalism with civic republicanism, see Wallach.

12. For one version of liberalism, see John Rawls, *A Theory of Justice*.

13. See John R. Wallach, "Two Democracies and Virtue," and Mary Ann Glendon, *Rights Talk: The Impoverishment of Political Discourse*.

14. More problems have been raised concerning the historical sources of these paradigms. Appleby and Wallach are only a few among many scholars who attribute the "revival" of civic republican virtue toward the end of the twentieth century to a reaction against the dominance of liberal ideology. They go so far as to suggest that the notion of civic republican virtue invoked in contemporary scholarship is more accurately characterized as a scholarly invention of the 1960s. In the 1980s and 90s, civic virtue also appeared in the popular political movement of communitarianism influenced first by the work of Robert Bellah and later by Robert Putnam; it was also invoked by political figures, such as William Bennett, and academics, such as Gertrude Himmelfarb and Stephen Carter.

15. Stephen Browne offers an important study of civic virtue in his *Edmund Burke and the Discourse of Virtue*. It is not discussed here since I am limiting my discussion to interpretations of ancient Greek concepts of civic rhetoric. For another discussion of eighteenth-century virtue, see Shelley Burtt, *Virtue Transformed: Political Argument in English, 1688–1740*.

16. Yunis is, of course, aware of the limitations of the Athenian public sphere. Beyond its critical exclusion of women, he acknowledges that it "is part of the paradox of ancient Greek democracy that it arose in a social-political context in which class conflict and class prejudices were traditional and throve undiminished" (25).

17. See Arendt, *The Human Condition*, part 2 in particular.

18. Hauser further explains, "Unlike the tradition of civic virtue, in which one's merit was established by public conduct, the civil society tradition founded the quality of relations with strangers in the individual self rather than the individual's public being. Individual actions were seen and judged by others in terms of *propriety* rather than *virtuosity*" (23).

19. For discussion of Greek conceptions of the public/private opposition, see David Cohen, *Law, Sexuality, and Society: The Enforcement of Morals in Classical Athens*, and S. Humphries, "Public and Private Interests in Classical Athens."

20. This is my argument in *Rhetoric Reclaimed*.

WORKS CITED

Adkins, Arthur. *Merit and Responsibility: A Study in Greek Values*. Oxford: Clarendon, 1960.

Appleby, Joyce. *Liberalism and Republicanism in the Historical Imagination.* Cambridge, MA: Harvard UP, 1992.

Arendt, Hannah. *The Human Condition.* 2nd ed. Chicago: U of Chicago P, 1998.

Atwill, Janet M. *Rhetoric Reclaimed: Aristotle and the Liberal Arts Tradition.* Ithaca: Cornell UP, 1998.

Browne, Stephen. *Edmund Burke and the Discourse of Virtue.* Tuscaloosa: U of Alabama P, 1993.

Burtt, Shelley. *Virtue Transformed: Political Argument in English, 1688–1740.* Cambridge and New York: Cambridge UP, 1992.

Cairns, Douglas L. *Aidōs: The Psychology and Ethics of Honour and Shame in Ancient Greek Literature.* Oxford: Clarendon, 1993.

Cohen, David. *Law, Sexuality, and Society: The Enforcement of Morals in Classical Athens.* Cambridge and New York: Cambridge UP, 1991.

Cole, Thomas. *Democritus and the Sources of Greek Anthropology. Philological Monographs,* no. 25. Cleveland: Western Reserve UP, 1967.

Farrar, Cynthia. *The Origins of Democratic Thinking: The Invention of Politics in Classical Athens.* Cambridge: Cambridge UP, 1988.

Fraser, Nancy. "Rethinking the Public Sphere: A Contribution to the Critique of Actually Existing Democracy." *Social Text* 25/26: 56–80.

Glendon, Mary Ann. *Rights Talk: The Impoverishment of Political Discourse.* New York: Free Press, 1991.

Habermas, Jürgen. *The Structural Transformation of the Public Sphere: An Inquiry into a Category of Bourgeois Society.* Trans. Thomas Burger. Cambridge, MA: MIT P, 1991.

Hauser, Gerard. *Vernacular Voices: The Rhetoric of Publics and Public Spheres.* Columbia: U of South Carolina P, 1999.

Humphries, Sarah C. "Public and Private Interests in Classical Athens." *Classical Journal* 73.2 (December/January 1977/78): 97–104.

Liddell, Henry George, Robert Scott, and Henry Stuart Jones. *A Greek-English Lexicon.* Rev. ed. 1940 Rpt. with supplement. Oxford: Clarendon, 1968.

Loraux, Nicole. *The Invention of Athens.* Trans. Alan Sheridan. Cambridge, MA: Harvard UP, 1986.

MacIntyre, Alasdair C. *After Virtue: A Study in Moral Theory.* 2nd ed. U of Notre Dame P, 1984.

Pocock, P. G. A. *The Machiavellian Moment: Florentine Thought and the Atlantic Republican Tradition.* Princeton: Princeton UP, 1975.

Rawls, John. *A Theory of Justice.* Cambridge, MA: Harvard UP, 1999.

Vlastos, Gregory. "Solonian Justice." *Classical Philology* 41 (1946): 65–83.

———. "Equality and Justice in Early Greek Cosmologies." *Classical Philology* 42 (July 1947): 156–78.

———. "Isonomia." *American Journal of Philology* 74.4 (1953): 337–66.

———. "Isonomia Politiké." In *Isonomia: Studien zur Gleichheitsvorstellung im griechischen Denken.* Ed. Jürgen Mau and Ernst Gunther Schmidt. Amsterdam: Hakkert, 1971.

Wallach, John R. "Two Democracies and Virtue." In *Athenian Political Thought and the Reconstruction of American Democracy*. Ed. Peter Euben, John Wallach, and Josiah Ober. Ithaca: Cornell UP, 1994.

Williams, Joan. "Virtue and Oppression." *Virtue* (Nomos XXXIV). Ed. John W. Chapman and Williams Galston. New York: New York UP, 1992. 309–37.

Wood, Ellen Meiksins, and Neal Wood. *Class Ideology and Ancient Political Theory: Socrates, Plato, and Aristotle in Social Context*. Oxford: Basil Blackwell, 1978.

Yunis, Harvey. *Taming Democracy: Models of Political Rhetoric in Classical Athens*. Ithaca: Cornell UP, 1996.

PART TWO

Possibilities:
Contemporary Rhetorical
Occasions and the Tradition(s)

SIX

A Human Measure

Ancient Rhetoric, Twenty-first-Century Loss

Susan C. Jarratt

From the chain of memory, cities are built.
—Herbert Muschamp, "The Memorial
Would Live in the Architecture"

THIS COLLECTION ADDRESSES the disciplinary tensions and struggles within rhetoric studies by posing questions about tradition: *the* tradition, multiple traditions, or the lack of a continuous tradition. In an active engagement with traditions, we preserve and value our rhetorical heritage but also view practices and institutions with the critical distance provided by our historical remove. A critical engagement with traditions calls into play the historiographic skills of recontextualization, selection, and recombination. In this chapter, rather than applying these processes in pursuit of educational projects or theoretical foundations, I ask how the rhetorical materials we have inherited can be called into service in a time of national crisis and public trauma. Where within our panoply of rhetorical materials (histories, theories, pedagogies, and practices) can we find explanatory power, guides for response, or even consolation for the events of September 11? For this purpose, I will be calling on familiar materials of ancient Greek rhetoric but construed more broadly than the canon of legal and political tools codified so effectively by Aristotle. That choice in itself implies a position in the debates about what defines "rhetoric" and its tradition.[1] Working from a view of rhetoric as both deliberative and performative, I look to ancient materials as resonant analogues for contemporary uses of public spaces as sites of contestation about violence and as scenes of mourning. This chapter is an attempt to capture a fleeting rhetorical moment, and in so doing, not to encompass or close off with understanding, but to measure, which is, according to Protagoras, the human purpose.

A Rhetorical Public

The availability of public space for deliberation over collective concerns can be considered a central legacy of the rhetorical tradition, a bequest manifest in the days and weeks after September 11. The immediate aftermath of the event produced a flood of rhetorical responses in every available medium, producing a national "public" of remarkable vividness, immediacy, and intensity. Of course the mass media (tv, radio, newspapers, periodical press) were fully mobilized. Commentary poured onto the internet; in a matter of days, lists of sites were circulating to organize and make sense of the flood.[2] Visual rhetoric found its most poignant expression in the fliers going up in New York, seeking news of lost friends and family members, and its repetition compulsion in the hypnotic replay of the eerily beautiful video images of planes colliding with buildings in an achingly blue sky.[3] Hastily arranged memorial services, teach-ins, lectures, and religious services were staged, followed by demonstrations against the coming war on terrorism. The occasion of September 11 has drawn huge numbers of people into a public, the features of which may be outlined through the terms offered by current theorists of the public sphere: it generates distinctive *topoi* of discussion (Eberly); it commands the attention of people brought together as strangers, involving them through both personal and impersonal modes of address (Warner); it is radically situational and action-oriented rather than stable and preexisting (Wells), although it often operates through familiar media. As both Bruce Robbins and Gerard Hauser point out, contemporary publics cannot be judged solely in terms set by the fifth-century Athenian precursor: an ancient civilization with only a few thousand members, a common culture, and a habit of deliberating orally in face-to-face settings. But neither are they as "phantasmagoric" as some twentieth-century commentators have suggested (see Robbins vii–xii). An argument for the viability of a September 11 public rests on the evidence of rhetorical resistance to the voice of the leader.[4]

Public discourse after September 11 was powerfully shaped from above. George W. Bush set the terms of rhetorical struggle from the outset along what would have been comically reductive lines (in other circumstances), firing up the patriotic engine, demanding without a moment's hesitation a military response, and driving rhetorical exchanges into Manichean oppositions:

good and evil, pro- and anti-American, for us or against us. Charlotte Bunch reminds us that it did not have to be that way: "[O]ur government's responses [to September 11] were not inevitable. This event could have taken the country in other directions, including toward greater empathy with what others have suffered, toward more concern for human security and the conditions that give rise to terrorism, and toward recognition of the importance of multilateral institutions in a globally linked world" (36). But, as she notes with understatement, "that would have required a very different national leadership" (46). Given the leadership with which we were saddled, one of the most notable rhetorical achievements of the year following September 11 was the insistence from many voices, including popular ones, on keeping questions open in the face of an overwhelming effort of control and containment on the part of the administration.[5] In this rhetorical field, another kind of heroism came into play, to draw on the language of Hannah Arendt, when people spoke and wrote about September 11 in terms other than those commanded by the president. Citing ancient Greek "self-understanding," Arendt claims that "to command rather than persuade [was] a prepolitical [way] to deal with people characteristic of life outside the *polis,* of home and family life, where the household head ruled with uncontested, despotic powers" (26–27). Refusing subjection under a patriarchal rhetoric of command, those who spoke out confirmed the "plurality [which] is the condition of human action" (8), inserting themselves into the world (175–76). The Athenian "crucible" providing Arendt with the framework for her vision of a public realm counts as one among many possible sites of ancient Greek rhetorical practice that, brought into conjunction with contemporary events, create a critical resonance. Hearing echoes of ancient rhetorical tropes, arguments, or rituals in September 11 rhetoric, we may ask what is being reproduced, what changes, and to what effect.

Over the course of a year, the rhetorical window narrowed considerably. Daily bombardments of government-generated rhetoric telling us not only what kind of sense to make of September 11 but how to mourn entered a public sphere shaped as well by efforts from many quarters to resist a centralized control of the public discourse. This chapter explores tensions created by this resistance, each of which finds its echoes in ancient Greek scenes. More specifically, it examines struggles to define the space of the nation and the rhetorical possibilities released by acts of mourning.

THE SPACE OF THE NATION

The attacks of September 11 mark only the second violation of U.S. national boundaries by an act of aggression. As such, they provoked a jarring re-cognition of national space and identity. Postmodern theorists of the political have argued for the decline of the nation as a center of power in the twenty-first century (Hardt and Negri), and yet September 11 drove the United States under the administration of George W. Bush into a frenzy of hyperbolic nationalist rhetoric.[6] "America" and "Americans" were under attack and must retaliate. The multiple targets, including the Pentagon and presumably, the White House along with the World Trade Center towers, suggested to most a symbolic merging of all industrialized, developed "Western" civilizations and economies into the sole remaining first-world power. We *are* the world, as the song goes, predicting the synecdoche that Bush's National Security Strategy document offers without apologies: the United States is demonstrably and justifiably dominant in the world theater and will use its power accordingly. This geopolitical ideology has not gone unchallenged in the spatial rhetorics generated by September 11.

In his influential study of nationalism, *Imagined Communities,* Benedict Anderson offers a spatially oriented explanation for the cultural roots of nationalism through which, by reading him somewhat aslant, we may gain perspective on the rhetorical orientations of national space post-September 11, as well as an angle of vision on ancient rhetorical parallels. Anderson sets the formation of Western European and North American nation-states in the eighteenth century in relation to two preceding, large-scale cultural formations: religious community and dynastic realm (9–22). Within both of the earlier political organizations, a sacred language with a written script created an imagined cosmic centrality, despite the geographical realities of widely spread territories. Membership was open to others who learned the language regardless of their "race" or other kinds of "otherness" (13). By contrast, "[i]n the modern conception, state sovereignty is fully, flatly, and evenly operative over each square centimetre of a legally demarcated territory. But in the older imagining, where states were defined by centres, borders were porous and indistinct, and sovereignties faded imperceptibly into one another" (19). Presumably the United States would fit the description of the modern state with its clearly demarked borders, yet George Bush's language after the attacks sketched a different picture. Adopting a cosmological and highly polarizing rhetoric from the very outset—a rhetoric that he has only slightly modified in the year since the attacks, Bush articulates an ideological space akin to the cosmology Anderson designates "religious community": "America" is the center, both geographically and ideologically, a geographic center that is simultaneously a moral center, moral clarity coming down on command of the leader, not to be challenged. The effect, enforced overtly through censures of any questioning of government decisions, is an attempt to block the rhetorical participation of a public inhabited by citizens with the capacity for independent judgment.[7]

The most prominent sign of a premodern, cosmological rhetoric is Bush's immersion in a moral world divided into good and evil. A search of the almost

900 speeches archived on the White House website (as of early December 2002) produced 315 containing the word *evil*. The number of references indicates that resorting to a simplistic, dualistic moral framework was for Bush not a momentary impulse indulged in the depths of grief and rage but is rather a deeply held world view. In his first address to the nation after September 11, at the National Day of Prayer and Remembrance in the National Cathedral, the president initiated the pattern:

> Just three days removed from these events, Americans do not yet have the distance of history. But our responsibility to history is already clear: to answer these attacks and rid the world of evil. War has been waged against us by stealth and deceit and murder. This nation is peaceful, but fierce when stirred to anger. This conflict was begun on the timing and terms of others. It will end in a way, and at an hour, of our choosing.[8]

A few days later, the president reiterated the theme in more spontaneous language:

> Nobody can threaten this country. Oh, they may be able to bomb buildings and obviously disrupt lives. But we're too great a nation to allow the evil-doers to affect our soul and our spirit. (September 18, 2001, Rose Garden)

Prompt reactions to Bush's apocalyptic rhetoric generated a discussion of the difference between modern and premodern world views and moral systems. In a *Los Angeles Times* article of September 18, 2001 ("When Evil Itself Becomes the Primary Foe"), Mary McNamara and Lynell George describe Bush's language as "epic," "biblical," and "even mythic." Placing him within the history of presidential rhetoric, they report that historians can find no other example of a president "naming evil itself as his primary opponent." Interviewing religious scholars and leaders, the journalists discovered a substantial measure of alarm and a hope that Bush would modify and quantify his accusations at a later time. Professors of comparative religion identified Bush's language with the Crusades, and one (Diane L. Eck of Harvard) made the simple yet profound observation that "to rid the world of evil is not a response that is possible by human beings" (column 2). A few people interviewed believed that the situation called for hyperbolic language. A scholar of the French Revolution, Simon Schama, pointed out that the attackers had basically rejected Enlightenment values of tolerance. Bush himself, speaking at a mosque in support of Muslims, is quoted at the end of the article citing the Koran to the effect that evil will come to those who do evil. The irony of Bush's evocation of a fundamentalist pronouncement following the distinction made by Schama is not pointed out by the journalists, but the placement of the quotation at the end of the article strongly suggests such a reading.

Only a few days after the events, Indian novelist and activist Arundhati Roy published an opinion piece in *The Guardian* picking up similar themes. Roy makes explicit what was implicit in the *Los Angeles Times* article: Bush and Bin Laden "borrow" each other's rhetoric, both trading on "loose millennial currency" of good and evil (8). Roy interprets America's response to the attacks as an indirect expression of unbounded national space. America's grief, she writes, is "immense and immensely public." Locating the events of September 11 within a global context of ongoing acts of terror of greater and lesser magnitude, Roy observes that Americans "usurp the whole world's sorrow to mourn and avenge only their own." Despite the fact that Bush's speeches are laced with Enlightenment concepts of 'liberty,' 'tolerance,' and 'human dignity,' his rhetorical actions—driven by the vision of evil-doers to be banished—emerges from a cosmic sense of national presence—a national vision whose frame is filled by a center fading to the dimly perceived boundaries Anderson describes.[9] When Roy advises that America must acknowledge "that it shares the planet with other nations, with other human beings," she offers a critique of Bush's cosmological world picture (6). The most damning example in her essay is the government's first marketing label for the action against Afghanistan: "Infinite Justice." Once again, not a mission to be achieved by humans, this plan, Roy argues, is a particular insult to Muslims, "who believe that only Allah can mete out infinite justice." "Bush can no more rid the world of evil-doers than he can stock it with saints," Roy writes. In her working out of the algebra of her title, Roy asks, to balance Bush's demand for the extradition of Bin Laden, for the extradition of Warren Anderson, chairman of Union Carbide at the time of the Bhopal gas leak that caused sixteen thousand deaths in 1984. The tension here, then, is between different spatial constructs, each accompanied by a moral vision. Over against the cosmological space of "America," and a black and white moral clarity, many other participants in the September 11 public posed a radically different geographical configuration. In the words of Schama, "Americans are, for the foreseeable future, fated to live inside, rather than alongside, the imperfect, dangerous world" and must cultivate capacities of moral judgment of adequate complexity to encompass that geographic disposition.

Which rhetorical traditions might be brought to bear in assessing questions of space and national identity? Although the "rational"(Havelock) democratic political culture of fifth- and fourth-century Athens is substantially different from the civilizations of Southeast Asia and China on which Anderson bases his formulations, it nonetheless provides notable examples of rhetoric wherein the imagined *polis* is grounded in a mythical past. The ideology of ethnic purity attached to geographic identity is captured in the concept of 'autochthony' and articulated powerfully in epideictic oratory presented on occasions of national ritual: the consummately Greek institutions of the state funeral and the Olympic games. But the broad sweep of ancient

Greek rhetoric serves as a uniquely flexible source for reflection on these questions because of its history as a tool of imperial power (during the emergence
of a pragmatic political Athenian rhetoric in the fifth century BCE) and later
as the practice of a spatially colonized, geographically dispersed, but culturally
privileged population during centuries of Roman rule. In addition to those
sources providing models of a political ideology of greatness connected with
the geographical centrality of Athens, later Greco-Roman sources present a
more complex spatial rhetoric.

The rhetoric of boundless global mastery appears in the famous funeral
oration attributed to Pericles in Thucydides' history. Delivered at the height
of Athens' power (II.31), just at the outset of the war with Sparta (431 BCE),
the oration records reactions to the shock of territorial violation similar to
those after September 11: "But when they saw the [Spartan] army at Achar-
nae, only seven miles from Athens, they could no longer put up with the situation. Their land was being laid waste in front of their very eyes—a thing the
young men had never seen happen" (II.23). In an oration renowned for its
articulation of democratic principles, Pericles, in this threatening moment,
does not fail to assert Athens' imperial dominance before an audience composed of both citizens and foreigners (II.36): "Mighty indeed are the marks
and monuments of our empire which we have left. . . . For our adventurous
spirit has forced an entry into every sea and into every land" (II.41). Further,
he urges his listeners not to demand a rationale for continuing to risk the lives
of young men in battle but rather to immerse themselves in blinding patriotic
passion: "I could tell you a long story (and you know it as well as I do) about
what is to be gained by beating the enemy back. What I would prefer is that
you should fix your eyes every day on the greatness of Athens as she really is,
and should fall in love with her" (II.43). We might imagine, from these brief
passages, that we had entered the unbounded geography and temporality of
Anderson's cosmological episteme, were it not for the rich record of debate
during the century and a half of Athenian hegemony.

In an example from the later Greco-Roman period, on the contrary, we
find a city rhetoric that celebrates a widely diverse and mixed genealogy (both
mythic and historic) and a concrete geographic location at the periphery of
the Roman Empire rather than at its imagined center. Libanius, a fourth-century CE "Greek" rhetor, praises his home city of Antioch in such terms in an
Olympic oration, adapting a by-then archaic classical language and traditional
rhetoric of praise to a colonial context: "My attitude, I must confess, will not
be like that of others, who force themselves to demonstrate that the place
whose praises they sing, whichever it may be, is the centre of the world
[chôrion meson]" (Norman, para. 14). Despite this gesture of displacement, the
rhetor argues that Antioch is, in fact, the best or finest in every other way.
Libanius' language associates geographical centrality—being in the middle—
with a kind of superiority gained through force or violence (kratos, suggesting

strength, might, and prowess), subtly calling to his audience's mind the power of Rome (the obvious but unnamed candidate for "center of the world"). But by minimizing reference to Rome itself, he diminishes its importance in a combined gesture of casual acquiescence and disregard. The empire becomes an only faintly perceived ground against which the surpassing beauties of Antioch are sketched as the figure. Introducing the topos of the best, first, or finest, the Greco-Roman rhetorician implicitly places Antioch at what might be termed an "aesthetic" or "cultural" center without having to argue for its geographic or political centrality in relation to Rome. In this complex *ekphrasis*, spatial description shades into an ideological gesture, but one that differs decidedly from the classical orators' assertions of the centrality of Athens. An ancient Greek rhetorical tradition including both Pericles and Libanius leaves a legacy not only of bombastic nationalistic aggrandizement but a complex record of memory practices that take on renewed significance under the current conditions.

MEMORY

> It is hard no doubt to offer consolation to those borne down with griefs like these. For sorrows are not stilled by word or law; only the individual's temper, and the measure of his feeling for the dead, can set the limit to his mourning.
> —Hyperides, "Epitaphios"

Many people died on September 11 in a very contained space. The fall of the World Trade Center towers brings to mind the grisly story underlying Roman rhetoricians' memory tricks. The Greek poet Simonides, so the story goes, was rewarded for his praise of the gods by being called out of a banquet hall just before the roof fell in, killing the revelers inside. The poet could identify the bodies, crushed beyond recognition, because he remembered where they were sitting.[10] The process of coming to know who died on September 11 became a massive work of public memory. In ancient rhetoric, memory work merges seemingly pedestrian *techne* for memorizing speeches with deeper reflections on the relationships among personal loss, social connection, and public life.[11] Some of the memory discourse after September 11 could be styled expressive: outpourings of personal grief at the loss of friends and relatives and at the destruction of places of living and working in one of the world's great cities. But, as Casey Nelson Blake observes in a reflection on the political possibilities of modernist memorial architecture, "[c]ivic spaces can begin with mourning" (46). Analyzing the rhetoric of mourning and memory reveals something about the nature of such civic spaces under construction after September 11.

It is worth noting that Bush's first major address concerning the attacks was given on a day of Prayer and Remembrance. The September 11 dead were not soldiers, though they have been called "heroes." That they died in an event defining the nation subjects them to rhetorical appropriation for projects of national ideologizing and war making. Anderson argues that nations, like the religious systems that precede them as major systems of cultural organization, arise out of and renew themselves through anonymous death and memorials. The Athenian funeral oration offers the prime example of this civic work: the nameless soldier being buried in a mass grave is essential to the ideological tasks of validating warrior citizenship over any other affiliation or identity, guaranteeing the reproduction of soldiers, the pacification of the women who bear them, and the timely willingness of all to perpetuate the processes of war, death, and memorializing. If one of the homogenizing ideological impulses of the nation is turning multitudes into "a people" (Hardt and Negri 103), then the spontaneous, random, and populist character of memorializing that took place in New York's Union Square in the first weeks after the events could be counted as a triumph of counterpublic rhetoric:

> Flags and patriotic songs, antiwar and antiracist banners, signs demanding vengeance and signs imploring forgiveness, prayer cards, poems and letters written to loved ones and strangers alike, handmade models for monuments, heartbreaking "missing" posters, the intense perfume of scented candles, incense and mounds of flowers, rhythmic drumming by Buddhist monks, performances by Julliard cellists and the sounds of quiet weeping briefly claimed the park as a site for collective grief and reflection. (Blake 46)

Who controls the power to describe? In times of war, that power is negated (Dawes). The lack of coordination, of a single identifiable "argument" or identity in this scene, gives support to those public sphere theories that value the performative.[12] Tracking the rhetorical power to describe and define the nature of loss through the weeks and months after September 11 takes us down a path of narrowed rhetorical possibilities. This pull between multiple, personal acts of mourning and the nationalistic efforts at homogenization is a second significant tension of the post-September 11 public.

Inspired by the homemade missing persons fliers that began appearing almost immediately, the *New York Times* began running a series of brief obituaries with photos called "Portraits of Grief." Begun on September 14 and continued as a daily feature until December 31, 2001, the series published "informal and impressionistic" accounts of people who lost their lives on September 11: for each, not a resumé but a snapshot, in the words of the article published at the end of the daily run of the series (Scott).[13] The series gave faces and names to the WTC victims, offering a way of mourning persons rather than an anonymous mass. Journalist Scott claims the feature became "a sort of national shrine."

What kind of memory is being crafted through this journalistic inspiration? The victims of September 11 did not die in battle, but the circumstances of their death—and the ways they are mourned—placed them in the middle of a struggle over national identity. By what means is it possible to take account of an individual death, or of all of them, somehow disentangled from the national discourse? Marita Sturken's analysis of the NAMES Project AIDS Memory Quilt provides an informing parallel to the difficulties of this effort.[14] She describes the quilt as a project in cultural memory with national significance, which began, like the first responses to September 11, as a spontaneous and disorganized performance of grief. By 1985, the magnitude of the devastation that would be wrought by AIDS began to be felt in San Francisco. On the occasion of the annual commemoration of the murders of Mayor George Moscone and Harvey Milk, San Francisco's first gay supervisor, people mounted placards bearing the names of people who had died of AIDS on buildings along the route of the memorial walk. The placards suggested to activist Cleve Jones the need for a memorial and the form it might take. He created the first panel with a national audience in mind and organized the NAMES project; he wanted it to "call upon the conscience of the nation" (qtd. in Sturken 186). Like the Portraits of Grief, the NAMES project enacts a singular process of mourning, of recognizing the person who had lived, in the context of a fraught public issue of national significance. "Each panel responds to the question: How can this person be remembered? What elements will conjure up their presence?" (188). The need for people to grieve publicly post-September 11 was often expressed through the *topos* of connection. Of the AIDS quilt, Sturken remarks, "[T]he creation of an object in the face of death is an act of connection" (98). The events, it was repeated again and again, brought people together. Uncoordinated acts of mourning responded to the human need for intimacy and connection outside the bounds of established rituals.[15]

Both the September 11 fliers (and their more coordinated off-shoot, the Portraits of Grief series) and the NAMES Project can be considered contemporary examples of epideictic rhetoric. In the epigraph for this section, we see an ancient Greek rhetor, some hundred years after Pericles, cracking open the solid facade of collective mourning most characteristic of the funeral oration to allow for the particularity of grief. Hyperides offered this funeral oration in 332 BCE at the very end of Athens' attempts to avoid conquest by Macedonia. Perhaps it was the desperation of the historical moment and the inevitability of defeat that enabled an opening within such a heavily coded nationalistic genre. Even George Bush touched this chord briefly in his first public address after the events: "We will read all these names. We will linger over them, and learn their stories, and many Americans will weep" (Day of Prayer and Remembrance, September 14, 2001). What is most valuable about unscripted acts of mourning, so briefly untouched by "word and law," their temporality seemingly unlimited, becomes painfully apparent later, when we see the state apparatus channeling and choreographing grief in patterns of ritual that enlist grief and connectedness to nationalistic ends.

The one-year memorial, a full-day affair broadcast on all the network tv channels, went a long way toward coopting the particularity of public grieving. The official events began at the Pentagon and ended at Ellis Island, on which occasions the president offered remarks. In the morning service, he denied both the capacity to measure grief and the possibility of understanding: "The 184 whose lives were taken in this place—veterans and recruits, soldiers and civilians, husbands and wives, parents and children—left behind family and friends whose loss cannot be weighed. The murder of innocence cannot be explained, only endured." The rhetorical trope of incalculable loss can be understood as a highly conventional gesture through which a speaker respectfully does not presume to be able to take such a measure for another, to mark an arbitrary limit for another's loss. But the very next phrase—"murder of innocents"—in fact offers its own implicit calculus, filling in enthymematically the explanation denied by the predicate but fully worked out in the administration's relentless rhetoric of retaliation through war promulgated over the past year. The terms of grieving set here deny the audience what Simon Schama terms "the educative power of melancholy," for the last thing the administration wants is a populace thinking through a range of causal factors on terms other than those already determined by the state. At the end of the day, Bush more directly alludes to those terms, suggesting that the fitting memorial for every person lost could be encompassed within national identity and policy: "We resolved a year ago to honor every last person lost. We owe them remembrance and we owe them more. We owe them, and their children, and our own, the most enduring monument we can build: a world of liberty and security made possible by the way America leads, and by the way Americans lead our lives" (September 11, 2002, Ellis Island). The ideological filaments of the classical funeral oration enmesh their newest audience.

At the center point of this event, a service in New York at "Ground Zero," the nation was embodied in the president, who walked among the survivors, wordlessly, praying with them, touching them. Through this performance, Bush, accompanied by his wife, enacted what Jürgen Habermas describes as the feudal mode of representative publicity. In the premodern era, the lord and lady appear before the people, creating through their appearance rather than through language an aura that expresses power (Habermas 5–12). The semiotics of dress and decoration communicate its presence. On September 11, 2002, red, white, and blue were mandatory dress for subjects as well as rulers in a mode of publicity carried forward from the prenational and premodern province of medieval aristocrats.[16]

Even though survivors, the press, and the government went to lengths to proclaim the personalization of the "tragedy," the memorial event effectively homogenized rather than particularized memory. The reading of the names on September 11, 2002, in a layering of two modes of publicity, produced a public "private" for national consumption. The "individuals" named are not citizens except in a nonspecific way; that is, as the naming was folded into the ritual of representative publicity, the dead become tokens rather than deliberative agents.[17] Despite the differences among victims—made much of in a celebration of America, the melting pot—the rhetorical force of the performance collapsed them into a single identity as "American." NPR radio commentator Scott Simon, in his editorial on Saturday, September 14, 2002, remarked on the international flavor of the names: "[I]n any ten you could here echoes from all over the world." He noted the variety of occupations among the victims, a recital of which began to sound like the children's chant: butcher, baker, Indian chief. But he reassures his listeners that, ultimately, they are "just names," with nobody adding information such as sex, occupation, or nationality in the recital. For Simon, there is "something reassuringly American in that toll of names rolling on." Even though they had come to America from all corners of the world (here he names a number of countries with violent histories, some involving U.S. military involvement), they have become "an assembly of names" that will "rest in the soil of one nation, indivisible." No more lingering is necessary: a single memorial gesture consolidates the power of a great nation.

CONCLUSION

In the analysis of a time-bound, public scene of rhetorical performance, ancient rhetorical materials—of space, memory, nation—have made a return, as John Bender and David Wellbery might say—not a repetition but a dynamic recasting. Even if one accepts the historiographical argument that "rhetoric" as a central organizing cultural force and *paideia* is no longer in operation (Bender and Wellbery's thesis), its elements remain at hand, disarticulated into a polyvocal array of resources. The brief touchpoints offered here establish that in both ancient Greece and the United States of the twenty-first century, rhetoric has been used to define and consolidate the power of an imperialist polis and to organize mourning in its service but that, at the same time, both operations have been resisted and disrupted by counterdiscourses and practices. There is no returning to a golden age of ancient rhetoric. But the rhetorical responses to a national trauma verify that a twenty-first-century public is not entirely phantasmagoric and that rhetorical traditions continue to prove their viability as a measure of a most human experience.

NOTES

1. See Patricia Bizzell and Bruce Herzberg for a theory-based definition of rhetoric. Richard Graff and Michael Leff (this volume) argue for reorienting the tradition around pedagogy. In a related debate, Jeffrey Walker makes a strong case (against, e.g., Edward Schiappa) for locating rhetoric's Western origins in a wide field of epideictic practices, including ceremonial rituals, epic, and lyric poetry, rather than in the influential but short-lived political rhetoric of Athenian democracy.

2. Such resources are difficult to document because of their ephemeral nature, but one example of a site that brought together a range of materials in the weeks following the attack is the London-based, English language global forum "opendemocracy" (www.opendemocracy.net).

3. Although the visual rhetorics of September 11 are deserving of extensive analysis, I will confine this short chapter to verbal texts. Slovoj Zizek's "Welcome to the Desert of the Real," available electronically within days of the attack and published later in print format offers reflection on the semblance of reality and the reality of semblances in American life that were shattered—or at least seriously disordered—by the video footage of the World Trade Center towers collapsing into rubble.

4. Any such judgment is of necessity somewhat arbitrary within a humanistic frame of scholarly argument. Louis Menard, for example, in a lengthy review of books published about September 11 within the first year, complains about the lack of resistant discourses. Perhaps for dramatic effect, he overlooks vast quantities of periodical journalism. Charlotte Bunch cites the same question asked by non-U.S. feminists in the international scene about feminist voices from within the United States. In this case, the questioners may not have had access to the steady stream of feminist commentary on September 11 by journalists, academics, students, and ordinary citizens (see, e.g., Ehrenreich, Pollit, Terrell). Perhaps future studies of a quantitative nature will be able to confirm or refute the claim made here that September 11 provoked a remarkable range of divergent discourses from citizens, journalists, and even prominent government figures. Democratic politicians were notably and almost universally absent from this counterpublic-in-process.

5. For a small sample of citizen response, see Ansary, Hurley, and Nees.

6. The debates about geopolitics in the postmodern, neocolonial, or neoliberal era are too complex to rehearse in this brief chapter. See Hardt and Negri for the case against "nations." From another perspective, Hommi Bhabha notes that more traditional political ideas of nationhood cannot be understood as "definitively superseded by those new realities of internationalism, multinationalism, or even 'late capitalism,' once we acknowledge that the rhetoric of these global terms is most often underwritten in that grim prose of power that each nation can wield within its own sphere of influence" (1). For the purposes of this analysis, the barrage of nationalist rhetoric, along with the power of the United States to unilaterally wage war in its own name, will be taken as evidence that the nation continues to wield both symbolic and material power in the twenty-first century.

7. The suppression of dissent by the government after September 11, as well as the erosion of civil liberties via new laws such as the USA PATRIOT act, are subjects worthy of separate treatment and can only be alluded to briefly here. For a small sample, see Fears, Glenn, and Lancaster.

8. References to presidential speeches were obtained originally from multiple sources (newspapers, radio and television broadcast, etc.). For ease of reference, I will cite them parenthetically in the text by date and location of the speech. Full texts (and in some cases audio replays) can be obtained from the White House website (http://www.whitehouse.gov/). On President Bush's role as "national chaplain" in the wake of September 11, see Silberstein.

9. Some readers may recall a parodic map circulating in the 1980s of Reagan's distorted Amero-centric imaginary featuring a globe-hogging United States with a red tide lapping at the Rio Grande River in Texas. The *New Yorker* cover of December 10, 2001, "New Yorkistan," made one of the first humorous interventions in post-September 11 popular culture, lampooning both New Yorkers' city-bound geographic consciousness and a nationwide ignorance of the geography of Central Asia. Needless to say, such distorted geographic imaginaries have somewhat different consequences as, on the one hand, a background for foreign policy decisions, and on the other, a measure of the general geographic ignorance of the American people.

10. The Simonides tale can be found in Cicero's *De Oratore* II.lxxxvi–lxxxviii and Quintilian's *Institutio Oratoria* XI.ii.

11. I explore these issues as they appear in an era prior to the institutionalization of ancient Greek political rhetoric in "Sappho's Memory."

12. See Robbins' discussion (xvii) of Negt and Kluge's *Public Sphere and Experience;* see also Warner.

13. Portraits were published as names became available and families gave permission. They continued to appear periodically after the end of the daily feature.

14. The information that follows is drawn from chapter 6 of Marita Sturken's fine study *Tangled Memories: The Vietnam War, the AIDS Epidemic, and the Politics of Remembering.*

15. A personal anecdote supplies another example of unscripted grieving and memorializing: A friend living in New York at the time of the events did not know anyone killed in the attack, but after the subways were rerouted around the damage, and she began making her daily trip from Brooklyn to New Jersey, she noticed a flier go up on the subway wall she walked by daily. As she saw it every day, she began to think of that person as "her" loss and developed a sense of attachment to the person whose face she now knew and whose lost life she now mourned, particularly and personally, but outside the scripts for both public and private mourning.

16. The illusion of power shared across gender in this aristocratic scenario is refuted by many other facets of administrative rhetoric. The White House website, for example, currently houses several pages related to the one-year memorial. One, called "Spirit of Freedom Tribute," begins with five photographic images emphasizing heroic masculinity. Four of the images represent men in postures of power and

control—the president, firefighters, soldiers, and rescue workers—and the fifth shows young girls offering money as evidence of their "patriotism" (the caption below this image; http://www.whitehouse.gov/911/tribute.html). In both the contemporary setting and the ancient Athenian funeral oration, women are fixed as bearers of children and survivors of heroic deaths of husbands and sons, their mourning contained by state ritual (see Holst-Warhaft, especially chapters 4 and 5; see also Jarratt and Ong).

17. The listing of names on the Vietnam Memorial was a condition of design decided upon by the group of veterans who initiated the project, conducted the design competition, and raised funds for its construction. In the case of Maya Lin's wall, the conditions of viewing enable ongoing personal acts of mourning in a multiplicity of forms (physically touching the name, grieving alone or with small groups at any time, leaving memorial objects such as personal property of the person mourned, letters, flowers, etc.) See Sturken's detailed and illuminating discussion of the monument (44–84). While the practice of calling out individual names in the September 11, 2002 event mimics the Vietnam memorial, its effect, because of the heavily scripted ceremonial context, carries only a negligible opportunity for each mourner to seek, in the words of Hyperides, the limit of her or his grief.

WORKS CITED

Anderson, Benedict. *Imagined Communities. Reflections on the Origin and Spread of Nationalism*. Rev. ed. London: Verso, 1991.

Ansary, Tamin. Untitled letter. 13 September 2001.

Arendt, Hannah. *The Human Condition*. Chicago: U of Chicago P, 1958.

Bender, John, and David E. Wellbery. "Rhetoricality: On the Modernist Return of Rhetoric." In *The Ends of Rhetoric: History, Theory, Practice*. Ed. John Bender and David E. Wellbery. Stanford: Stanford UP, 1990. 3–39.

Bhabha, Hommi, ed. *Nation and Narration*. London: Routledge, 1990.

Bizzell, Patricia, and Bruce Herzberg, eds. *The Rhetorical Tradition*. 2nd ed. Boston: Bedford, 2001.

Blake, Casey Nelson. "Mourning and Modernism After 9/11." *The Nation* 23 September 2002: 40, 42–43, 46, 49.

Bunch, Charlotte. "Whose Security?" *The Nation* 23 September 2002: 36–38, 40.

Connor, W. Robert, ed. "The Funeral Oration of Hyperides." Trans. J. O. Burtt. *Greek Orations: Fourth Century B.C.* Prospect Heights, IL: Waveland P, 1987. 210–19.

Dawes, James. *The Language of War: Literature and Culture in the U.S. from the Civil War through World War II*. Cambridge, MA: Harvard UP, 2002.

Didion, Joan. "Fixed Opinions, or The Hinge of History." *New York Times Review of Books* 16 January 2003: 54–57.

Eberly, Rosa A. *Citizen Critics: Literary Public Spheres*. Urbana: U of Illinois P, 2000.

Ehrenreich, Barbara. "Veiled Threat." *Los Angeles Times* 4 November 2001: M1, 4.

Fears, Darryl. "Deep Distrust of Government Still Simmers." *Washington Post* 29 October 2001: A2.

Glenn, David. "The War on Campus. Will Academic Freedom Survive?" *The Nation* 3 December 2001: 11–12, 14.

Habermas, Jürgen. *The Structural Transformation of the Public Sphere: A Category of Bourgeois Society.* Trans. Thomas Burger in association with Frederick Lawrence. Cambridge, MA: MIT P, 1989.

Hardt, Michael, and Antonio Negri. *Empire.* Cambridge, MA: Harvard UP, 2000.

Hauser, Gerard A. *Vernacular Voices: The Rhetoric of Publics and Public Spheres.* Columbia: U of South Carolina P, 1999.

Havelock, Eric A. *The Literate Revolution in Greece and Its Cultural Consequences.* Princeton: Princeton UP, 1982.

Holst-Warhaft, Gail. *Dangerous Voices: Women's Laments and Greek Literature.* London: Routledge, 1992.

Hurley, Adrienne. "Stop the Violence; Kids Are Watching." *Los Angeles Times* 16 December 2001: B17.

Jarratt, Susan C. "Sappho's Memory." *Rhetoric Society Quarterly* 32.1 (2002): 11–43.

Jarratt, Susan C., and Rory Ong. "Aspasia: Rhetoric, Gender, and Colonial Ideology." In *Rhetorica Reclaimed: Essays on Women in Rhetoric.* Ed. Andrea A. Lunsford. Pittsburgh: U of Pittsburgh P, 1995. 9–24.

Kolhatkar, Sonali. "'Saving' Afghan Women." *Z Magazine* 9 May 2002.

Lancaster, John. "'Bully Remark Earns Biden a Lesson in Wartime Rhetoric." *Washington Post* 29 October 2001: A15.

Loraux, Nicole. *The Invention of Athens: The Funeral Oration in the Classical City.* Trans. Alan Sheridan. Cambridge, MA: Harvard UP, 1986.

McNamara, Mary, and Lynell George. "When Evil Itself Becomes the Primary Foe." *Los Angeles Times* 18 September 2001: A3.

Menard, Louis. "Faith, Hope, and Clarity. September 11th and the American Soul." *New Yorker* 16 September 2002: 98–104.

Muschamp, Herbert. "The Memorial Would Live in the Architecture." *New York Times* 22 December 2002, sec. 1: 2, 43.

National Security Strategy Statement. September 2002. http://www.whitehouse.gov/nsc/nssall.html.

Nees, Greg. "An Open Letter to President Bush from a Former U.S. Marine Sergeant: Can America Help Lead the World to Peace and Justice?" *New York Times* 9 October 2001: A22.

Norman, A. F., trans. *Antioch as a Centre of Hellenic Culture as Observed by Libanius.* Liverpool: Liverpool UP, 2000.

Pollit, Katha. "Put Out No Flags." *The Nation* 8 October 2001: 9.

Robbins, Bruce. "Introduction." *The Phantom Public Sphere.* Ed. Bruce Robbins. Minneapolis: U of Minnesota P, 1993.

Roy, Arundhati. "The Algebra of Infinite Justice." *The Guardian* 29 September 2001. http://www.guardian.co.uk/saturdayreview/story/0,3605,559756,00.html.

Schama, Simon. "Mourning in America; A Whiff of Dread for the Land of Hope." *New York Times* 15 September 2002, sec. 4: 1.

Schiappa, Edward. "*Rhetorikê:* What's in a Name? Toward a Revised History of Early Greek Rhetorical Theory." *Quarterly Journal of Speech* 78 (1992): 1–15.

Scott, Janny. "Closing a Scrapbook Full of Life and Sorrow." *New York Times* 31 December 2001: B6.

Silberstein, Sandra. *War of Words: Language, Politics, and 9/11.* New York: Routledge, 2002.

Simon, Scott. Commentary. National Public Radio. 14 September 2002. http://www.npr.org/20020914.wesat.12.ram.

Sontag, Susan. "War? Real Battles and Empty Metaphors." *New York Times* 10 September 2002: A25.

Sturken, Marita. *Tangled Memories: The Vietnam War, the AIDS Epidemic, and the Politics of Remembering.* Berkeley: U of California P, 1997.

Terrell, Valerie. "The Pathos of the Pregnant Woman in the Rhetoric Following Sept. 11th." Speech. Student Forum: Contrasting Perspectives on 9/11. University of California, Irvine. 5 March 2002.

Thucydides. *History of the Peloponnesian War.* Trans. Rex Warner. Middlesex, England: Penguin, 1954.

Walker, Jeffrey. *Rhetoric and Poetics in Antiquity.* New York: Oxford UP, 2000.

Warner, Michael. "Public and Counterpublics." *Public Culture* 14 (2002): 49–90.

Wells, Susan. *Sweet Reason: Rhetoric and the Discourses of Modernity.* Chicago: U of Chicago P, 1996.

Williams, Patricia J. "Pax Americana." *The Nation* 1 October 2001: 9.

Zizek, Slovaj. "Welcome to the Desert of the Real!" *South Atlantic Quarterly* 101 (2002): 385–89.

SEVEN

Teaching "Political Wisdom"

Isocrates and the Tradition of Dissoi Logoi

Arthur E. Walzer

AMONG THE MORE BENIGN effects of the recent public pressure on universities to become politically responsive is the addition to the curriculum of courses structured around citizenship. Such courses have as goals to enable students to understand the ethos of the citizen and to enable and encourage students to participate in politics. Surely the rhetorical tradition has something to teach us about such courses, for it is not an exaggeration to characterize the history of rhetoric as a twenty-four-hundred-year reflection on citizen education. From this perspective, no figure within the tradition is more important or more perplexing than is Isocrates. What can we learn about citizen education and its relationship to rhetoric from Isocrates' work? This chapter is an inquiry into that question. It focuses on two of Isocrates' speeches—*Archidamus* and *On the Peace*—that, taken together, constitute a single case in how Isocrates might have instilled political judgment in his students.

In contrast to the questionable coherence of Isocrates' moral philosophy, his views on education and on teaching are coherent and clear. If it is too much to credit him with a philosophy of education, it is not extravagant to grant him an identifiable educational program. First, Isocrates identifies political judgment as a type of cognition that he would develop and sets this against theoretical knowledge—what we might place under political science today. The political judgment he would develop he defines as the ability, by "the powers of conjecture, to arrive generally at the right course" in contingent matters (*Antidosis* 271), and he opposes this type of political knowledge to the abstract, transcendent theory that was the goal of Plato's Academy (*Against the Sophists* 3). Respect for situational elements as crucial to judgment and the recognition of a radical contingency that put political skill beyond the reach of system is fundamental to Isocrates' view (*Antidosis* 184). Second, Isocrates understands that if he is to inspire students to achieve the political leadership that he sets as the practical goal of his curriculum he must change attitudes—inspire his students. To this end, Isocrates maintains that political oratory is "the highest kind," dealing with "the greatest affairs" (*Panegyricus* 4) and predicts that those who pursue it will be thought "wiser and better and of more use to the world" than those who study forensic rhetoric and aspire to careers in the law (*Antidosis* 48). Third, Isocrates identifies a focus on rhetoric as both a means of developing the skills needed to lead and as a complementary means to developing judgment, for effective rhetorical choice, as also political judgment, depends upon a sense of what is appropriate to say in a given case, at a particular time, to a particular audience—a skill that, like political judgment, is too subtle for the crude generalizations of a handbook (*Against the Sophists* 13). It is not too much to identify this set of views—that includes a type of knowledge and a goal and addresses both the fostering of an attitude and the development of skills—as a program.

Regrettably, we know much less about the methods Isocrates used to enact this program than we do about its aims. At the point in *Against the Sophists* where it appears that Isocrates is to describe his approach (section 22), the text ends.[1] Ignorance, however, is an opportunity as well as an obstacle and in this case leaves room for the speculation that Isocrates' speeches, which he claimed never to have delivered (*To the Rulers of Mytilenaeans* 7), were central to his method and composed for pedagogical purposes—that they served as models for analysis and imitation. That is my hypothesis in the analysis of two speeches, the *Archidamus* and *On the Peace*.

The *Archidamus* is a fictional speech written in the voice of Archidamus III, the son of the ruling king of Sparta, Agesilaus. The speech is set as a response to a crisis facing Sparta in the years following defeat at the battle of Leuctra and the Theban invasions of the Peloponnesus, including the invasion of Sparta itself in 369 BCE. In 366, Sparta had sued for peace with Thebes. As a condition of peace, Thebes insisted that Messene, a Spartan colony, be granted independence. Sparta's allies, including most prominently Corinth, urged that Sparta comply. In the speech, Archidamus III urges the Spartan Assembly to refuse to accept the Theban demand, to resist the Corinthian pressure, and to maintain Messene as a colony. The rhetorical situation for the second speech, *On the Peace*, is parallel. The context is Athens following the Social War, in which Athens fought against some of its former colonies who had withdrawn from the Second Athenian Confederacy and who now sought their independence. A peace treaty had been drawn up. The speaker (presumably Isocrates) urges the Athenians to accept it. Indeed, the speaker urges the Assembly that Athens should give up its imperial ambitions, its "sea empire," entirely.

The speeches are strikingly similar. Both are deliberative: a speaker addresses a political assembly that must make a decision about the future in a situation of uncertainty. In both speeches, the speaker attempts to persuade a resistant Assembly to reject (in the case of the *Archidamus*) or accept (in the case of *On the Peace*) a peace treaty offered by a seemingly more powerful opponent. Moreover, in both speeches the speaker uses the occasion of the particular treaty to reflect more generally on the broader question of the benefits and costs—both spiritual and material—of imperialism. But the two speeches are addressed to different city-states, with different ideologies and different national characters. And the speakers advance contrary theses about imperialism.

The parallel quality of the speeches has suggested to Phillip Harding that the speeches are *dissoi logoi* or antilogies, that is, speeches that present opposite sides of the same issue. Harding speculates that Isocrates created them as a rhetorical exercise, to be read together. He proposes his thesis against the theory advanced in nineteenth-century German scholarship that argued that Isocrates wrote his speeches to influence Athenian politics, that print versions circulated as political pamphlets and were influential (Harding 137). Although subsequent scholarship argued that this reading of Isocrates' purpose was too grandiose, the speeches were still understood as having a direct political purpose, though a more modest one: Isocrates was trying to influence his students' political views (138–39). Harding goes further at least with regard to *Archidamus* and *On the Peace:* he claims these speeches have no direct political purpose. They are companion pieces—antilogies presenting opposite theses on the same themes.[2]

Assuming the speeches are antilogies (and once our eyes are open to the possibility that these are companion pieces, it is virtually impossible to see them differently), what lessons might Isocrates have expected his students to take from analyzing them? The Sophistic lesson that an education in eloquence allows one to argue toward any conclusion? The relativist's view, that the "wise decision" necessarily differs relative to cultural and situational factors? The patriotic, propagandistic conclusion that the Athenian position espoused in *On the Peace* is superior to Archidamus' view? Something else? These possibilities foreground not only the interpretive complexities of the two speeches but also the complexities of the meaning of *dissoi logoi* within the rhetorical tradition. One way of exploring the richness of this tradition and of the possibilities it presented to Isocrates, who was perhaps uniquely prepared to appreciate the tradition's complexities, is to examine the two speeches in light of Isocrates' educational program. My analysis will focus on the contrasting ways in which the two speeches treat three values that were of considerable importance to Greeks in the fourth century BCE—justice, honor, and patriotism.

Justice is treated in both speeches in the context of a consideration of the relationship between what is advantageous and what is right. In both speeches, the Socratic ideal is honored: the speakers insist that what is not just cannot be advantageous. Although Archidamus acknowledges that considerations of the consequences of policy and action must weigh heavily in deliberations about an uncertain future, he nonetheless insists that "no man could ever persuade me that one should ever deem anything to be of greater consequence than justice," and he goes on to detail the practical benefits of doing what is just, including that "in general the life of man is destroyed by vice, and preserved by virtue" and that those who fight in a just cause fight better (35–36). In a like vein, the speaker in *On the Peace* maintains the extreme folly of those who "hold the view that, while injustice is reprehensible, it is, nevertheless, profitable and advantageous in our lives . . . and that, while justice is estimable, it is . . . disadvantageous [to] . . . those who practice it" (31).

We can infer from the two speeches that Isocrates' students would be led to conclude that, regardless of the circumstances, justice should have a priority in political deliberation. The wise counselor must first establish that an action is just as a necessary precondition of a consideration of the advantages of the recommended course. But this conclusion, reassuring as it is to those in search of a nonrelativist Isocrates, assumes that the meaning of "justice" is the same in the two speeches, and it is not. As Aristotle observes in the *Nicomachean Ethics,* justice is an ambiguous word with at least two meanings: that which is lawful and that which is equal or fair—this latter sometimes called "commutative" justice (V.i.7–9).[3] These two meanings correspond to the different meanings of justice in the two speeches. In the *Archidamus,* what is just is what is lawful. Archidamus maintains that Messene is lawfully the possession of Sparta—that Sparta acquired Messene by conquest, a common and accepted way of gaining possession, he points out. Nor has Sparta's claim to Messene ever been contested in the four hundred years that it has held it, not even by its enemies, which is de facto confirmation of the legality of Sparta's claim. In addition, Sparta's right to Messene is attested to in Messene's founding myth and confirmed by oracles (*Archidamus* 16–30).

In contrast, in *On the Peace* justice is defined in relational, not legal or contractual, terms. Athens' present rule over its colonies is unjust, according to the speaker, because of the quality of this rule: Athens oppresses and exploits its colonies. There is a type of "dominion which is greater than just" (89). In the past, the empire met the standard of justice because Athens attended to its colonies' interests, as well as its own. It liberated and protected the Hellene colonies and did not ignore their welfare. As a result, the colonies did not object to being ruled. For in former times "as the result of keeping our city in the path of justice and of giving aid to the oppressed and of not coveting the possessions of others we were given the hegemony by the willing consent of the Hellenes" (30). Today, Athens dominates and exploits its colonies, which make its rule unjust: "For it is the duty of those who rule to make their subjects happier through their care for their welfare, whereas it is a habit of those who dominate to provide pleasures for themselves through the labours and hardships of others" (91). This definition of justice is relational; that is, it depends on how the stronger treats the weaker.

An analysis of the appeals to honor in the two speeches leads to a similar conclusion: both speakers insist that the state's honor is at stake—that adopting the policy that the speaker recommends is the honorable course—but the meaning of honor is different in the two speeches. Throughout his speech, Archidamus contends that yielding to the threats of Thebes and the pressure of Sparta's allies to give up Messene could only be indicative of Sparta's preference for security over risk, fear over honor, which would be shameful: "I had rather die this moment for not complying with the dictates of the foe than live many times my allotted span of life at the price of voting what the Thebans demand. For I should feel disgraced" (8). And so should all Spartans who would agree to such terms in light of Sparta's history and traditions: "Is it not shameful, finally, that other cities have endured the last extremities of siege to preserve our empire, while we ourselves see no reason why we should bear even slight hardships to prevent our being forced to do anything contrary to our just rights, but are to be seen even at this moment feeding teams of ravenous [race] horses, although, like men . . . in want of their daily bread, we sue for peace in this fashion?" (55).

It is clear from this speech that Archidamus thinks of honor as a preference for risk over security: "Indeed, honours and distinctions are wont to be gained, not by repose, but by struggle, and these one should strive to win sparing neither our bodies nor our lives nor anything else which we possess" (105). Honor in this sense is a matter of motives and is objective: the courage to risk what is dear is honorable regardless of the consequences. But although honor depends on motives, it is conferred by others—by other Hellenes, by the Olympian national assembly, by humankind (95).

The speaker of *On the Peace* also appeals to honor, but the honor he invokes is virtually the opposite of that invoked by Archidamus. In *On the Peace* honor is not a matter of motives but of tangible effects and is secured not by sacrificing material gain but by prosperity:

> Let me ask, then, whether we should be satisfied if we could dwell in our city secure from danger, if we could be provided more abundantly with the necessities of life, if we could be of one mind amongst ourselves, if we could enjoy the high esteem of the Hellenes. I, for my part, hold that with these blessings assured us, Athens would be completely happy. Now it is the war . . . [that] has given us a bad name among the Hellenes. (18–19)

Moreover, honor is conferred first and primarily by those affected by an action who give it freely; only subsequently is it given by spectators: "And we ought not to emulate those who hold despotic power nor those who have gained a dominion which is greater than is just but rather those who, while worthy of the highest honours, are yet content with the honours which are tendered them by a free people. For no man nor any state could obtain a position more excellent than this or more secure or of greater worth" (89).

Finally, an analysis of the appeals to patriotism in the two speeches yields a similar conclusion: both speakers insist that they proceed from patriotic motives but the signs of patriotism are contrasted in the speeches. For Archidamus, patriotism means doing all that one can to increase respect for Sparta's power. Once Archidamus has satisfied himself that rejecting this humiliating treaty does not violate his definition of justice and proven that Spartan resistance has at least a chance of success, he is passionate in his insistence that relinquishing what is Sparta's would be "to fasten disgrace" upon the fatherland (38) and must for that reason be resisted. No sacrifice is too great: "[M]onstrous above all things would be our conduct" if we were unwilling to make any sacrifice necessary to resist the enemy (83). Failing to prosecute the war would be a betrayal of the legacy that our forefathers secured for our children (110).

Although for Archidamus, patriotism is measured by the personal sacrifice one is willing to make to increase the respect for Sparta's power, for the speaker of *On the Peace*, the measure of patriotism is the courage to give wise, even if unpopular, counsel, counsel that will win the friendship of other states. The speaker acknowledges the unpopularity of his recommendation that Athens grant independence to the colonies but insists that the patriotic response is to state the truth:

> I am at a loss what I should do—whether I should speak the truth as on all other occasions or be silent out of fear of making myself odious to you. For while it seems to me the better course to discuss your blunders, I observe that you are more resentful towards those who take you to task than towards those who are the authors of your misfortunes. Nevertheless, I should be ashamed if I showed that I am more concerned about my own reputation than about the public safety. It is therefore my duty and the duty of all who care about the welfare of the state to choose, not those discourses which are agreeable to you, but those which are profitable for you to hear. (39)

The speaker insists on a distinction between admonishing, which is loyal speech, and denunciation, which is not: Although those "who admonish and those who denounce cannot avoid using similar words," their "purposes are the opposite as they can be." The Assembly "ought to commend those who admonish you for your good and to esteem them as the best of your fellow citizens" (72). In contrast to Archidamus, respect for power is not the measure of patriotic commitment. The course he recommends, which he insists is the

patriotic one, will lower taxes and increase prosperity (20–21)—precisely the
motives that Archidamus saw as contemptible, dishonorable, and unpatriotic.
Granting independence to the colonies would put Athens in a friendly relationship—not one based on fear—with its allies: "And, what is most important of all, we shall have all mankind as our allies—allies who will not have
been forced, but rather persuaded, to join with us, who will not welcome our
friendship because of our power . . . but who will be disposed towards us as
those should be who are in very truth allies and friends" (21). As does Archidamus, the speaker in *On the Peace* claims loyally to put his city's interest above
his own, but the signs of patriotism—the values that underpin it and the policies that express it—contrast.

What lessons would Isocrates want his students to learn from a comparison of these speeches? Three possibilities occur to me that, in the spirit of
the *dissoi logoi,* I offer as three antilogies. In doing so, my analysis necessarily
reflects also on our understanding of the *dissoi logoi* tradition. The antilogies
confront us, then, not only with alternative understandings of the speeches
but also with alternative understandings of antilogy as a rhetorical and educational method.

FIRST POSSIBILITY

If *Archidamus* and *On the Peace* are companion speeches created as a pedagogical exercise, students could learn from comparing them that rhetoric is,
indeed, a powerful art. In the hands of a master orator, such as Isocrates,
rhetoric can make justice, honor, or patriotism be one thing in Sparta and
quite another in Athens. Let us take justice as an example. In the persona of
Archidamus, Isocrates equated the just with the legal because he had evidence
to show that Sparta held its colonies legally. Justice means "not illegal," and
Sparta's rule is just. But he could not show that Spartan rule met the standard
of fairness, so this potential definition of justice does not materialize in
Isocrates' speech. Indeed in *On the Peace,* Isocrates argued that Spartan rule
could *not* meet the standard of commutative justice that he held out for
Athens to meet, for, he claims, Sparta treated its citizens and colonies even
worse than did Athens:

> For, tell me, against which of the cities of Hellas did [the Spartans] fail to
> take the field? Which of them did they fail to wrong? Did they not rob the
> Eleans of part of their territory, did they not lay waste the land of the
> Corinthians, did they not disperse the Mantineans from their homes, did
> they not reduce the Phliasians by siege, and did they not invade the country
> of the Argives, never ceasing from their depredations upon the rest of the
> world and so bringing upon themselves the disaster at Leuctra? (99)

In Athens, rhetoric can transform justice into something quite different from its reality in Sparta: here legality is no longer relevant to justice. To prove that granting the independence of the colonies is the just course, Isocrates must accordingly create a new "justice" (or "injustice"). Rhetoric is equal to the task.

On this account of Isocrates' understanding of antilogy and his uses of the speeches, Isocrates' students would learn that reality is what rhetoric presents it to be. This is how Phillip Harding understands Isocrates' intentions. Harding sees the speeches as teaching the "power of the logos, which was demonstrated by Gorgias in the fifth century and later on many occasions by Isokrates, his pupil. Isocrates is saying, 'Give me a theme, give me two opposite situations and I'll show you how to argue both sides of the question. On the one hand, peace at any price; on the other, naked imperialism'" (147). Isocrates follows his teacher; he is a Gorgian Sophist primarily interested in displaying his own rhetorical virtuosity for the admiration, edification, and imitation of his students, and antilogy is the premier device for such a lesson.

SECOND POSSIBILITY

That the two speeches are companion pieces, that they were created for teaching purposes, and that justice, honor, and patriotism have different meanings in them does not license the inference that they are demonstration pieces intended to display Isocrates' rhetorical virtuosity. *On the Peace* expresses some of Isocrates' most deeply held ideas, ideas that are present throughout his corpus. As Takis Poulakos has argued in *Speaking for the Polis: Isocrates' Rhetorical Education*, Isocrates' educational agenda emphasized the specific virtues that constitute good citizenship—most prominently justice, temperance, and piety, virtues that must be enacted by leaders and ordinary citizens alike (Poulakos, chapter 2). In *On the Peace*, Isocrates faults Athenian rule, its sea empire, as failing precisely these tests of virtue (31–35, 63–64). In exploiting its colonies, Athens' rule has been unjust; in its reckless, imprudent excess, it has been immoderate; in not husbanding the legacy of its ancestors, it has been impious and brought dishonor on its ancestors. These themes appear in *Nicocles, Panegyricus, Areopagiticus,* and *Panathenaicus.* Isocrates speaks in his own voice in *On the Peace;* referring to "the speaker" is misleading. Although we cannot know for certain how Isocrates used these speeches with students, that he presented *On the Peace* as exemplary and foil to the flawed *Archidamus* is the most likely hypothesis, a hypothesis that is strengthened by his criticism of Spartan rule as also unjust and excessive in *On the Peace* (99).

On this understanding of Isocrates' purposes, antilogies recognize the ambivalent nature of abstractions, which are always capable of yielding two conflicting interpretations. But we need not, nor would Isocrates' students, conclude from this that the preferable in a given case cannot be discerned or is a matter of rhetorical presentation only. Isocrates' goal was to foster political judgment; this judgment was prior to eloquence. For the Athenians at the time of the Social War, the just, honorable, and expedient course was to make peace with other Greek states, to make them allies, not subjects—generally a superior philosophy for Greeks, according to Isocrates. Because it reflects the nature of reality, *dissoi logoi* must be the starting point for wisdom, but wisdom involves judgment and manifests in the wise choice.[4]

THIRD POSSIBILITY

Whatever speculations we make about how Isocrates used the speeches he created should be grounded in what we know of his educational program. We know that Isocrates' aim was to teach "political discourse." We should think of this aim as the *telos* that informs his teaching, to which all other aims are instrumental. This assumption dictates an analysis focusing on content more than style. Of course Isocrates, an accomplished stylist himself, would have had students attend to style, but as Erika Rummel has argued, the substance of the speeches was more important to him (150). Isocrates made modest claims for what instruction could do in helping students develop political judgment, placing instruction behind both natural ability and experience in importance. But he did insist on a heuristic value for instruction. He maintained that "formal training makes such men more skilful and more resourceful in *discovering the possibilities of a subject;* for it teaches them to take from *a readier source the topics* that they otherwise hit upon in haphazard fashion" (*Against the Sophists* 15; my emphasis). This passage is crucial to an understanding of how the analysis of the speeches probably functioned in Isocrates' system. With the goal of invention in mind, an analysis of these speeches would readily yield the special topics that are the basis for the political judgment that was the goal of Isocrates' program—such topics as what constitutes a just relationship between states? What are the constituents and measures of utility and self-interest? How do justice and utility relate to rationality? Because the purpose of the instruction is heuristic, the goal would not be to reconcile the different views presented in the different speeches but to discuss the salience of each response in different circumstances as a way to increasing the fullness of students' experience.

　　This third possibility is the one I embrace because it seems consistent with the bent of Isocrates' mind and the aims of the mission he set for himself. Isocrates should be seen primarily as a teacher and moralist. While from the point of view of moral philosophy, Isocrates' thought is muddled, incoherence rarely deters a moralist. But a moral aim does disqualify one from being indifferent to the moral implications of language or the positions that one espouses, and Isocrates meets this test. As Stephen Halliwell points out (120), in *Helen,* Isocrates rejects the radically subjectivist view of those who claim "it is impossible to say or gainsay what is false" or "who argue on both sides of the same questions" for no apparent purpose except to display a rhetorical virtuosity (*Helen* 1). Isocrates contrasts the purposes of these sophists from what teachers should do: "pursue the truth, to instruct their pupils in the practical affairs of our government" (5).[5] Harding's dismissal of the speeches as mere display pieces mocks the serious purpose that Isocrates claims for his educational program and misses the serious purpose that Isocrates thought antilogies could serve in fostering political judgment: "How can men wisely pass judgment on the past or take counsel for the future," Isocrates asks, " unless they examine and compare arguments of opposing speakers, themselves giving an unbiased hearing to both sides?" (*On the Peace* 13).[6] With regard to the second possibility, if Isocrates' primary goal were to instill his Panhellenic ideals in his students, the most efficient way to achieve this goal would have been to have them analyze only those of his speeches that advance this program.

This third position—that sees the two speeches as an effort to identify the archetypal, conflicting positions on the topoi of political philosophy—also has two other benefits. First, it denies that the *dissoi logoi* technique is irrational. Within the rhetorical tradition *dissoi logoi* has often been not only an effective way to generate reasons but also a way of generating a critique—all as a means to coming to the best decision in situations of uncertainty. Cicero celebrated arguing both sides *(in utramque partem)* for these reasons, and in the title of his recent book calling for its revival, Thomas Sloane identifies pro and con arguing as the protocol of rhetoric.

Finally, I prefer this third possibility because it addresses our present need for a critical, civic education and our present intellectual climate. When viewed from the perspective of Isocratic contingency, the meanings of justice, honor, and patriotism in the two speeches seems incommensurable. This sense was felt in Athens of the fourth and fifth centuries, as Sophocles' *Antigone* shows, and it is widely felt today, as the title of Alasdair Macintyre's *Whose Justice? Which Rationality?* attests. A course in civic education with the contested topoi of political philosophy as its focus and *dissoi logoi* as its method would speak to our needs as it did to the needs of Isocrates and his students.

NOTES

I thank Richard Graff for his help with this essay.

1. Scholars have long maintained that this section of *Against the Sophists* is lost, but recently some have advanced the theory that Isocrates intended the abrupt ending. See Michael Cahn, 137, who cites an earlier argument advanced by Christoph Eucken, 5, 32; also Yun Lee Too, 194–99.

2. R. A. Mosey has challenged Harding's view, especially the later dating of *Archidamus* that Harding's thesis entails. Yun Lee Too reviews the controversy, concluding that, regardless of the date of composition, Isocrates intended the two speeches to be read as antilogies (Too 66–69).

3. See Janet Atwill, "Rhetoric and Civic Virtue," in this volume.

4. See Takis Poulakos, "Isocrates' Civic Education and the Question of *Doxa.*" Professor Poulakos sent me a prepublication version of this paper. He also read and commented very helpfully on my chapter in draft. I thank him for sharing his work and for the time and attention he gave to mine.

5. Of course, Isocrates makes this claim in a foreword to his own encomium to Helen. But Isocrates' *Helen* does emphasize political themes, at least in comparison to other encomia to her.

6. Michael Gagarin has maintained that sophistic antilogies do not intend to persuade to a particular thesis but typically attempt to display the sophist's ingenuity. But Gagarin does acknowledge the possibility that the purpose of the anonymous *Dissoi Logoi* may have been "to clarify ways of thinking or speaking about such paradoxes" (286). We might agree that, yes, Isocrates' *dissoi logoi* is not intended to persuade— except to this thesis: that the best way to develop political judgment is through a rhetoric-centered education that includes the analysis of antilogies.

WORKS CITED

Aristotle. *Nicomachean Ethics.* Trans. H. Rackham. Cambridge, MA: Harvard UP, 1994.

Cahn, Michael. "Reading Rhetoric Rhetorically: Isocrates and the Marketing of Insight." *Rhetorica* 8 (1989): 121–44.

Eucken, Christoph. *Isokrates: Seine Position in der Auseinandersetzung mit den zeitgenössischen Philosophen.* Berlin: De Gruyter, 1983.

Gagarin, Michael. "Did the Sophists Aim to Persuade?" *Rhetorica* 19 (2001): 275–91.

Halliwell, Stephen. "Philosophical Rhetoric or Rhetorical Philosophy? The Strange Case of Isocrates." In *The Rhetoric Canon.* Ed. Brenda Deen Schildgen. Detroit: Wayne State UP, 1997. 107–25.

Harding, Phillip. "The Purpose of Isokrates' *Archidamos* and *On the Peace.*" *California Studies in Classical Antiquity* 6 (1973): 137–49.

Isocrates. *Archidamus.* Trans. George Norlin. *Isocrates,* vol. 1. Cambridge, MA: Harvard UP, 1928. 343–411.

———. *Panegyricus.* Trans. George Norlin. *Isocrates,* vol. 1. Cambridge, MA: Harvard UP, 1928. 116–241.

———. *Against the Sophists.* Trans. George Norlin. *Isocrates,* vol. 2. Cambridge, MA: Harvard UP, 1929. 160–83.

———. *Antidosis.* Trans. George Norlin. *Isocrates,* vol. 2. Cambridge, MA: Harvard UP, 1929. 181–365.

———. *On the Peace.* Trans. George Norlin. *Isocrates,* vol. 2. Cambridge, MA: Harvard UP, 1929. 2–97.

———. *Helen.* Trans. Larue Van Hook. *Isocrates,* vol. 3. Cambridge, MA: Harvard UP, 1945. 54–97.

———. *To the Rulers of Mytilenaeans.* Trans. Larue Van Hook. *Isocrates,* vol. 3. Cambridge, MA: Harvard UP, 1945. 459–467.

Jaeger, Werner. *Paideia: The Ideals of Greek Culture.* Trans. Gilbert Highet. Oxford: Oxford UP, 1945.

Mosey, R. A. "Isokrates' On the Peace: Rhetorical Exercise or Political Advice." *American Journal of Ancient History* 7 (1982): 118–27.

Poulakos, Takis. *Speaking for the Polis: Isocrates' Rhetorical Education.* U of South Carolina P, 1997.

———. "Isocrates' Civic Education and the Question of *Doxa.*" In *Isocrates' Civic Education.* Ed. Takis Poulakos and David Depew. Austin: U of Texas P (forthcoming).

Rummel, Erika. "Isocrates' Ideal of Rhetoric: Criteria of Evaluation." *Classical Journal* 75 (1979): 25–35. Reprinted in *Landmark Essays on Classical Greek Rhetoric.* Ed. Edward Schiappa. Davis, CA: Hermagoras, 1994. 143–54.

Sloane, Thomas O. *On the Contrary: The Protocol of Traditional Rhetoric.* Washington DC: Catholic University P, 1997.

Too, Yun Lee. *The Rhetoric of Identity in Isocrates.* Cambridge: Cambridge UP, 1995.

EIGHT

On the Formation of Democratic Citizens

Rethinking the Rhetorical Tradition in a Digital Age

William Hart-Davidson, James P. Zappen, and S. Michael Halloran

IN HIS FINAL WORK James Berlin signaled his movement away from rhetoric and toward cultural studies. Berlin maintained that cultural studies offers a better theoretical perspective than the rhetoric that has become predominant in American higher education for achieving the educational goal he thought English as a discipline should embrace: to form citizens capable of sustaining a democracy. On his analysis, rhetoric is ill-equipped for forwarding this goal because it lacks (1) an ability to locate, name, analyze, and ultimately influence the relations of power that make up our society; (2) an ability to adopt a view of social formations as historical enterprises; (3) an ability to call attention to and influence circumstances that have led to the empowerment of some groups and the oppression of others through a network of discursive relations. Some critics of rhetoric might go further and argue that rhetoric as a discipline has been complicit in sustaining an oligarchic society. Quintilian's "citizen orator" on this view is a mystifier who cloaks the actualities of power in a fog of fine verbiage.

Berlin's argument, grounded in a historicized understanding of rhetoric in the English studies tradition, tends to render both rhetoric and cultural studies as a priori systems. The first is deficient, the second preferable in virtue of a specific set of intellectual tools it ought to bring to the analysis of symbolic action. There's nothing particularly unusual in this way of thinking. Belletrism, for example, is dismissed by many historians of rhetoric because it lacks tools for thinking about invention, emphasizing instead a meticulous attention to niceties of style. (One of us can recall a conference discussion at which the Nietzschean question of what might be "forgotten" in the rhetorical tradition was raised. After a brief silence someone suggested, "Blair, Campbell, and Whately." No one rose to defend them.) Berlin simply brings this line of thinking to a higher level of generality, indicting not some particular rhetoric(s) but rather the entire tradition of rhetorical studies for its failure to direct our attention a priori to questions about how discourse inscribes historically contingent power hierarchies. Cultural studies in Berlin's view is a stronger theoretical framework because it gives us the missing tools.

We do not disagree with Berlin's critique of the rhetorical tradition, though we do point out that he never meant this to be his last word on the matter. What turned out to be his final statement should have been one leg of a longer journey. We do wish to make two points at the outset. First, the rhetorical tradition need not be understood as an a priori set of analytic tools. Gerard Hauser, for one, insists on what he calls an "empirical attitude" that he identifies with a "Ciceronian sense" of rhetoric, an attitude that "draws its inferences . . . from actual social practices of discourse" rather than from "a priori assumptions about what is real or true" (275). Hauser's Ciceronian or "vernacular" rhetoric is a complex and messy business, extending beyond "the podium, printed page, legislative chamber, or executive office" and including "the everyday dialogue of symbolic interactions" in which active citizens "share and contest attitudes, beliefs, values, and opinions" (12, 14, 36, 67). Our second point, and one that we think Berlin would agree with given the thrust of the latter chapters of *Rhetorics, Poetics, and Cultures,* is that rhetoric and cultural studies need not be seen as mutually exclusive alternatives among which one must choose one and only one. We prefer to see them as simultaneously competing and complementary intellectual frameworks. Here too Hauser can serve as a useful example. His study of publics and public spheres draws heavily on Habermas while rejecting both Habermas's idealization of the discourse situation and his concomitant antipathy toward rhetoric.

For Hauser, the rhetorical situation "is marked by elements of novelty and possibility for refiguring the meaning of experience and human relations" (115). Such a rhetorical situation is populated not by isolated individual agents but by interdependent and competing social actors whose experience is shaped in an "ongoing *struggle* between permanence and change, tradition and transformation," against the backdrop of history and cultural memory (112). According to Hauser, this struggle is a "self-structuring activity" through which our "publicness" is formed in a seemingly endless process of negotiation

(113). This self-structuring activity "inevitably encounters competing inter-pretations that must be negotiated, so that inventing publicness invariably poses the problem of integrating conflicts" (113). In this context, society's dis-courses—its stories, its memorials, its rituals—are complex negotiations by which society makes and remakes its political and social relations—"which is to say that rhetoric is among the social practices by which society constitutes itself" (114–15). Though we are, as Hauser insists, active and self-reflective social agents, our stories are never just about ourselves but always encompass the other and are thus, necessarily, rhetorical achievements (115, 117). We agree, and we conclude that the rhetorical tradition is vital not as an a priori set of hermeneutic and inventive principles for application today, but as a record of social practices by which societies have constituted themselves throughout history, a record that can assist us in understanding and shaping the social practices by which our own society constitutes itself.

Hauser's vernacular rhetoric emerges from multiple arenas of public dis-course, and his analyses range from the contrasting narratives of hope and despair in post-Communist Poland and Yugoslavia, to the Meese Commis-sion's report on pornography, to the technological production of public opin-ion that shaped the Carter administration's rhetorical choices during the Iran hostage crisis, and to Franklin D. Roosevelt's vernacular exchanges with his publics through letters, speeches, and radio addresses at the time of his bid for a third term as president of the United States. We believe, however, that this vernacular rhetoric also emerges from small, local arenas of public discourse, arenas that are becoming ever more important as local communities appear to dissolve into the vast and growing electronic web of disparate and competing discourses. As illustration of the vitality of these local vernacular rhetorics, we offer—at the end of this chapter—the example of our own experience with a community information system, a database of youth-services resources and multimedia content that we are developing for our own local community of Troy, New York.

It is our view that the purpose of *rhetorica docens* has always been the for-mation of citizens, that is, of participants in human collectives. For Aristotle and Isocrates, rhetoric formed participants in the Greek polis. For Hugh Blair and Adam Smith, rhetoric formed participants in the provincial cities and towns of North Britain. For John Witherspoon and John Quincy Adams, rhetoric formed participants in a new democratic republic struggling to become something other than West Britain. When read from the empirical perspective that Hauser counsels, the works of these and others in the tradi-tional canon have much to tell us about the discursive construction of the Greek polis, the cities and towns of eighteenth-century Scotland, and the emerging political culture of the United States, which is to say that they have much to tell us about how discourse has operated to inscribe the historically contingent power hierarchies about which Berlin was concerned. It is *not* to say that these works offer explicit analyses of these matters, any more than the letters analyzed by Hauser in chapter 8 of *Vernacular Voices* develop an explicit theory of the class tensions to which they speak.

Berlin's critique of the rhetorical tradition and his recommendation of a cultural turn as the means for reinvigorating that tradition flowed from his belief that the telos of a rhetorical education should be the formation of a *postmodern* democracy. He saw that to simply appropriate the texts of Aristotle, Blair, and others as if their pedagogical prescriptions could work in the late twentieth century would be a futile attempt to reinscribe the polities of ancient Athens or eighteenth-century Edinburgh.

Berlin understood democracy as an articulation of cultural practices that exists and subsists in the social structures we build to encourage and perpetuate it. Influenced by Iris Marion Young's critique of distributive justice, or the impulse to model the distribution of responsibility and social "goods" among the members of society after the distribution of commodity goods, Berlin argues for a view of democracy that recognizes abstract social benefits as products of social relationships, and not vice versa. This view, according to Berlin, urges us to rethink what a social benefit such as "democracy" might look like:

> The postmodern conception of justice leads to a definition of democracy based on the recognition of difference . . . democracy requires "real participatory structures in which actual people, with their geographical, ethnic, gender, and occupational differences, assert their perspectives on social issues within institutions that encourage the representation of their distinct voices" (Young, 116). Traditional notions of civic discourse have constructed fictional political agents who leave behind their differences to assume a persona that is rational and universal in thought and language. In a postmodern world, no such subject exists. (99)

Berlin's view is consonant with Hauser's. Both call upon us as scholars and teachers to ground our understanding of civic discourse in the material conditions within which discourse arises. What stands out in Berlin's definition is the attention to participation in these concrete discourses as the foundation of democratic practice. This focus begs the question: by what means does participation occur, and by what means is it ensured? The answer lies in a certain perspective on rhetorical and poetic discourse. Berlin asserts that "rhetorics and poetics and rhetorical and poetical texts can be regarded as a technology [sic] for producing consciousness, social and material conditions, and discourse activities that will ensure their continuance" (111). But can we find examples of these "technologies" and social structures that Berlin alludes to in the world? Can we locate Democracy by observing discursive practices at work building and maintaining the kinds of technologies and institutions that embody and enable participation?

LITTLE DEMOCRACIES: PARTICIPATORY DESIGN AND THE ROLE OF DISCURSIVE RELATIONS IN DEVELOPING INSTITUTIONS AND TECHNOLOGIES

We believe that it is possible to see the rhetorical tradition at work, either in the past or in the present historical moment, at points where institutions and technologies are in process of being shaped. Both institutions and technologies are social structures that discursively position those who inhabit or use them, enabling and constraining people as they move into specific subject positions to participate in those social structures in specific ways. Both institutions and technologies tend to establish concrete presence in the world—social structures become bureaucracies housed in buildings, discursive relationships become physical connections via phone and data lines, work processes become software applications and network routing protocols. And both institutions and technologies exist and are observable, at bottom, as discursive exchanges.

The pivotal role of rhetoric in making both institutions and technologies has been recognized, at times with trepidation and at others with exuberance, by scholars ancient and contemporary. The more positive depictions tend to heap praise on rhetoric's role in establishing institutions. Cicero gives us just this sort of endorsement of rhetoric's power in the words of Crassus, whose appeal to the power of rhetoric to build nations ignites the debate on the character of the orator in *De Oratore:*

> [W]hat other power [oratory] could either have assembled mankind, when dispersed, in to one place, or have brought them from wild and savage life to the present human and civilized state of society; or, when cities were established, have described for them laws, judicial institutions, and rights? And that I may not mention more examples, which are almost without number, I will conclude the subject in one short sentence; for I consider, that by the judgment and wisdom of the perfect orator, not only his own honor, but that of many other individuals, and the welfare of the whole state are principally upheld. Go on, therefore, as you are doing young men, and apply earnestly to the study in which you are engaged, that you may be an honor to yourselves, an advantage to your friends, and a benefit to the republic. (C.vii, p. 14)

Cicero's Crassus was updating to his own cultural moment a commonplace about the institution-making power of rhetoric that went back at least as far as Isocrates (*Nicocles* 5–9). Looking to our own time, Porter and others propose that we remember the stuff of which institutions are made, arguing that "though institutions are certainly powerful, they are not monoliths; they are rhetorically constructed human designs (whose power is reinforced by buildings, laws, traditions, and knowledge-making practices) and so are changeable" (611).

Porter and colleagues' purpose in arguing for the mutability of institutions follows from a democratic aim in Berlin's sense of rhetoric, namely "to change the practices of institutional representatives and to improve the conditions of those affected by and served by institutions" (611). This view of institutions, moreover, makes clear that change is possible via participation in the rhetorical (re)construction that brings institutions into being and keeps them going.

The role of rhetoric in democratic institution building coincides in the information age with its role in creating technologies that foster participation. While both Hauser and Berlin express some support for a model of institutions as the products of rhetoric, neither seems enthusiastic about the prospect of technology as an outlet for or a product of public discourse. Both Berlin and Hauser tend to cast technology as a cultural force descendent from an Enlightenment project that famously diminished the value of rhetoric in favor of science, even in matters formerly recognized as squarely within the province of rhetoric. Hauser attacks the effort to "technologize public opinion" in the practice of opinion polling, which he sees as antithetical to the organic development of public consensus as a product of deliberation (197). Berlin levels a similar attack against the tradition of current-traditional rhetoric as a mode of writing instruction, characterizing it as a kind of technologizing of the rhetorical tradition for the purposes of "text production for the new scientific meritocracy" (28). Both opinion polling and the practices of current-traditional rhetoric share an assumption that truth emerges from the correct application of scientific methods of inquiry, rendering both the natural and the social worlds susceptible to what Hauser calls "instrumental rationality" (195). For both Berlin and Hauser, technology is the means by which instrumental rationality becomes concrete in the form of tools and techniques that, all too often, have been used to curtail public discourse by limiting access to deliberation, and most significantly, by concentrating power in the hands of an elite class of the technologically gifted (Berlin 30; Hauser 196).

But, while there is merit in these critiques, as the title of our chapter suggests, we also believe that technology is both inevitable and redeemable. The printing press was a profound technologizing of the word, and like the rhetorical *techne* invented by Aristotle it could be and has been used for both democratic and totalitarian purposes. Practices of technology development are discursive, and the products that these practices develop are themselves locations for discursive interaction. A nagging problem with so-called high technologies is to achieve democratic participation in those processes.

In *Rhetorical Ethics and Internetworked Writing*, Porter emphasizes that today rhetorical work is increasingly work at the "interface," the place where people and technologies intersect and interact with one another. He further makes clear that interfaces are not merely technical products but social spaces: "[B]y interface I am not talking about screen design elements only (trash cans and such), but rather larger spaces (what Foucault, 1986, might call a hetero-topia) in which the screen intersects with situated uses of the technology in the classroom, community, and workplace—a contextualized interface, in other words" (146).

This view of the "architectonic" function of rhetoric is not merely a product of the coming of age of "cyberspace" as social reality. In 1970, for example, *The Report of the Committee on Rhetorical Invention* included the following discussion of rhetoric's emerging role in a technologized world:

> We begin with the assumption that a vital aspect of man's [sic] experience is rhetorical. By this we mean that every man will find himself in circumstances in which he cannot act alone, in which he must seek to act cooperatively with others, or in which others will seek to make him act cooperatively. From his interactions with others, man finds that his ability to share symbols gives him the power to meet his rhetorical needs with rhetorical materials. Because of compelling social realities man's consciousness of his rhetorical environment is expanding. The technological revolution in media and in traditional forms of persuasion have significantly extended man's inventive needs and potentialities. These changes are critical to his ability to share and perceive symbols. (105)

The roots of this discussion lie in an ancient debate about the nature of rhetoric as a practical or productive art (cf. Aristotle, *Nichomachean Ethics* 6.4; Quintillian, II.xviii.1–5). The underlying questions in this ancient debate are germane today: Is rhetoric a way of acting, a way of making? Might it be a way of "making ways of acting" that are then inscribed and normalized in the technologies we employ? Is the development of technology a "rhetorical project" in the sense that it builds concrete tools out of fundamentally discursive relations? Political scientist Langdon Winner argues precisely this point in an article whose title, "Citizen Virtues in a Technological Order," implies his thesis that technologies are enactments of a prevailing social order, much as our public institutions are. But Winner reminds us that individuals typically do not enjoy as "citizens" rights to shape technology design or policy, despite our belief that a similar level of participation in the shaping of our public institutions is vital to our democratic goals as a society.

A major obstacle to a truly democratic ideal of citizen participation is the apparent ineffability of technology, its presumed origin in esoteric and logocentric arenas in which average citizens are neither prepared nor particularly interested to participate. In insisting that the development of technology is a rhetorical project, we seek to disrupt this view and suggest that there are always moments in the development of a technology when the social relations that constitute it are in play, open to and indeed dependent upon the participation of those who would use that technology (Feenberg). Can we find one of those moments? More specifically, can we find a burgeoning democratic moment in the development of a technology?

Following Hauser's lead in adopting an empirical attitude, we turn our attention to a project that undertakes the ambitious goal of building social relationships and technologies simultaneously—though on a small scale, in a local community, "a little democracy." This project, a community information system called Connected Kids (http://troynet.net/connectedkids/, April 20, 2002), shows how vernacular rhetorics function as complex processes of negotiation in which social actors make and remake (and are in turn made and remade by) both their social relationships and the technologies that support and sustain them.[1] A collaborative effort initiated by Teri Harrison, State University of New York at Albany, and Jim Zappen and Sibel Adali, Rensselaer Polytechnic Institute, Connected Kids is developing an interactive database of youth-services resources. (We adopt the somewhat awkward convention of making "Connected Kids" a grammatical agent to acknowledge the radically collaborative nature of a project whose strategy and purposes include turning the proposed users of a technology into designers of it.) The proximate goals of Connected Kids are to permit youth-services organizations to disseminate information about themselves and their programs and events and simultaneously to enlist young people as participants in the development of information and multimedia content for the database. The project illustrates Hauser's vernacular rhetoric as a process of negotiation, a "self-structuring activity" in which social actors make and remake themselves in concert and sometimes in conflict with others (112–13). It is a rhetorical process of negotiation among programmers, designers, and users participating in the development of the database and among teachers, parents, and young people engaged in the production of multimedia content for storage in the database and display on the World Wide Web.

PRACTICING DEMOCRACY: THE CONNECTED KIDS PROJECT

In his analysis of letters written to Franklin D. Roosevelt during his bid for a third term as president, Hauser documents the overwhelming support for the president expressed in these letters, the confidence of ordinary people that he was the person most capable of handling the threat of war and also the person who cared most about them. Hauser's analysis of these letters reveals "a *moral America* . . . dedicated to peace, patriotism, and decency" and "a *virile America* devoted to self-sufficiency and self-sacrifice" (260–61). Our analysis of the Connected Kids project reveals similar cultural values. Users of the developing database seek and indeed insist upon self-sufficiency but are apprehensive about both their own technical expertise and resources and the performance capabilities of the database. Young people show both a remarkable self-confidence and self-sacrifice and an equally remarkable dependence upon contemporary social and family values. Both groups are engaged in ongoing self-structuring activities in negotiation with themselves and others.

But while the cultural values revealed in our analysis of Connected Kids are in important ways similar to those that Hauser observed in the Roosevelt letters, we found far less unanimity of opinion than he did. We can only speculate about this diversity, but we suspect that it is a product of the differences in the particular historical (and rhetorical) moments that we have chosen, respectively, to study. Hauser selects a moment near the end of Roosevelt's second term, a moment at which public opinion has coalesced around the threat of a world war and the evident benefits of the New Deal to masses of ordinary people. We have selected a moment very near the beginning of the development of a large and complex community information system, a point at which the local community participants are unconvinced of the benefits of the project and skeptical of the professed good intentions of their academic neighbors. We are interested in observing the process of negotiation by which we academics and our partners from local youth-services agencies build the technical system, but also and more especially the process of negotiation by which we build a social community of shared interest—a process that Hauser aptly calls a "self-structuring activity" (113). We are equally interested in observing the process of negotiation by which young people participate in this endeavor, creating their own images of themselves, exploring their own identities, and sharing them with others via the World Wide Web—another "self-structuring activity" but one that is always and everywhere unfinished.

Still in its early stages of development, Connected Kids has engaged representatives from youth-services organizations in participatory design processes to develop specifications for the database, to assess the progress of the design team, and, where necessary, to redefine the system specifications. Connected Kids has also conducted focus-group meetings with students in the middle and high schools and with parents to determine how and why they use—and would like to use—World Wide Web resources. In addition, Connected Kids has involved Rensselaer graduate and undergraduate students in a variety of activities directed toward the creation of a social and physical infrastructure to ensure convenient access and ease of use of the database, especially among underserved and underprivileged populations. These activities include rebuilding recycled computers, installing computers and networking equipment in local youth-services facilities and after-school programs, and conducting on-site training in basic computing, image processing, and Web design in the after-school programs. In these collective social activities, representatives from youth-services organizations, graduate and undergraduate students, and young people are making and remaking their social relationships and the technologies that support them in discursive practices by which they negotiate their basic cultural values and beliefs both within themselves and with others.

We offer two examples of these processes of negotiation: one from the participatory design meetings with representatives from the youth-services organizations, another from computer-training sessions in the local after-school programs.

In the participatory design meetings, partner organizations expressed conflicting needs. All felt a need to be self-sufficient, and most felt some apprehension about their own technical capabilities and the capabilities of the proposed database. Initially envisioning a system that would provide little more than a calendar of events, the design team learned that as a group the youth-services organizations wanted to present a much more complex array of organizational and programmatic information. Some larger organizations already had Web-based information systems and were apprehensive about duplicating their efforts. Smaller organizations, worried about their limited resources and technical expertise, doubted their ability to maintain these systems for themselves. Some had had discouraging previous experiences with student-designed technical resources. Recalling her previous experiences with these students, one representative from a small organization observed (with a smile): "Sometimes we can't get rid of them." Teri and Jim acknowledged this problem and its complement: students who disappeared once their classes were over, leaving a small organization with a technically sophisticated and aesthetically pleasing Web that the organization was unable to maintain.

The participatory design meetings demonstrated the need for ongoing processes of negotiation between designers and partner organizations—self-structuring activities in which all parties actively reconstitute or reinvent both their social relationships and the technologies that sustain them. To address the needs of both large and small organizations, the design team is now developing a database and World Wide Web interface capable of providing both a port of entry to the existing Web-based information systems of larger organizations and a self-sufficient Web-based information system for smaller ones. For the smaller organizations, the design team is attempting to provide ongoing support of several kinds: Web design and maintenance, computer reconstruction and/or purchases of new computers or components, computer troubleshooting, and negotiations with Internet service providers. On the academic side, students and professors continue to struggle with institutional structures (courses, credit hours, and calendars) that make it difficult for students to provide the ongoing support the smaller organizations need. The degree of self-restructuring required to enable Rensselaer students to be full and continuing partners in this project remains allusive, but participants are confident that progress is being made.

The computer-training sessions in the local after-school programs show young people similarly engaged in the process of negotiating both their social relationships and the technologies they are just beginning to learn to use. Connected Kids designers initially speculated that the database system would be more appealing to parents, teachers, and young people if they could see something of themselves in it—a speculation confirmed by initial meetings with students in the middle and high schools. The designers have therefore launched a series of learning experiences in which young people are developing informative and visually appealing content for the database: art galleries representing the work of students in local schools, science and technology information modules for middle and high school students, and artwork and storytelling by kids in the after-school programs.

The after-school computer-training sessions are especially instructive as processes of negotiation between and among social actors and technical systems. Like the representatives from the partner organizations, the young people in these programs experience conflicts in cultural values and engage in complex processes of negotiation with their families, within themselves, and with the computer technologies that are new to most of them. On the one hand, the young people seem to be remarkably self-confident about themselves and their futures; on the other hand, they seem to be just as remarkably dependent upon contemporary social and family values. Most are in the lower grades and just beginning to learn to write. In one of their activities, the teachers asked the children to draw a picture and tell a little story in answer to the prompt: "If I could be anything in the world, I would be. . . ." The students developed their responses in conversations with their teachers, in processes of negotiation in which they discovered what they thought by talking through their ideas and then writing them out in stories. Their responses reveal the complexity of their developing social relationships. Clearly they felt confident that they could be anything that they wanted to be. But equally clearly they were powerfully influenced by larger social values as represented in the mass media. Many wanted to be successful sports figures or entertainers. Others wanted to be veterinarians, wedding planners, bakers, and teachers. Some just wanted to be rich and famous. Others wanted to care for animals or to make other people happy, for example, by planning their weddings (like the wedding planner in the movie, perhaps?). Some just liked muffins and pastries. Some seemed confused or conflicted. One wanted to be a teacher because she thought that she would enjoy correcting papers and watching movies with the other teachers. Another wanted to be a scientist rather than a cashier because he would rather look through a microscope than take people's money from them.

It is not surprising that the kids were also influenced by their own family values. Some who wanted to be sports figures or entertainers hoped to be rich or famous. But one acknowledged that she would give the money to her mom because she herself would not know what to do with it. Another wrote that she was inspired by her own mother to become a foster mom. But she also noted that she would be a foster mom to only two children because three would be much too great a challenge!

Strikingly, these young people seemed not to be tied to traditional gender roles. One girl wanted to be Michael Jordan, and another wanted to be a New York Yankee. A boy wanted to be Aaliyah. These stories illustrate the complexity of their negotiations with the world—wanting money, for example, but not knowing what to do with it. They also illustrate the openness to new possibilities and new social relationships in which girls can do "boy things" and boys can do "girl things." As Hauser observes, our stories are deeply rooted in history and cultural memory, but they are also "a means for meeting the challenge of a past and future moving in opposite directions" and thus a means of not only reporting history but also transforming it (112).

The after-school programs are also instructive as processes of negotiation with the computer technology, which was new to most of the kids. To ensure access and use of computers among underserved populations, Connected Kids has involved Rensselaer students in rebuilding computers with free Linux software (Red Hat 7.2), installing and networking the computers in the after-school programs, and offering instruction in the use of the software. Although some of the older kids seemed comfortable with Linux, probably as a result of their experience in the schools, most of the kids in the lower grades—those who attended the after-school programs—were just beginning to learn to use it. The kids proved to be quick and eager learners, but they were schooled in some conventions of print literacy that seemed to work at cross-purposes with the computer technology. Connected Kids teachers sometimes asked young people to write out their stories before typing them into the computer. The students were meticulous about their handwriting, checked their spelling with the teachers and other kids, and rewrote whole words rather than replacing individual letters when correcting errors. These habits carried over to their use of the computers, with curious results. At the computers, they typed slowly, often searching at length for the correct letter. When the software underlined misspellings in red, the kids would routinely erase and retype whole words, again searching at length for each letter. If the underlining persisted, they would replace a word, even if it were actually spelled correctly. When the students were telling Halloween stories, one group included the figure of Frankenstein, whose name was underlined in red. Despite several attempts to correct the spelling, the underlining persisted, presumably because the Linux spelling tool did not recognize the name. The kids changed the name to Jack and were obviously very pleased with the result. With time, the kids learned to ignore the red underlining, but they persisted in correcting whole words rather than individual letters, and they seemed willing to correct or edit only their most recent text, the habits of print literacy apparently carrying over to the keyboard and screen. Presumably, they will eventually learn to take a stronger stance in their negotiations with the computers. But we suspect that they will need to learn most of these lessons for themselves, as they, like all of us, negotiate a past and future moving in opposite directions.

Beyond the Sublime: Two Directions
for Rhetorical Inquiry in the Digital Age

We conclude this chapter with a roadmap of sorts, pointing the way to a vital and, we hope, newly relevant rhetorical tradition in the age of the Internet and the World Wide Web. In particular, we want to highlight two important paths rhetoricians might take in order to pursue not merely a sustained critique of the rhetorical tradition but also a reconstruction of that tradition in the interest of making and remaking "little democracies." The first path is a familiar one: pedagogy and curriculum. We will spend little time elaborating on this path, except to note that with our use of the terms *pedagogy* and *curriculum* we hope to point to moments like those discussed in the foregoing description of the Connected Kids project: opportunities to remake the entrenched aims and modes of rhetorical instruction. Connected Kids has undoubtedly fostered pedagogy and curriculum but has done so through what Hauser has identified as "processes of negotiation" rather than through the more traditional, institutional exercises of offering courses, programs, and so on. This sort of "vernacular pedagogy," as we might call it, is one promising new direction for the rhetorical tradition that recalls, and perhaps reimagines, a Sophistic tradition of situated learning, challenging, and broadening the borders of the polis.

The second path we recommend reflects a relatively unexplored trajectory in the recent history of American rhetorical inquiry: the design of communication technologies. As we have tried to show in the case of the Connected Kids project, pedagogy and design become intertwined and mutually informing when they are pursued in the spirit of Hauser's vernacular voices. Connected Kids demonstrates how the voices of the children of Troy along with the voices of adults—parents, teachers, social-services personnel, city officials—are actively articulating the institutional and technological connections that create "subject positions" we can actually see, even point to: in the database, on the network, and in the community. Shaping democratic citizens in our increasingly networked environment calls for a stronger-than-ever commitment to clarifying the discursive positions, functions, and forms that permit participation in the practice of democracy. A rhetorical education is, of course, a valuable way to foster such a commitment. But pedagogy and curriculum are not enough. The communication technologies that increasingly influence and, in some cases, actively (re)form institutions are built of the same stuff as any rhetoric. In Berlin's words, both rhetoric and communication technology qualify as "device[s] to train producers of discourse" (137). As we saw in the examples of the Connected Kids design meetings and in the words and artwork of the students being introduced to computer technology for the first time, the devices trained everyone involved to utter an "appropriate" discourse, even when deliberations about what were and were not "appropriate" utterances never became explicit. The Connected Kids project reveals the tremendous potential for rhetoricians to intervene in the making of communication technologies with an explicit agenda: ensuring that a participatory model of discursive practice prevails. In fact, we ignore this opportunity at our peril. Rhetorics of one sort or another will prevail, training the future producers of discourse in such matters as who can and cannot enter conversations about matters of material and social importance and how these conversations should proceed. Increasingly, these rhetorics will not appear in any textbook, but instead will be integral to the devices, software, and networks that give physical form to our social environments.

We might recognize in the model of tacit rhetorical training that our communication technologies impart a familiar combination of fear and fascination. What software developers sometimes refer to as "elegant solutions" we might just as readily call "the sublime," an idea that hearkens back to the cultural moment in which American democracy first emerged and thus reminds us of the role of Hugh Blair in spreading the rhetorical tradition in antebellum America. In the view of many historians of rhetoric, Blair's views on such matters as invention and the sublime constituted a powerful reinscription of the predominant white, male, upper-class subject position (see, e.g., Golden and Corbett; Halloran), to whose authoritative genius women and the middling classes were supposed to defer. And yet as Ferreira-Buckley and Halloran argue in the introduction to their forthcoming new edition of Blair's *Lectures on Rhetoric and Belles Lettres,* Blair's overtly elitist and colonialist rhetoric could be put to liberatory purposes in specific local contexts. The uses of traditional rhetorical texts may be as much a matter of negotiation as are the vernacular voices attended to by Hauser.

Built into our cutting-edge technologies of communication are tacit assumptions about the ability of the average citizen to "invent" that are as elitist and antidemocratic as anything purveyed by the much-maligned Hugh Blair. For the vast majority of ordinary citizen "users," the appropriate activity is "browsing"—a metaphor more bovine than human. At best, browsing invites us to participate in what amounts to an emerging stylistics of online discourse. Those who would engage in *inventio* ("designers") or even *dispositio* ("developers") of online systems and the "content" that flows over them are supposed to meet higher levels of technical expertise. And yet as the Connected Kids project suggests, there are gaps in the Wizard's curtain through which ordinary citizens may poke their noses, even at this primitive stage of the digital era. The challenge for those who would defend rhetoric is to establish a strong participatory tradition with/in the network: a tradition where citizens do not merely browse, but invent, discuss, and negotiate.

NOTE

1. This material is based upon work supported by the National Science Foundation under Grant No. 0091505. Any opinions, findings, and conclusions or recommendations expressed in this material are those of the authors and do not necessarily reflect the views of the National Science Foundation. The Connected Kids project is supported by the City of Troy; Rensselaer County; Academic and Research Computing, the School of Humanities and Social Sciences, and the School of Science, Rensselaer Polytechnic Institute; the 3Com Urban Challenge Program; the National Science Foundation; the Rubin Community Fellows Program; Salerni and Boyd; Time Warner Cable; the Troy and Lansingburgh public schools; and numerous youth-services organizations.

WORKS CITED

Aristotle. *On Rhetoric: A Theory of Civic Discourse.* Trans. George A. Kennedy. New York: Oxford UP, 1991.

Berlin, James A. *Rhetorics, Poetics, and Cultures.* Urbana, IL: NCTE, 1996.

Blair, Hugh. *Lectures on Rhetoric and Belles Lettres: The Rhetoric of Blair, Campbell, and Whately.* Ed. James L. Golden and Edward P. J. Corbett. Carbondale: Southern Illinois UP, 1990.

Cicero, M. T. *De Oratore.* Trans. J. S. Watson. Carbondale: Southern Illinois UP, 1970.

Connected Kids. 20 April 2002. http://troynet.net/connectedkids/.

Feenberg, Andrew. *Critical Theory of Technology.* New York: Oxford UP, 1991.

Ferreira-Buckley, Linda, and S. Michael Halloran. Editors' Introduction. *Hugh Blair's Lectures on Rhetoric and Belles Lettres.* Carbondale: Southern Illinois UP, forthcoming.

Foucault, Michel. "Of Other Spaces." *Diacritics 16* (1986): 22–27.

Halloran, S. Michael, "Hugh Blair's Use of Quintillian and the Transformation of Rhetoric in the Eighteenth Century." In *Rhetoric and Pedagogy, Its History, Philosophy and Practice: Essays in Honor of James J. Murphy.* Ed. Winifred Bryan Horner and Michael Leff. Mahwah, NJ: Lawrence Erlbaum, 1995. 183–95.

Harrison, Teresa M., James P. Zappen, and Christina Prell. "Transforming New Communication Technologies into Community Media." In *Community Media in the Information Age: Perspectives and Prospects.* Ed. Nicholas W. Jankowski with Ole Prehn. Cresskill, NJ: Hampton, 2002. 249–69.

Harrison, Teresa M., James P. Zappen, Timothy Stephen, Philip Garfield, and Christina Prell. "Building an Electronic Community: A Town-Gown Collaboration." In *Communication and Community.* Ed. Gregory J. Shepherd and Eric W. Rothenbuhler. Mahwah, NJ: Lawrence Erlbaum, 2001. 201–16.

Hauser, Gerard A. *Vernacular Voices: The Rhetoric of Publics and Public Spheres.* Columbia: U of South Carolina P, 1999.

Isocrates. "Nicocles or the Cyprians." *Isocrates*, vol. 1. Trans. George Norlin. Cambridge, MA: Harvard UP (Loeb Classical Library), 1928. 73–114.

Porter, James E. *Rhetorical Ethics and Internetworked Writing*. Greenwich, CT: Ablex, 1998.

Porter, James E., Patricia Sullivan, Stuart Blythe, Jeffrey T. Grabill, and Libby Miles. "Institutional Critique: A Rhetorical Methodology for Change." *College Composition and Communication* 51 (2000): 610–42.

Quintillian. *Institutio Oratoria, Books I–III*. Trans. H. E. Butler. Suffolk, UK: St. Edmundsbury Press.

Red Hat Linux. Vers. 7.2. 28 April 2002. http://www.redhat.com/software.

"Report of the Committee on the Nature of Rhetorical Invention." In *Contemporary Rhetoric: A Conceptual Background with Readings*. Ed. W. Ross Winterowd. New York: Harcourt, Brace, Jovanovich, 1975. 104–11.

"Thompson Will Shut Down Harcourt's Online College." *The Chronicle of Higher Education*. 10 August 2000. http://www.chronicle.com/weekly/v47/i48/48a04901.htm.

Winner, Langdon. "Citizen Virtues in a Technological Order." In *Technology and the Politics of Knowledge*. Ed. Andrew Feenberg and Alastair Hannay. Bloomington: Indiana UP, 1995.

Young, Iris Marion. *Justice and the Politics of Difference*. Princeton, NJ: Princeton UP, 1990.

NINE

Civic Humanism, a Postmortem?

Thomas J. Kinney and Thomas P. Miller

IN THEORY AND PRACTICE, the rhetorical tradition has been defined as the history of theories of public discourse, the principles of which have generally been defined in civic humanist terms.[1] Public-speaking courses, history of rhetoric seminars, and the occasional humanistic composition course have looked to the Athenian Assembly and Roman Senate for classical models. Such a historical orientation has stopped making sense for many of us. We have worked through the recognition that "the good man speaking well" served to give virtue to power by making educated white men of property the spokesmen for the public good. Insofar as it relied on such rhetoricians as Aristotle, Cicero, and Quintilian for its sense of purpose, the rhetorical tradition depended upon the vision of a few good men as representatives of history in a manner that reproduced the ideology of civic humanism. As these figures have lost their representative authority, the rhetorical tradition has lost its coherence, and it has become difficult to get from the ancient Greeks to the first college composition courses at Harvard with any clear sense of where we are going, or who "we" are to be when we get there. Our disciplinary identification with such civic ideals has been cited as evidence that the purposes served by our discipline are an anachronism. Wayne Booth, for example, has been ridiculed for offering a civic humanist jeremiad on behalf of "a lost republican virtue that never was" (Fusfield 268). Is rhetoric so imbued with doctrines of the purposeful individual speaking for public virtues that it can only serve as a subject of nostalgia, as such postmodern critics as John Bender and David E. Wellbery have maintained?

Rhetoric may be so invested in civic values that it will pass into history with them, or it may jettison them and become just another area of cultural studies. Without a sense of the civic to provide a purposeful engagement in political action, what really distinguishes the *rhetorical* in "the rhetorical tradition," "rhetorical hermeneutics," "rhetorical criticism," or rhetoric and composition for that matter? Rhetoric has already ceased to be central in most communication departments, and the conjunction in rhetoric and composition may be losing its locutionary force as composition studies becomes fully established and less in need of an ancient heritage to legitimate itself.[2] Without a collective sense of purpose, rhetoric is little more than a theory of speaking and writing, with conceptions of audiences and intentions that provide just another set of hermeneutical categories, interesting historically, though somewhat mundane and rather outdated, if not downright pernicious. After all, civic humanism has pretty much lost its appeal to us, for what is still relevant in the ideal of the purposeful agent speaking with reason for the common good to the assembled public who will decide what is right according to the force of a good argument? Such a figure has become little more than a straw man to be set up on occasions when one needs some fireworks. And even that purpose has dimmed, for few are left to be surprised by seeing the republican orator lit up as a representative of the classism, sexism, and ethnocentrism that made rhetoric the power apparatus of the Western Tradition.

How can a sense of the *civic* offer more than nostalgia for republicanism? The civic tradition offers conceptions of praxis and *phronēsis,* or practical wisdom, that have been invoked against the instrumental rationality of scientism by such figures as Heidegger, Horkheimer and Adorno, Gadamer, Habermas, and others who have shaped the frameworks within which we work. The modern opposition of humanism to scientism has shaped the positions and purposes of rhetoric on both sides of that institutional divide. As "service" courses positioned at the bottom of humanities and social science hierarchies, college writing and public-speaking courses have been pressed to define themselves in utilitarian terms by confining themselves to the mechanics of basic skills, though more humanistic justifications have been sustained in some places. Humanism and vocationalism have both been rejected by teachers who have adopted more materialist and collectivist approaches to discourse (see the Normal Research Collective, for example). A richer sense of such alternatives may open up from a critical reassessment of the ethnographic dimensions of the civic tradition. If we can look past the modern conceptions of individual agency that have been overlaid on that tradition, we may be able to use its problematics as heuristics to explore the technologies that are transforming literacy. Our attempt to reimagine the civic in this chapter will begin with rethinking rhetoric as a *technē,* and then we will consider science and technology studies as a space of civic possibilities. This line of inquiry seems timely to us, for as we were writing this chapter, deliberative assemblies around the world were calling upon our government to justify its preparations to make war on Iraq with evidence that it had technologies of mass destruction. Discussions "at home" routinely ignored the role our nation plays in creating such technologies and the profits that multinational corporations make from their distribution, in part because Americans do not generally think of business as politics. If we mean to, a retooled and redeployed sense of the civic may be useful because it presents a pragmatic ideology with popular currency that can be appropriated to develop broadly based coalitions among public agencies to resist the imposition of the values of the market on civic life.

RECLAIMING A SENSE OF THE CIVIC

One of the paradoxes of the humanist tradition is that it began by making a philosophy of the *technē* of rhetoric and perhaps ended when all such philosophies became reinterpreted as rhetorical. The "fact that the humanities were born in a rhetorical manger" was an article of faith among such founders of rhetoric and composition as James Kinneavy ("Restoring" 20). As Kinneavy discussed with the sort of excitement that only civic rhetoricians still feel for him, Isocrates was the first professor of the humanities; the first recorded use of *humanitas* was in the *Rhetorica ad Herennium;* and the first documented use of *artes liberales* was in Cicero's *De Inventione*. More recent scholarship has focused on the differences that get effaced by sweeping from classical *paideia* and Renaissance humanism through the liberal arts to general education. Positioned above the utilitarian concerns of the mechanical arts, the liberal arts were reserved for those who could take a liberal interest in education because they were freed from having to work for a living. We have often glossed over the political differences contained within the humanities in the same way that we have assumed that classical rhetoric could be used to teach composition and communication or that ancient theories could explain modern democracy.

Janet Atwill's *Rhetoric Reclaimed: Aristotle and the Liberal Arts Tradition* offers an analysis of the pre-Aristotelian sense of *technē* that provides us with the basis for a richer understanding of rhetoric (see also Walker). Rather than socializing subjects toward the customary, Atwill reconceives *technē* as an intervening into and challenging of the customary. In so doing, she identifies the *technē* of rhetoric with the contingencies of time and place. Rhetoric is, under this analysis, an art of "intervention and invention" in the here and now (2). In this way, Atwill refigures one of the oldest of rhetorical questions: if rhetoric is an art, what is it the art of? Atwill answers by developing a sense of *technē* that combines the artistic and the technological to treat *making* as instrumental but indeterminate, as different in kind from theoretical and practical modes of knowing and doing. As a technology for reinterpreting received beliefs to make sense of changing situations, rhetoric is integrally involved with *ethnography* because the "writings of a tribe" or *ethnos* set out the terms in which it understands its pragmatic possibilities. By "reclaiming" a creative understanding of rhetoric as a technology, Atwill traces the universalist pretensions of humanism back to their source, in the collective making of meaning, which is redefined as a pragmatic process whose ends cannot be set in advance. Rhetoric thus becomes a social capacity rather than a prescribed methodology set up to serve a prescribed system of values, and humanistic *topoi* can then be treated as heuristics for "the negotiation and invention of diverse standards of value, subjectivity and knowledge" rather than generalized into the virtues of humanism and humanity (172). This line of analysis presents a more useful, a more rhetorical sense of the liberal arts as historically constituted and constitutive.

This dialectical understanding of the conventions of the liberal arts is evident in perhaps the most influential paeon to the civic virtues of rhetoric, Cicero's *De Oratore,* which identifies rhetoric with the conventions of daily life, "common usage and the custom and language of all men" (9). This ethnographic sense of the humanities as concerned with practical morality, reasoning, and language was fundamental to rhetoric as the art of the commonplace. According to *De Oratore,* the highest achievements and basic principles of other arts tend to be "drawn from recluse and hidden springs . . . remote from the knowledge and understanding of the illiterate," but in rhetoric "the greatest of faults" is to vary from common language and popular beliefs (9). While Cicero advised rhetoricians to study prevailing "laws, customs, and equity," Aristotle was most systematic about ethnographically surveying popular opinions, whether they be codified in social conventions or political constitutions, and then reasoning through them dialectically to develop practical wisdom or *phronēsis.* One need not adopt Aristotle's hierarchical epistemology to reclaim the *technē* of rhetoric as a civic hermeneutic for exploring sites of controversy and making use of commonplaces to compose enthymemes that audiences will fill out from their experiences. Discussions of "rhetorical hermeneutics" have sometimes maintained that rhetoric has been too concerned with the production of discourse to provide interpretive categories for our use, which may very well be true if they are used just to interpret individual texts rather than to explore contested beliefs to assess the pragmatics of collective action. The pragmatics, or *pragmatikon,* of deliberative action were formalized as the three genres of public discourse that have been central to the arts of rhetoric, as discussed in Walker's *Rhetoric and Poetics in Antiquity* (7–10).[3]

Atwill's analysis of *technē* also provides a way of thinking about technologies that could help us to rethink the modern opposition of the arts and sciences. Drawing on the civic humanism of Isocrates, Aristotle, and Cicero, Atwill reconceives rhetoric as a situated technology of collaborative deliberation that treats differences as generative. This conception can help us see our differences as productive resources in knowledge making. If we are to make democracy practical, we need pragmatic alternatives to the hierarchy of scholarly research and technical expertise that have established the academy as a center of knowledge making, but that also made humanistic inquiry appear impractical. Atwill shifts the grounds of humanistic resistance to utilitarianism by reframing the locus of value around *technē* as technologies of making and thereby creating a more productive response than hermeneutical accounts of praxis alone.[4]

Technology has been divested of civic value by the ideology of scientific exceptionalism that has exempted science from the contested domain of public rhetoric. Inverting without transforming the modern subordination of the arts to the sciences, the humanities have reduced rhetoric to mechanical techniques devoid of intellectual value and creative possibility. Reclaiming a dialectical sense of the civic potentials of rhetoric is vital to the very viability of the humanities because the practical arts of composition and interpretation provide the most compelling arguments for more holistic philosophies of public education. The surest way to make such a philosophy less persuasive to the public is to continue to try to set its methods of inquiry apart from the technologies of communication that are transforming what it means to be literate. The humanities have pragmatic value precisely because they provide one of the best ways for people to understand that communications are never univocal or uncontested, that their effects are not as inevitable as they may be made to feel, and that the pragmatics of communication are not merely an instrumental matter. As we learn each day anew, studies of composition and interpretation can enrich our practical sense of the virtues of difference by enabling us to imagine alternative modes of experience and expression. In this pragmatic process, collaborations with those who come from different cultural and social backgrounds can teach us the values of double-voicedness, but only if we can make ourselves listen.[5] By devaluing the practical art of intervening in public debates over popular values, the humanities have contributed to their isolation from broader publics and to the replacement of civic by professional ethics. According to Kinneavy, terms of engagement such as *scientific objectivity, academic freedom,* and *the marketplace of ideas* have worked to exempt educators and the educated from attending to their "rhetorical obligation" to broader public interests ("Exile" 110).

A CIVICS FOR CYBORGS

We have recently come to recognize that we are part of the technologies we use to express ourselves. From this posthumanistic perspective, the individual is situated not at a critical distance but rather in the midst of the machine. As N. Katherine Hayles notes, "[T]he posthuman subject is an amalgam, a collection of heterogeneous components, a material-informational entity whose boundaries undergo construction and reconstruction" (3). Through the popular influence of the writings of Donna Haraway, this posthuman subject has become represented as a cyborg. The (wo)man as machine brings the death of one strain in humanism, for he/she/it is fabricated from the fictions of science and appears terminally disfigured when assessed in terms of the organic imagery and spiritual imaginings of literary classics. The cyborg is an artifact of technoscience, a fusion of artistry and facticity that embodies living with technology. From this perspective, *technoscience* (Haraway's term for the merging of science and technology) is "civics, in the strong sense, at the heart of what can count as knowledge" (*Modest_Witness* 114). In this sense, "civics" is understood not as an abstraction from but a hacking into codified conventions—a critical appropriation that creates an alternative not written into the code. A civic sense of technoscience recreates the technologies and economies of knowledge that constitute our political and ethical possibilities, particularly the technologies of collective engagement that have effaced traditional distinctions between public entities and private individuals. The civic dynamics of these collective forms of agency have become a subject of discussion in the works of such figures as Steve Fuller, Richard Sclove, and Haraway, as well as others who have set out the civic possibilities of technoscience.

The cyborg personifies posthumanism by representing personal identity itself as a collective form of agency interpellated by a proliferation of electronic, informatic, and cybernetic technologies. In its most elemental form, the cyborg fuses human and machine. In its more conceptually elaborated form, it is a trope for the synthetic character of postmodern identity—the provisional fabrication of parts picked up from here and there in the process of making do. As Haraway notes, in "our time, a mythic time, we are all chimeras, theorized and fabricated hybrids of machine and organism; in short, we are cyborgs" (*Simians* 150). Human beings have been cyborgs ever since we began using tools and engaging in systems that enable us to exchange what we make and do for what we desire and need. Insofar as our physical needs and cultural aspirations are mediated through technology, we "all live in a 'cyborg' society" (Gray, Mentor, and Figueroa-Sarriera 3). Technoculture "is our nature," according to Laughlin, a nature that does not hold out an alternative to convention but that values artifice as part of the pragmatics of becoming (2). As technologies have transformed our sense of our world and our selves, the modern opposition between knowers and known, subjects and objects has become a contrivance to be critiqued rather than a foundation to be assumed. "The emergence of the cyborg," writes Laughlin, "is a process of progressive technological penetration into the body, eventually replacing or augmenting the structures that mediate the various physical and mental attributes that we normally considered "natural" to human beings" (3–4). As humanity has been retooled at an intensifying rate, the disinterested spectator has become a figure not of reason but of boredom, arising from the failure to connect.[6] Indeed, the shift in vantage point from scientist to cyborg marks the historical transition from the objective observer to engaged participant as a civic ideal for transactional modes of inquiry.

Insofar as postmodernism represents not an end but a turn in the history of modernity (as Lyotard and others have discussed), posthumanism is not simply the postmortem of humanism but a transformation of the humanistic understanding of *techné* along the lines of Atwill's reappropriations of classical rhetoric.[7] More traditional humanists such as Walter Ong have amply detailed how the discursive technologies we use constitute us and that understanding reaches back through the civic humanist tradition that includes such figures as Vico who have predicated their whole conceptions of history and culture on the assumption that we are creatures of our own making, not in the modern sense of self-made men and women but in the humanistic sense of creative creatures who come to know by making use of tradition. The civic tradition provides useful heuristics for exploring such ethnographic questions about technologies of self-fashioning. To highlight the possibilities that open out from this disjuncture, we would like to configure the political possibilities it presents in terms of *civic* posthumanism.

As an awareness of our interdependence with technology has replaced modern conceptions of the autonomous individual, we have come to understand our freedoms from and duties to others in more mediated ways. Civic posthumanism has been concerned with "technoscientific liberty," which as Haraway discusses, "takes shape in strong, contestatory democratic practice, and in the creation of technoscientific ends achieved by citizen activity" (*Modest_Witness* 113). The obvious place to begin considering such practices is in public policy deliberations. Unfortunately, studies of science and technology policy making, as Aant Elzinga and Andrew Jamison note, "occupy a weak and rather fragmented position within the broader STS [science and technology studies] community" (572). This position needs to be bolstered, they argue, for "science studies are naive if not informed by a science and technology policy perspective" (573). Elzinga and Jamison characterize science and technology policy making as an integral part of the ideological program of legitimation aimed at enabling "those in power—the political, industrial, military establishments—to use knowledge to achieve their goals" (574). However, policy changes have sometimes been shaped by public debates and social movements provoked by technological developments ranging from nuclear bombs to gene splices. As Elzinga and Jamison discuss, the ideological frameworks in which institutional reforms and regulatory innovations have been debated have been shaped by popular activists and writers. Deliberations upon science and technology policies hold civic possibilities because such deliberations function as "a rhetorical struggle over the ways that science and technology are interpreted" (Elzinga and Jamison 574). And when civic rhetoricians fail, "policymaking has been reduced to a technocratic instrument for rationalization and planning in an established framework whose basic assumptions go unquestioned" (Elzinga and Jamison 575). In such venues, one can see how scientific exceptionalism has functioned to exempt changes in technology from deliberations upon their civic implications in ways that have mirrored how we understand technologies as simple tools rather than as extensions of ourselves.

If universities are to function as institutions of public learning and not just the credentialing apparatus for the technical and managerial class, they need to form coalitions with citizen groups to address disjunctures in legitimations of technoscience. English and communication departments need to see themselves as a site for such collaborations. Few scientists are currently prepared to debate matters of science and technology policy, and general education courses in science studies often view public policy debates from the perspective of the consumer rather than the participant. This lack of preparation in the rhetorical craft of collective deliberation is itself a product of scientific exceptionalism. While critics have made the rhetorical strategies of influential scientists a topic of study, scientific research and education are not generally understood to be deliberative processes. Given the requisite facts, any trained professional can reach the correct conclusion, and others can do little more than check the calculations. While such assumptions have become unsustainable in theory, they remain a pervasive part of scientific work, including teaching novices that one simply does research and then writes up the results. In the laboratory, as in the public forum, the appropriate conclusions should be obvious to anyone with the expertise to read the data. Such assumptions have been increasingly contested, but scientists are not generally taught to debate the civic dimensions of science any more than other citizens are. As Steve Fuller discusses, "it is not clear that the 'experts' are competent in the area where we tend to want their advice, namely, the 'public sphere'" (285). Science and technology policy makers, whose job it is to be a liaison between science and the government, "still operate with what is properly seen as a 'folk theory' of how science itself works" (Fuller 230). Functioning as tacitly conveyed common sense, such norms become naturalized as facts that can then be deployed as evaluative criteria, as with the universalism of humanism and the exceptionalism of scientism. Critical rereadings of such tacitly accepted assumptions are needed to intervene in the tendency of policy makers to "equate statistically normal behavior with normatively desirable action" (Fuller 275). Funding and accounting for technoscience might then be more broadly deliberated upon, and practitioners could "be shaken from their unreflective stances of presuming that the 'is' and the 'ought,' facts and values, are fused together in some 'implicit norms' or 'natural trajectory' of knowledge production" (Fuller 275). They might therefore be more inclined to treat science and technology as rhetorical arts of "intervention and invention" (Atwill 2).

While those with power will inevitably resist making its uses a subject of public debate, treating science and technology policy making as a civic genre of rhetorical *technē* opens it up to thinking more creatively about how it works.

In his book, *Toward a Democratic Science: Scientific Narration and Civic Communication,* Richard Harvey Brown argues that thinking of science as a type of storytelling calls into question the normative claims of technoscience because scientific authority is compromised when we respond with rhetorical analyses of the stories it makes for us about the means and ends of progress. In the absence of a rhetorical understanding of such civic discourse at work, we are left "to choose between the amoral rationality of science and the seemingly irrational moralism of storytelling, with little confluence of the two in reasoned public moral action" (ix). We are left with an impoverished sense of the civic because "when moral discourse and action become exclusively emotive or private, and when actions taken in the public arena are governed purely by the functional efficiency or irrational stories, then the space for reasoned public moral action is drastically reduced" (ix). By failing to engage with the domain of technoscience as a civic space for collective action, we enable private businesses and state officials to speak for the public interest. A civic alternative emerges, according to Brown, when we begin "to construe science as a kind of narration and to understand narration as a form of reason" (x). This redefinition moves technoscience "from a technocist practice, accessible only to a specialized priesthood, to a rhetorical practice in which all competent adults can engage" (194). In this way, the *technē* of rhetoric becomes a heuristic for treating technoscientific deliberations as part of the craft of citizenship.

CIVIC INTERVENTIONS INTO TECHNOSCIENTIFIC DELIBERATIONS

The rhetoric of science may be moving "inward" to focus on the writings of influential scientists, as Gaonkar has concluded, but broader political possibilities open up if we move dialectically between disciplinary conventions and civic applications. David Dickson's "Towards a Democratic Strategy for Science: The New Politics of Science" positions these possibilities within the broader history of science studies: "[T]he first postwar generation of science critics demonstrated the need to develop a political debate around the applications of science; the second generation shifted focus to the other end of the spectrum, namely the conditions under which science was produced" (473). Today, the need is "to integrate these two perspectives into a single critique of the whole spectrum, from the most fundamental science through to its most sophisticated high-technology applications" (473). Dickson examines three domains for intervening in the deliberative processes that make up technoscience: (1) the procedures and work practices of the scientific community, (2) the institutions that decide how research funds should be allocated, and (3) technological research, design, and development. At such junctures, the issue of agency comes into focus, as is evident in Dickson's case studies of the Lucas plan and the science shop. The Lucas plan was developed in the 1970s by the

Lucas Aerospace Company in the United Kingdom when workers pushed their company to redirect their technical expertise from the manufacturing of military technologies, which had been the main product line, to the manufacture of more socially useful products such as equipment for disabled people and public transportation. The science shop was pioneered in Holland in the 1970s as a means to involve community members in the deliberations upon science and technology policies (475). Both the Lucas plan and the science shop demonstrate that technoscience can be democratized if alternative forms of agency can be articulated and enacted. The pragmatic conditions and political consequences involved in such alternatives present a civic subject worthy of study.

Such cases provide practical instantiations of how agency can be exercised collectively. Attending to such sites moves our work beyond studies of purposeful individuals to make it into a civic discipline that has some hope of resisting the hierarchies of technoscience. As Haraway stresses, the question at issue is "who gets to count as a rational actor, as well as an author of knowledge, in the dramas and courts of technoscience" (*Modest_Witness* 89). Traditionally, she argues, three groups have controlled how technoscience gets done in the United States: the Department of Defense, technoscientific experts, and multinational corporations. Among these groups is "the conspicuous absence of serious citizen agency in shaping science and technology policy" (*Modest_Witness* 95). "The capacity for multisided, democratic criticism and vision that fundamentally shape the way science is done," she continues, "hardly seems to be on the political agenda in the United States, much less in the R&D budget of universities, in-house government labs, or industries" (*Modest_Witness* 94). Rhetorical studies of the collective exercise of agency in varied civic fora are needed to redress the cynicism that often shadows postmodern theorizing. As Haraway discusses, even expressing a hope for democratic alternatives can be seen as "evidence of hopeless naïveté and nostalgia for a moment of critical, public, democratic science that never existed" (*Modest_Witness* 94). If the civic hope for public participation and critical discourse has any chance of being realized, we rhetoricians will need to seek out sites where it can be enacted and articulate their values.

Haraway describes such sites as the "technoscientific commons" (113–14). For historical examples, she cites some of the commonplaces of the civic tradition: New England town meetings, the self-governing Swiss cantons and trial by a jury of peers, as well as the civil rights movements and the Polish solidarity movement. Such points of reference have popular currency, but they can also play directly into the republican ideologies that gave virtue to power by making men of property the voice of the public good. An attempt to realize democratic alternatives was undertaken in Denmark, which was then imitated in the United States by the Loka Institute, the executive director of which is Richard Sclove. Sclove's book, *Democracy and Technology*, articulates the civic vision of this project in terms of "strong democracy," a concept drawn from

Benjamin Barber. Strong democracy "envisions extensive opportunities for citizens to participate in important decisions that affect them" (Sclove 26). As Sclove discusses, to create a more democratic society, citizens must become involved in policy making on technoscience. In order to achieve "outcomes that are substantively democratic," "democratic design criteria" must be implemented (30, 31). These principles of design enact a pragmatic understanding of democracy as a way of life: (1) democratic communities need to be fostered by seeking a balance among various nonauthoritarian technologies; (2) democratic work involves a diverse array of flexible technological practices; (3) democratic politics requires the full participation of all citizens; (4) democratic self-governance is used to develop technologies that promote local economic self-reliance; and (5) these democratic social structures are assessed against broader environments to ensure ecological sustainability (Sclove 98).[8]

A practical example of such civic principles in collective action is provided by Sclove's work at the Loka Institute. The Loka Institute is "a non-profit research and advocacy organization concerned with the social, political, and environmental repercussions of research, science, and technology" (Loka Institute). According to the Loka Institute, there are two fundamental shortcomings in science and technology policy. First, "although strongly attentive to technology's role as an economic factor . . . current policies are insufficiently attentive to technology's profound range of environmental, social, and political effects" (Loka Institute). Second, for the most part, "policies are being formulated and implemented without the involvement of public-interest, grassroots, and workers organizations" (Loka Institute). In order to remedy these shortcomings, the Loka Institute has implemented a variety of programs: (1) listservs and "Loka Alerts," which distribute information on technoscience; (2) community research networks, which provide links among universities, government agencies, nonprofit organizations, and community organizers; (3) citizen panels on science and technology policy, in which citizens participate in the making of science and technology policy; and (4) publications such as articles, books, and reports. In all, the Loka Institute seeks to establish a technoscientific commons. Other examples of a democratic politics of technology include the Dutch science shops and the Danish "consensus conference model" (Sclove 217). This model involves bringing together groups of nonscientists to deliberate upon technoscientific knowledges and practices based partly on the testimony of competing experts.

HOW CAN SUCH STUDIES HELP US UNDERSTAND OUR CIVIC DUTIES AS PUBLIC EDUCATORS?

These innovations may seem to be but isolated examples, but the global trends at issue are broadly based and quite advanced. Technoscience has become

increasingly contested as technology has changed our lives at a rate so
intense as to become visible. The economic sustainability of major technoscience projects has been threatened by public indifference and outright
hostility, with developments in such areas as fetal research and genetically
modified foodstuffs arousing noted public opposition. Fraud in laboratories
and licensings has raised public suspicions of the professional ethics of
experts. Our aging population has come to understand that the technologies
they depend upon are governed by economics that do not account for their
needs, and when scientists and other experts have been called upon to
defend their thinking in deliberative and forensic fora, the public has come
to realize that we are not as disinterested as we had been led to believe (see
Nelkin 34). These developments have created a booming market for communications graduates with public relations expertise. Perhaps it is time we
went to work for the opposition. Such public works projects can be supported by writings such as this, perhaps, but we need to do more than pub-
lish for fellow specialists. We need to get out more. We need to become
involved in the localities where we live and to work to make a difference
there as well as here. The purpose of rhetoric, at least in a civic sense of the
art, is not simply to explain how different discourses work but to use discourse to make a difference. The classroom is a good place to start, but our
civic engagements cannot end there.

    At this point in our history, technology is central to all sorts of human
rights issues—issues ranging from our duties in war time to the rights of the
yet to be born and the soon to die. We need to reflect not just on technology
but through it, to the technological forms of thinking that limit civic discourse. The utilitarian calculations of technological rationality are clearly at
work in military experts' thinking that it is in their best interest to keep the
public ignorant of what they do. As Jacqueline Sharkey discusses, such rhetorical strategies may enable the military to accomplish its purpose in an unhin-
dered manner, but they disable democracy by preventing a society from learning from the history that it makes for itself. Technological rationality divests
public controversies of their civic value as opportunities to reflect upon how to
make productive use of our differences. This divestment can arise from an
instrumental mindset that focuses on technical matters concerned with
achieving a predetermined purpose. Such a mindset devalues the critical
insights that arise from the process of making it so—which in the case of war
entails coming to terms with the killing of thousands of men, women, and
children who have nothing to do with the technologies of making war. In this
way technological rationality disables pragmatic deliberations by denying the
possibility that the process of doing something may enable us to reevaluate
what we set out to achieve and how it is to be made so. We tend to think about
technology in an instrumental manner because our society is heavily invested
in believing that technological advances inevitably produce not just profits for

the few but broader benefits for all. As the public ceases to think like that, we need to consider alternatives with popular currency.

A civic sense of rhetoric can provide a broadly articulated pragmatic alternative to the market-driven ideologies that are being imposed on higher education as a part of a historic divestment in public institutions that has been accelerated by increased investments in technologies of mass destruction. In rhetoric and composition, which is where the two of us work, a civic philosophy of rhetoric provides a historically informed vision of the discipline that could provide coherence to some of our most promising projects: community literacy and service learning; other activist modes of inquiry such as ethnography, action research, science and technology studies; and histories of the rhetorics of social movements. These projects could enable us to expand the institutional base of our work with writing and teaching, especially comprehensive composition programs' partnerships with public schools, literacy centers, writing across the curriculum programs, teaching with technology initiatives, and writing centers that foster collaborative learning and critical thinking. Technical writing courses are particularly open to a civic reinvisioning of technology and to rethinking how rhetoric can be of critical use in serving public needs (see Moeller and McAllister; Bowdon and Scott). Such civic reimaginings of the technical have broad implications for the possibilities that are opening up with the reestablishment of rhetoric as a field of study in the humanities, as evident for example in the internships in writing at work that are being added to some expanded English majors. A vital distinction emerges when we view such internships as opportunities not merely to gain experience in the corporate sector but also to work with public agencies to learn the rhetoric of collective action. By helping us articulate the practical values of such differences, a civic philosophy could serve as a pragmatic alternative to the vocationalism to which higher education is being held accountable. Of course these diverse concerns are a lot to try to bring into a coherent framework, especially with an ill-defined term such as *civic*. Despite the vagaries of the term, defining *rhetoric* in civic terms at least foregrounds its historical engagement with public debates over popular values. Reclaiming that historical engagement can help us to speak in broadly appealing ways for social justice. We hope that our critical analysis of the historical dynamics of virtue and power within the rhetorical tradition can contribute in a small way to this civic project.

NOTES

We would like to thank Janet Atwill and Arthur Walzer for their help with the revisions of this chapter. Of course we retain responsibility for the argument and its implications.

1. The civic humanist tradition of Isocrates, Aristotle, and Cicero can be defined by these assumptions: first, man is by nature political (with "man" limited to citizens, ideally those with enough property to rise above feminine refinements and self-interested private business to take a liberal interest in public duties); second, this nature is evident in the human ability to persuade and be persuaded, to rule and be ruled in turn; third, this natural faculty enables civilization and civil society to develop through deliberations upon justice; fourth, in such public deliberations, men achieve their highest potential by exercising their collective judgment; and finally, citizenship is thereby a noble duty, for which one prepares by studying the "shared" tradition of the humanities.

2. For example in a recent collection devoted to the expansion of composition studies beyond English departments, Kurt Spellmeyer has questioned whether the discipline ought to define itself in terms of *rhetoric,* which "has never really managed to free itself from the ponderousness of the Classics" (278). For an alternative critique of rhetoric in the teaching of writing, see Knoblauch and Brannon.

3. In *Rhetorical Hermeneutics: Invention and Interpretation in the Age of Science,* Dilip Parameshwar Gaonkar and his respondents explore his argument that classical rhetoric provides too "thin" a set of interpretive categories to support the sort of rhetorical criticism of "institutionally driven discursive formations" such as science that we will be advocating later in this chapter. According to Gaonkar, "Aristotelian/Ciceronian" critics cannot develop classical categories such as practical wisdom and decorum into "a language of interpretation" because neoclassicists are too invested in outmoded assumptions about "human agency" and tend to treat interpretation and composition as reciprocal processes (343). While effectively critiquing the modern emphasis on individual authorship as the source of discourse, Gaonkar's position demonstrates the need to attend to agency while denying it. In our assessment, to be *rhetorical,* rhetorical criticism must attend to the possibilities for "intervention and invention" and not simply practice textual studies as an end in itself, as Gaonkar does by making the distinction of interpretation from production his definitive concern. For an alternative sense of rhetorical hermeneutics, see the works of Steven Mailloux.

4. Within rhetoric and composition, the most influential proponent of the Gadamerian response to scientism has been Louise Wetherbee Phelps. Her discussion of teachers' practical knowledge as combining technical know-how and reflective know-what-for provides an incisive example of the potentials of rethinking productive and practical modes of knowing in civic terms. With "reflective practice" as a model, Phelps argues that teachers resist theory not simply because they are uninformed but because they do not understand practice as "applied science" and refuse to be characterized as "technicians" (863). In this and other ways, Phelps aptly distinguishes the routinization of procedural knowledge in scientism from the pragmatics of experimental accounts of collective inquiry in practice.

5. These are the points where a reinterpretation of the civic has come to terms with the politics of difference, as articulated most incisively by Iris Marion Young. Atwill's analyses of the universalizing tendencies of humanism are congruent with Young's moral philosophy. As with other types of ideological critique, Atwill's analysis

is a form of demystification, and as such an example of what Cornel West calls "prophetic criticism," which begins with a critique of prevailing values and attempts to set out an inevitably "partisan, partial, engaged, and crisis-centered" alternative while seeking to avoid "dogmatic traps, premature closures, formulaic formulations, or rigid conclusions" (213). Such reenvisionings of the potentials of pragmatic conventions are basic to critical ethnography.

     6. Here are a few dates that can serve as benchmarks for this process: in 1948, Norman Wiener established "cybernetics" as the study of the regulatory properties of complex systems; in 1950, ENIAC began distributing the UNIVAC, the first mass-produced computer; in 1960, neuroscientists Manfred Clynes and Nathan Kline implanted an osmotic pump into a laboratory rat and coined the term *cyborg* to describe it; during the 1960s ARPANet, the forerunner to the Internet, was developed by the U.S. Department of Defense; in 1972 Noland Bushnel invented the video game; in 1982, Robert Jarvik patented the artificial heart; and in 1998, Kevin Warwick becomes the first person to have a microchip surgically implanted into his body.

     7. For a discussion on the relationship between the ideals of posthumanism and the ideals of humanism, specifically Renaissance humanism, see Hardt and Negri 91–92.

     8. The "democratic politics of technology" includes three areas of concern for strategic thinking: awareness and mobilization, core activities and institutions, and supporting macroconditions (206). Awareness and mobilization are concerned with (1) mapping local needs and resources, (2) educating, and conducting and publicizing research, (3) building coalitions with other political movements, and (4) creating more time for politics. The core activities and institutions are (1) initiating democratic research and development and design, (2) seeking civic technological empowerment, (3) strengthening democratic governance, and (4) promoting supportive institutions. Supporting macroconditions include (1) democratizing the government and corporations, (2) Subordinating the military to democratic prerogatives, and (3) evolving world political and economic relations that are more compatible with strong democracy.

WORKS CITED

Atwill, Janet M. *Rhetoric Reclaimed: Aristotle and the Liberal Arts Tradition*. Ithaca: Cornell UP, 1998.

Barber, Benjamin. *Strong Democracy: Participatory Politics for a New Age*. Berkeley: U of California P, 1984.

Bender, John, and David E. Wellbery. "Rhetoricality: On the Modernist Return of Rhetoric." In *The Ends of Rhetoric: History, Theory, Practice*. Ed. John Bender and David E. Wellbery. Stanford: Stanford UP, 1990. 3–39.

Bowdon, Melody, and Blake Scott. *Service Learning in Technical and Professional Communication*. New York: Longman, 2003.

Brown, Richard Harvey. *Toward a Democratic Science: Scientific Narration and Civic Communication*. New Haven: Yale UP, 1998.

Cicero. *De inventione. De optimo genere oratorum. Topica*. Trans. H. M. Hubbell. Cambridge, MA: Harvard UP, 1949.

———. *De Oratore*. In *Cicero on Oratory and Orators*. Trans. J. S. Watson. Carbondale: Southern Illinois UP, 1970.

[Cicero]. *Ad G. Herennium: De ratione dicendi (Rhetorica ad Herennium)*. Trans. Harry Caplan. Cambridge, MA: Harvard UP, 1954.

Dickson, David. "Towards a Democratic Strategy for Science: The New Politics of Science." In *The Racial Economy of Science: Toward a Democratic Future*. Ed. Sandra Harding. Bloomington: Indiana UP, 1993. 473–83.

Elzinga, Aant, and Andrew Jamison. "Changing Policy Agenda in Science and Technology." In *Handbook of Science and Technology Studies*. Ed. Sheila Jasanoff, et al. Thousand Oaks, CA: Sage, 1995. 572–97.

Fuller, Steve. *Philosophy, Rhetoric, and the End of Knowledge: The Coming of Science and Technology Studies*. Madison: U of Wisconsin P, 1993.

Fusfield, William D. "Refusing to Believe It: Considerations on Public Speaking Instruction in a Post-Machiavellian Moment." *Social Epistemology* 11 (1997): 253–314.

Gadamer, Hans-Georg. *Truth and Method*. Trans. Joel Weinsheimer and Donald Marshall. New York: Crossroad, 1975.

Gaonkar, Dilip Parameshwar. "The Idea of Rhetoric in the Rhetoric of Science." In *Rhetorical Hermeneutics: Invention and Interpretation in the Age of Science*. Ed. Alan G. Gross and William M. Keith. Albany: State U of New York P, 1997. 25–85.

Gray, Chris Hables, Steven Mentor, and Heidi J. Figueroa-Sarriera. "Cyborgology: Constructing the Knowledge of Cybernetic Organisms." In *Cyborg Handbook*. Ed. Chris Hables Gray. New York: Routledge, 1995. 1–16.

Habermas, Jürgen. "Technology and Science as 'Ideology.'" In *Toward a Rational Society*. Trans. J. Shapiro. Boston: Beacon, 1970. 81–122.

Haraway, Donna J. *Simians, Cyborgs, and Women: The Reinvention of Nature*. New York: Routledge, 1991.

———. *Modest_Witness@Second_Millenium.FemaleMan©_Meets_OncoMouse™: Feminism and Technoscience*. New York: Routledge, 1997.

Hardt, Michael, and Antonio Negri. *Empire*. Cambridge, MA: Harvard UP, 2000.

Hayles, N. Katherine. *How We Became Posthuman: Virtual Bodies in Cybernetics, Literature, and Informatics*. Chicago: U of Chicago P, 1999.

Heidegger, Martin. "The Question concerning Technology." In *The Question concerning Technology and Other Essays*. Trans. William Lovitt. New York: Harper and Row, 1977. 3–35.

Horkheimer, Max, and Theodor W. Adorno. *Dialectic of Enlightenment*. Trans. Edmund Jephcott. Ed. Gunzelin Schmid Noerr. Stanford: Stanford UP, 2002.

Kinneavy, James. "Restoring the Humanities: The Return of Rhetoric from Exile." In *The Rhetorical Tradition and Modern Writing*. Ed. James Jerome Murphy. New York: Modern Language Association, 1982. 19–28.

———. "The Exile of Rhetoric from the Liberal Arts." *Journal of Advanced Composition* 8 (1988): 105–12.

Knoblauch, C. H., and Lil Brannon. *Rhetorical Traditions and the Teaching of Writing.* Upper Montclair, NJ: Boynton/Cook, 1984.

Laughlin, Charles. "The Evolution of Cyborg Consciousness." 1 December 2002. http://www.carleton.ca/~claughli/cyborg.htm.

Loka Institute. "The Loka Institute." 7 January 2003. http://www.loka.org.

Lyotard, Jean François. *The Postmodern Condition: A Report on Knowledge.* Trans. Geoff Bennington and Brian Massumi. Minneapolis: U of Minnesota P, 1993.

Mailloux, Steven. *Rhetorical Power.* Ithaca: Cornell UP, 1989.

———. *Reception Histories: Rhetoric, Pragmatism, and American Cultural Politics.* Ithaca: Cornell UP, 1998.

Moeller, Ryan, and Ken McAllister. "Playing with *Techne:* A Propaedeutic for Technical Communication." *Technical Communication Quarterly* 11 (2002): 185–206.

Nelkin, Dorothy. "The Evolution of Science Studies." In *Technoscience and Cyberculture.* Ed. Stanley Aronowitz, Barbara Martinsons, and Michael Menser. New York: Routledge, 1996. 31–36.

Normal Research Collective: Elizabeth Hatmaker, et al. "Postmodern Pedagogies and the Death of Civic Humanism." *Social Epistemology* 11 (1997): 339–48.

Ong, Walter, S. J. *Interfaces of the Word: Studies in the Evolution of Consciousness and Culture.* Ithaca: Cornell UP, 1977.

Phelps, Louise Wetherbee. "Practical Wisdom and the Geography of Knowledge in Composition." *College English* 53 (1991): 863–85.

Sclove, Richard. *Democracy and Technology.* New York: Guilford, 1995.

Sharkey, Jacqueline. *Under Fire: U.S. Military Restrictions on the Media from Grenada to the Gulf War.* Washington, DC: Center for Public Integrity, 1991.

Spellmeyer, Kurt. "Bigger Than a Discipline." In *A Field of Dreams: Independent Programs and the Future of Composition Studies.* Ed. Peggy O'Neill, Angela Crow, and Larry W. Burton. Logan: Utah State UP, 2002. 278–94.

Vico, Giambattista. *The New Science of Giambattista Vico.* 3rd ed. Trans. T. G. Bergin and M. H. Fisch. Ithaca: Cornell UP, 1991.

Walker, Jeffrey. *Rhetoric and Poetics in Antiquity.* New York: Oxford UP, 2000.

West, Cornel. *The American Evasion of Philosophy: A Genealogy of Pragmatism.* Madison: U of Wisconsin P, 1989.

Young, Iris Marion. *Inclusion and Democracy.* New York: Oxford UP, 2001.

TEN

Rhetoric in the Age
of Cognitive Science

Jeanne Fahnestock

THE LAST FEW DECADES have seen the creation, expansion, or renaming of
departments, institutes, programs, and centers around the world dedicated to
studying the brain, the mind, and "cognition." Researchers and students now
pursue "cognitive studies" or "cognitive science" in places such as the Institute
for Research in Cognitive Science of the University of Pennsylvania, the Keck
Center for Integrative Neuroscience at UCSF, the Doctoral Program in Neuroscience and Cognitive Science at the University of Maryland, the Riken
Brain Science Institute in Japan, the Centre de Recherche Cerveau et Cognition in France. Journals have been founded, conferences held, grants
bestowed, and books published, including a large number of popularizations
ranging from primers describing how the brain works to highly speculative
accounts of consciousness.[1] In the United States, George Bush declared the
nineties the "decade of the brain" in a Presidential Proclamation, July 17,
1990. The impetus for this attention came in part from a growing awareness
of the prevalence of diseases of the brain such as Alzheimer's, schizophrenia,
autism and chemical dependency, but such medical interests drive basic
research. An unprecedented amount of funding for individuals and research
programs has stimulated progress on one of science's last great frontiers:
understanding how the brain produces the mind.

In a history of the "cognitive revolution" written in 1985, Howard Gardner traced the "cognitive turn" to a disenchantment with behaviorism in the
fifties and to the subsequent synergy among several disciplines, including linguistics, psychology, and anthropology, that began to investigate the mental

processes behind the phenomena they studied.² At the same time, computer science and especially artificial intelligence research offered an apparent model for cognitive processes, while neurophysiologists became more sophisticated in their probing and imaging of the physical brain. Decades later, researchers on brain and mind can be roughly divided into a speculative subdiscipline that usually appropriates the term *cognitive science* or *cognitive studies,* and a "hard" science subdiscipline that gathers under the term *neuroscience* or *cognitive neuroscience.* The whole enterprise, however, seeks to understand how mental processes such as sensation, classification, memory, language, and ultimately consciousness itself are produced from a biological system. Pieces of the puzzle such as visual perception are known in some detail, and research on other areas is being produced prodigiously. Yet despite all the activity and prestige surrounding cognitive science, researchers at the beginning of the twenty-first century acknowledge that little is firmly known about how the brain works overall, and there are fundamental disagreements on the mental processes that enable basic human abilities such as memory or language.

Why should rhetoricians, and especially historians of rhetoric, be interested in cognitive science? Cognitive scientists certainly are not and have not been interested in rhetoric. Surely these two enterprises inhabit opposite sides of the humanities/science dichotomy despite the work of a few intrepid scholars such as Mark Turner (e.g., *Reading Minds; The Way We Think*). Rhetoricians are interested in phenomena on an interpersonal scale—complex human interactions, historical trends, contextual factors, ideological issues. They have not typically, or at least recently, been concerned with what might happen in an individual mind as it produces or responds to a text or an image. And cognitive scientists have not been interested in phenomena that involve groups or in complex cognitive skills that concern functions such as the perception of plausibility or the generation of lines of argument. Indeed the neuroscientists, more interested in the physical brain, often devote their research to primates other than humans. Yet there is an area of overlapping concern for both rhetoricians and cognitive scientists, and that area is language. Though admittedly in very complex manifestations, language in use is the object of study for rhetoricians, and language is absolutely central in studies of brain and mind by both cognitivists and many neuroscientists.

If cognitivists and neuroscientists ever reach agreement on a model of the brain and mental processes, and particularly of how people produce and use language and images, that model should be compatible and even continuous with the characterizations of human communication available in the rhetorical tradition. The specific answers that cognitive scientists or neuroscientists come up with are not likely to be interesting to rhetoricians. Knowing that the concentration of a certain neurotransmitter in a certain area of the brain affects attention is not likely to be cited as a satisfactory explanation of the kind of phenomena rhetoricians usually study. Nevertheless, these two disciplines, because they deal with dovetailing or overlapping phenomena, should eventually be compatible. They should "touch" at certain points, the one handing off its accounts to the other, cognitive science to rhetoric, though they operate on different scales and answer to different systems of explanation. Ultimately an understanding of the brain should lead to a better understanding of language, and that in turn should lead to a better explanation of effective language, of persuasion, and hence of the complex behaviors and historical processes, mediated by language, that rhetoricians study.

The purpose of this chapter is to make rhetoricians aware of the enterprise being conducted by their academic neighbors and in the process to revisit elements in the rhetorical tradition. No overview of cognitive science is attempted here. Instead, after acknowledging discontinuities between the assumptions and goals of cognitivists and rhetoricians, the discussion that follows examines elements from the rhetorical tradition that might be useful to cognitive neuroscientists. This chapter also considers a few of the findings in contemporary neuroscience that suggest the viability of rhetorical stylistics as it is embodied in the classical and early modern attention to language.

Assumptions about Language in Cognitive Science and the Rhetorical Tradition

There are many impediments to assessing potential connections between cognitive neuroscience and rhetoric, and these impediments reveal fundamental differences in basic assumptions.[3] To begin with, the terms that cognitive scientists use for fundamental mental skills or operations seem far removed from a rhetorical lexicon. They seek the neural substrates of sensation, attention, categorization, and learning, and none of these mental processes necessarily even involves language. Indeed categorization has been studied in monkeys where a surprisingly robust all-or-nothing response to different images by different neurons in the prefrontal cortex has been discovered (Freedman et al. 315; see also Thorpe and Fabre-Thorpe 260).

Furthermore, when cognitive scientists, particularly those of the speculative variety, describe mental operations overall, they often resort to the term *information processing*, and talk about input and output. These and other cognate terms show the influence of computer science and the governing analogy between the brain and the computer, an analogy that persists despite criticism.[4] This reductive analogy between the brain and a computer reveals a more serious discontinuity between rhetoric and cognitive science over the basic nature and purpose of language, a difference that can be traced to the influence of analytical linguistics, and particularly of Chomskyan lingusitics, on cognitive scientists.

As a theory of language, Chomskyan linguistics could almost be called "arhetorical" or even "antirhetorical." First, Chomsky posited a radical dissociation between competence and performance; he was after a person's innate "knowledge" of a language, not his or her actual use of it (Chomsky, *Knowledge* 9–10, 19–32). Second, given this orientation toward abstract competence, he emphasized a model of language that was formal and logical. The language system posited into a person's head had to conform to principles of mathematical logic, and he criticized other theories of language that lacked this presumed explanatory rigor (Tomasello 134). (Even though the ever-changing Chomsky is now in a "minimalist" phase, he and his followers still postulate some universal hard-wired, uniquely human syntactic component [Chomsky, "Chomsky's Revolution" 64]) Third, and most interesting ultimately for rhetoricians, Chomsky dismissed figures of speech from his competence modeling, relegating them to the less interesting category of language use (Lakoff 248).

Analytical linguistics then, of which Chomskyan linguistics has been the most widely known version, is not rooted in a theory of language as a communicative medium. It is rooted in a theory of language as a referential or representational medium or as a formal/logical or computational system. No one would deny that humans use language to refer to things or to express thoughts. But are referring and, as Pinker puts it in the opening of his recent *Words and Rules,* filling "one another's heads with so many different ideas" (1) the primary functions of language?

Any *rhetorical* theory of language will be rooted instead in the interactional and functional. Language, from a rhetorical perspective, cannot simply be a system for the unmotivated pairing of spoken or graphic symbols with referents, nor does it exist to exercise a "language module" in the brain that generates syntax. A mental lexicon and a mental grammar may be necessary constituents of the human language apparatus, but why do humans engage in pairing, referring, or syntax generating in the first place? Clearly, *homo rhetoricus* uses language as a means to satisfy needs and achieve intentions and purposes. This view of language makes sense to any observer of language in action in the world, and it also makes sense from an evolutionary perspective since one can readily imagine selective pressures on an instrument that enhances the survival of the organism. It may then be better to describe referring and expressing as secondary functions that serve primary functions such as securing cooperation, communicating danger, or establishing dominance.

To emphasize again impediments to mutual understanding, cognitive scientists have not typically investigated "language processing" in a way that connects directly to the purposes, goals, actions, and intentions of speakers, precisely the issues that concern rhetoricians. They concentrate instead on the processes that they assume must underlie these functions: for example, how the brain decodes speech signals or how seeing one word leads to the recognition of a similar word. This limitation to the basics of construal may be necessary for the psycholinguists and neuroscientists who are constrained by their experimental methods and devices. When human subjects are confined in an MRI apparatus, it is difficult to investigate natural language use, and in the interest of statistical rigor, psycholinguists have used highly artificial experimental protocols such as dichotic listening, that is, input to one ear and hence one hemisphere. But even if these researchers wanted to connect the basics of language processing to human purposes, there is no currently available rhetorical theory of language to bring to the attention of cognitive scientists in a form they could readily use.

If a rhetorical theory of language were available, what would it look like, and how could it serve cognitive science? Rhetoric arguably has a clearer grasp of the teleology of language than analytical linguistics. But an overarching conception of the purpose of language, while crucial, is not enough for a theory of language. A robust theory of language must also offer explanations connecting small-scale features to the attempted achievement of large-scale schemes. Such a theory must, therefore, also include some system of feature identification. We can call this system a "parser." Though that term has computer connotations, it also connects to the older notion of "parsing" a passage in Latin or Greek by identifying certain formal features. With a "parser" one can identify elements of a language. Any grammar—traditional, generative, construction—that identifies types of sentences, clauses, phrases and words is a kind of parser. No matter what elements are ultimately identified, a parser describes formal linguistic features irrespective of their content. A rhetorical parser would include higher level structures like the enthymeme and the *topoi*, and it would connect the features identified to their potential uses.

Language Theory in the Rhetorical Tradition

There once was a body of rhetorical theorizing on language that both provided a detailed parser for formal features and connected those features with their potential effects. This "theory" of language originates in classical rhetoric where it is tied to oral language, also considered the primary object of attention by linguists (Lamb 18). But its greatest development occurred in the early modern period, from the fifteenth through the seventeenth centuries. This age saw the production of full rhetorical treatises with expansive sections on style and of many separate treatises on the figures of speech. It is the age of curricular reform by humanist educators who emphasized mastery of Latin grammar, composition, and oral performance, as well as the close reading of ancient texts according to rhetorical principles of style.

What theory of language does the rhetorical tradition provide from the era of rhetoric's greatest interest in language that might be of use in the age of cognitive science? In particular, what does the traditional lore of the figures of speech, now largely absent from rhetorical theorizing, reveal about a rhetorical theory of language? Some answers to these questions can be provided by examining treatments of style and of the figures in the sixteenth and seventeenth centuries.[5] Elements of a rhetorical theory of language are implicit in the great sixteenth-century Latin style manuals such as Susenbrotus' *Epitome troporum ac schematum et grammaticorum et rhetorum* (1541) or Sturmius' *De universa ratione elocutionis rhetoricae libri tres* (1576), or in their English equivalents such as Sherry's *Treatise of Schemes and Tropes* (1550) and Peacham's *Garden of Eloquence* (1577, 1593). These early modern texts built on contemporary editions of Quintilian and Cicero as well as on the continued influence of the *Rhetorica ad Herennium* whose fourth book provided the model of a rhetorical description of language analysis and production. Peacham's *Garden of Eloquence* is particularly useful because it sums up earlier Latin works, gives detailed definitions, examples, uses, and warnings about individual figures, and is conveniently in English. Examples from Peacham will be used as representative in the discussion that follows.

As theories of language, both rhetorical stylistics and analytical linguistics share the categories of traditional grammar. (Rhetoric does by long historical association since grammatical and rhetorical pedagogy were intimately linked.) Both systems identify parts of speech (nouns and verbs) and phrases, clauses, and sentences, and both identify how words and concepts are paired and how arrangement (syntax) constitutes meaning. But the theory of language implicit in the style manuals offers several differences beyond these commonalities. For example, rhetorical stylistics places great emphasis on the sound dimension of linguistic choices, on patterns of arrangement beyond the isolated sentence, and on the overriding importance of communicating the speaker's intentions since in human communication the "why you are telling me" may often be more important than the "what you are telling me." Furthermore, all the formal features identified in a rhetorical style manual are ultimately linked to the potential achievement of the speaker's goals. Analytical linguistics (the words and rules equal input/output school) does not pay attention to these functional elements of language as it is used by humans with emotions and purposes. It therefore cannot offer a theory of language, general or detailed, that is likely to reflect the evolved organization of a brain that can support language.

PROCESSING LANGUAGE IN THE BRAIN

A rhetorical view of language then is likely to be a better resource for cognitive scientists. At the same time, cognitivists, and especially the neuroscientists, would be right to insist that elements of rhetorical stylistics correspond to what they already know with some confidence about how language is processed in the brain. Their discoveries will either reinforce or rebut the insights into language that are provided in rhetorical doctrine. Is there any evidence from research on the brain and language that would support the view of language implicit in rhetorical stylistics?

Early research on the physical brain concerned, first, the localization of brain functions, carried out initially by researchers who matched a known impairment with an underlying pathological condition in a specific area of the brain, whether produced by tumors, lesions, strokes, or injuries, as in the war victims examined by A. R. Luria or the hideously injured Phineas P. Gage made famous in Antonio Damasio's *Descartes' Error*. Neurosurgeons have added to this knowledge by direct electrical stimulation of the exposed cerebral cortex during surgery to remove the focal lesions of epileptics.

Recent research has investigated brain function from the nonpathological end of the spectrum, starting with normal or elicited behavior and observing the brain with newer imaging technologies. These techniques presumably reveal where the brain is receiving an increased flow of oxygenated blood (fMRI) or concentrating radioactively labeled tracers (PET) and hence what areas are active when a particular task is being performed. Still other imaging techniques use EEGs or MEGs, measuring electrical or magnetic changes from the outside of the skull. The most precise studies of brain localization are achieved by inserting tiny microelectrodes into individual neurons to record their electrical impulses. But such invasive surgery is usually performed only on animals, typically cats or monkeys. The result of all these various research fronts is, currently, a detailed functional topography that identifies areas of the brain devoted to processes as precise as judging the angular orientation of an object in the visual field.

The mapping of functions onto physical areas of the brain—the visual cortex here, the sensory-motor cortex there—has been criticized recently as a kind of neophrenology (Lieberman 23). While areas of ever-increasing specificity have been identified, much of the newer imaging evidence also demonstrates that large, diverse areas of the brain are involved when complex processes such as language production and comprehension are occurring. In other words, though there may be an area of the cortex associated with proper nouns (presumably because electrical stimulation of this area interferes with recall), that does not mean that only that area is used when someone recalls a name (Calvin and Ojemann 46–47, 120). Recent research also suggests the unsurprising conclusion that the more complex the language task, the more extensive the neural activity (although as usual this research was based on subjects reading lists of decontextualized sentences [Just et al. 114]).

While neuroscientists in the last twenty years have discovered that widespread areas of the brain are involved in different operations, they have also discovered that localized groups of neurons (minicolumns) are highly specialized and that specialized activities are handled at the same time in different regions. Neuroscientists, in their computer idiom, call this dispersed specialization "parallel processing," and the discovery of these simultaneous but distinct pathways has also led to the "binding problem," the process by which the brain presumably recombines what it first partitions.

The specialization involved in vision is the best known of the senses and provides the model for the others. A visual stimulus is analyzed into separate components: its color, shape, intensity, spatial position, and movement (Dubin 25). Signals from nerve cells in the retina go to the thalamus and specifically to a group of neurons called the "lateral geniculate nucleus" (LGN) and from there to the V1 or primary visual area of the cortex. Studies in animal brains show the exquisite sensitivity of neurons in this primary visual cortex. Some are so specialized that they respond differentially (i.e., in their rate of firing) according to the orientation of an object in the visual field, some responding to 45 degrees of rotation and others to 60 degrees, and so on, around the full 360 degree circle.

Speech is an aural phenomenon, and like visual stimuli, aural stimuli are broken down into constituent parts including loudness, pitch, duration, and direction of origin. Modern imaging techniques have demonstrated, again and again, the recruitment of different areas of the brain in responding to these separable features of speech. A study by Robert Zatorre and colleagues at the Montreal Neurological Institute demonstrates both how this research is done and what its typical conclusions and limitations are. Subjects in Zatorre's experiments were asked to press a button when they recognized first noises, then separate syllables, then pairs of syllables ending with the same phoneme, then pitch differences in a pair. PET scans during these discrimination tests revealed the successive involvement of different areas of the brain. The primary auditory cortex registered noise, the right and left temporal gyrus were involved in the "passive" recognition of a syllable, Broca's area in the left hemisphere, usually associated with speech production, became active when finer phonetic discriminations were made, showing that subjects had to "access an articulatory representation" when noticing the similar endings on syllables such as "big" and "bag" (Zatorre et al. 846, 848). Finally, when subjects were asked to make pitch discriminations, other areas of the right hemisphere showed activity. The authors conclude, "Our results, taken together, support a model whereby auditory information undergoes discrete processing stages, each of which depends on separate neural subsystems" (848). The separation revealed in such imaging studies suggests not only the evolutionary layering of language perception but also, and most important for an assessment of rhetorical stylistics, the manipulable parameters of a language, the features that can remain the same when others change.

Human speech presents the ear with a profile of sounds of differing durations at differing pitches and intensities producing the overall prosodic contour of an utterance. English speakers, for example, are familiar with the difference in meaning when an utterance ends in a rising tone versus a falling tone. The former converts a statement into a question, "He has a PhD" versus "He has a PhD?" Most language processing is done in the left hemisphere, but neuroscientists have discovered that the right hemisphere has the special role of analyzing the prosody of an utterance, the "tone" that is produced by variables of pitch, duration, and loudness.[6] The right hemisphere's analysis of prosody, of stressed syllables and rising and falling intonation, has been tied to decoding the emotional value of an utterance.[7] The right hemisphere's role in the affective dimension of language was suspected in the late nineteenth century when Hughlings Jackson noted that patients who had lost most of their speech through left hemisphere damage could still utter curse words (Borod, Bloom, and Santschi-Haywood 290).

The special role of the right hemisphere in emotional speech has since been repeatedly confirmed. In one type of experiment, subjects heard sentences in only one ear, each ear feeding its information to the opposite hemisphere. The words in some test sentences were then obscured, while the intonation was preserved. In these trials, "an le-RH [left ear, right hemisphere] advantage has been demonstrated for processing the emotional tone of natural speech, nonverbal vocalizations, and musical passages" (Borod, Bloom, and Santschi-Haywood 289). This hemispheric specialization has been confirmed repeatedly in humans; epileptics being evaluated for brain surgery are often anaesthetized in their right hemisphere, and the test for shutting down the right side of the brain is an inability to identify simple musical rhythms (Calvin and Ojemann 60). Also, patients who have had stroke damage in the right hemisphere tend to speak in a flat monotone (65). It is interesting that the right hemisphere areas involved in prosodic construal are the same as those identified in social monkeys who have a system of alarm calls for communicating various dangers to one another, creating a strong suggestion of the evolutionary origins of the brain's ability to decode sound patterns for their affective content (Deacon 54–57, 313).

Nothing could seem less useful to rhetoricians than knowing how many or which areas of the brain are involved in language comprehension or production. But while the details may not be useful, the overall results of these imaging studies do provide certain interesting insights into and even affirmations of traditional rhetorical stylistics. To begin with, they support the attention paid in traditional rhetorical stylistics to the sound dimension of phrasing. The fact that prosodic construal has a separate location in the brain suggests that this dimension of an utterance can be manipulated separately. The separate manipulation of prosody was thoroughly appreciated in classical and early modern rhetorical stylistics, but its importance in human language has been neglected by most linguists (Dwight Bolinger being a distinct exception) until recently when the results of brain imaging studies have forced its consideration (Tomasello 150).

Illustration: The Case of Parallelism

The case of syntactic parallelism illustrates the importance of prosody in rhetorical stylistics and hence the potential richness of the rhetorical tradition for contemporary cognitive studies. Attention to parallelism begins in Aristotle's discussion of equal cola in book 3 of the *Rhetoric*. His remarks can seem trivial or confusing, in part perhaps because, having lost a rationale for their significance, contemporary readers do not take his observations about the sound dimensions of language choices as seriously as he did. Aristotle, however, placed a great deal of importance on paired cola (i.e., paired phrases or sentences) that could produce an impression of segmented, equivalent units for a listener (Kennedy 243). One means of producing this impression of equal duration was to produce units of equal syllable length, or in the case of prose as opposed to rigorously metrical poetry, approximately equal syllable length. Harmonies between clauses could also be created by the repetition of opening or concluding sounds, or short of rhyming, two phrases could end with the same inflectional ending (see Fahnestock, "Verbal" 129–31).

These sources of aural parallelism were taken up separately in later catalogs of the figures, beginning with "isocolon" [compar] defined in the first century BCE in the *Rhetorica ad Herennium* as "that figure comprised of cola which consist of a virtually equal number of syllables" ([Cicero] 299); almost seventeen hundred years later, Peacham's *Garden of Eloquence* defines isocolon in precisely the same way (58–59). The recommendation of units of equal length is then consistent in rhetorical stylistics. The discovery of the right hemisphere's separate construal of prosody provides a potential rationale for why this feature was singled out.

From the perspective of brain processes, any utterance is analyzed simultaneously but separately for its syntax and semantics and for its prosodic contour, including the variables of duration (that is length), loudness, and pitch. Thus two phrases that have roughly the same length have at least one variable among several in common. They may be perceived (not necessarily consciously) as similar in at least one dimension in the brain, by duration. In addition, they may or may not have the same rising and falling intonation or the same syntactic pattern or make lexical choices from the same semantic categories. But the more of these potential variables they have in common, the more similar they will be and the more redundancy, and presumably efficiency, in their consecutive construal or processing in the brain.

Same syllable length:
    The blue jays chased the finches in the trees
    When the wind turned, the temperature fell.

Same syllable length and syntactic pattern:
   The blue jays chased the finches in the trees.
   The dentist pulled the tooth in her office.

Same syllable length, syntactic pattern, and semantic categories for lexical choices:
   The blue jays chased the finches in the trees.
   The sparrows woke the robins in the bush.

The second of each of these pairs is, to a lesser or greater degree, predicted or prepared for by the first. There are several ways to think about the effects of such patterning. First, similarity in at least one dimension (e.g., syllable length or duration as recommended under isocolon) can impose a connectedness on consecutive sentences, even when their content is different. Next, the more features that correspond, the more redundant the neural processing of the second sentence. Psycholinguists have in fact recorded quicker recognition time for highly constrained, predictable sentences (Faust 177). When two or more phrases or sentences in sequence share multiple features—prosodic, syntactic, semantic, in any combination—they are more likely to be construed as a set. Place these similar sentences in a text with variation around them, and the tendency to group them and to have them perform the same discourse function, as in the following famous example, will be increased.

   The attack yesterday on the Hawaiian Islands has caused severe damage to American naval and military forces. I regret to tell you that very many American lives have been lost. In addition, American ships have been reported torpedoed on the high seas between San Francisco and Honolulu.
      Yesterday the Japanese government also launched an attack
         against Malaya.
      Last night Japanese forces attacked Hong Kong.
      Last night Japanese forces attacked Guam.
      Last night Japanese forces attacked the Philippine Islands.
      Last night Japanese forces attacked Wake Island.
      And this morning the Japanese attacked Midway Island.
   Japan has therefore undertaken a surprise offensive extending throughout the Pacific area. The facts of yesterday and today speak for themselves. (Safire 142).

Franklin D. Roosevelt's situation before Congress on December 8, 1941, was unique, but the stylistic principles and the underlying mental processes he called on were not. By the time readers, or the original listeners, reach the third sentence opening "Last night," they are familiar with the pattern being used, the clauses of roughly similar length repeating the same opening words. They anticipate the reoccurrence of the pattern and participate in its fulfillment. Because of the verbal similarity of presentation, all these items become a single unit in the argument, parallel supporting examples of Japanese aggression in the Pacific. Basic features of human language construal are put to effective use.

RESIDUAL ORALITY

A critic might complain at this point about an emphasis on sound since in our culture important texts are read not heard, and the sound dimensions of written texts are unimportant. But brain imaging studies challenge that view by showing that reading has an aural and even an oral dimension. Indeed these imaging studies show a surprising involvement of the "output" areas of the brain in the decoding of different kinds of "input." In one experiment, subjects were instructed to move a finger and then to watch a moving finger in a movie. In both cases, doing and watching, the same area in the premotor cortex showed heightened activity. In fact, the same area was stimulated when a subject was told simply to imagine the finger movement (Dubin 41). It seems as though the brain "rehearses" motion even when only thinking about it.[8]

An overlap between reading and hearing, two means of consuming language, is perhaps not surprising. But an overlap between reading/hearing and speaking, that is between consuming and producing language, is. Formerly these activities were thought to be quite distinct. Their separation was based on the well-known and endlessly repeated midnineteenth-century findings of Paul Broca and Carl Wernicke who correlated their observations of language deficits exhibited by stroke victims with later autopsy findings showing areas of brain lesions. The result was the association of Broca's area (posterior part of the inferior frontal gyrus) with Broca's aphasia, a compromised ability to speak, and Wernicke's area (posterior half of the superior temporal gyrus) with Wernicke's aphasia, a compromised ability to comprehend. These findings created a tidy separation, or reinforced a preexisting antithesis, between the production and comprehension of speech.

However, recent brain imaging studies with the newer technologies have called into question the boundaries and dedication of these areas. Researchers using fMRI have demonstrated that some parts of Broca's area, presumably dedicated only to language production, are activated during comprehension. "An initial explanation of this finding was that silent, covert subvocalization was occurring as part of comprehension. That is, in trying to understand the words being heard, the person was rehearsing the speaking of those words without being aware of doing so" (Dubin 51). A new appreciation of this motor component in higher cognition has come with an increasing appreciation of the role of the cerebellum, which has long been understood as the part of the brain involved in posture, movement of the limbs, and skilled small muscle movements such as those involved in speaking and writing. Imaging studies have shown, for example, that "verbal working memory for letters, words and names utilized a strategy of silent, nonconscious rehearsal that involves some of the same parts of the brain as actually speaking these items. Studies showed activation of cerebellar regions that would normally be involved in the motor speech task, even though no actual speech occurred" (Dubin 45). Because for all nondeaf humans language is a heard and spoken system before it is a system of visual and written symbols, it persists in the auditory and motor areas of the brain even during silent reading. Hence language as revealed in brain imaging studies is always a residually aural phenomenon. Even an argument that is read is in some sense heard, and the aurally based effects of the figures can persist even in a written text that is read silently. This conclusion would not have surprised the early modern rhetoricians.

Why is this evidence that "production" areas are presumably involved in comprehension of any importance to rhetoricians? The research suggests that as someone listens to or reads a phrase or sentence, some part of the brain is also, in parallel, activated as though it were simultaneously constructing that phrase or sentence. If the relevant segment is constructed according to a pattern with which the language user is already familiar, perhaps because it is established by a figure of repetition in the text, it will be more easily constructed as it is construed. Though Burke would perhaps not be pleased with this source of evidence, these details about language processing in the brain do support his insight about "formal assent," about the ability of a listener to participate actively in the completion of an utterance. He attributed this phenomenon especially to the syntactic figures *antithesis* and *gradatio* because they so strongly predict the pattern for completing an utterance (Burke 58–59). The findings of neuroscientists seem to ratify his insight; they in turn might design a test for the predictability of these figures.

The simultaneous construction of phrases in the process of listening to them is also strengthened by current theories of "verbal working memory" originally developed by A. D. Baddeley and colleagues. Cognitive neuroscientists now postulate an "articulatory loop" as part of comprehension. While a sentence is being parsed, according to this theory, "words are subvocally maintained using neuroanatomical structures that regulate speech production" (Lieberman 70). In other words, listening for comprehension involves a simulated speaking of what is heard. The capacity of this verbal working memory has been tested by seeing how many final words from a series of sentences subjects were able to recall. Those who could recall the final words in four or more sentences were classified as having "high-span" memories; those who could recall less than three were "low-span" (71). Asking for the recall of the final word makes stylistic sense since this word presumably receives more stress from the falling intonation and pause at the end of a sentence. The end of the sentence also presumably features the new and salient information. However, these tests of the capacity of verbal working memory used a series of unconnected, decontextualized sentences, showing once again how far these typical research protocols are from natural language. The test sentences also ended in different words. Had this research been informed by a theory of figuration, subjects could also have been tested for the effects on verbal memory of *epistrophe*, the repetition of the last word or phrase in a connected series of sentences. A repeated final element in such patterned sentences should be more readily maintained in verbal working memory. Figure manuals recommend the figures of repetition for just this effect.

Illustration: The Case of Paronomasia

One intriguing result of the research on verbal working memory indirectly confirms the attention paid in rhetorical stylistics to another group of figures, those that recommend various forms of word play. Experiments on verbal working memory have shown, for example, that subjects have more difficulty recalling phonetically similar words when they are given lists of unconnected words to remember—hardly a natural task (Lieberman 70). Presumably, phonetic similarities lead to potential confusions; the words are harder to keep distinct in verbal working memory without an effort.

To this result can be added observations on different types of reading difficulties (dyslexias) that afflict patients with noncongenital brain damage, usually from strokes. In testing these reading defects, cognitive neuropsychologists distinguish among several types of words: regular words whose sound can be reliably interpreted from their spelling (e.g., *bat*); nonwords that could follow the same rules (e.g., *dag*); and exception words whose phonetic realization cannot be reliably interpreted from their spelling (e.g., *though*) and that therefore require, in common terms, "sight reading." One interesting group of dyslexics has few problems with words they were formerly able to read, whether regular or exceptional, but they have trouble with nonwords. Their ability to sound out unfamiliar words has somehow been compromised. However, these dyslexics do somewhat better with pseudohomophones (made up words that sound like real words) and with words that have some orthographic similarity to established words, such as *sayl* (Coltheart, Langdon, and Haller 30–33). This observation suggests that words that look or sound alike are somehow grouped together or processed in overlapping ways in the brain, in part because of a separate stage of phonemic processing (Dubin 53).

Still another interesting source of evidence that the brain groups sets of similar words comes from the phenomenon known as "priming." A technique used by psycholinguists, priming involves timing the recognition or recall of a target word after the subject first hears or sees another word, phrase, or sentence. Research on word-to-word priming has frequently demonstrated that related words are retrieved or identified more quickly than unrelated words (Faust 163). This finding has led to the assumption that the recognition of a word produces a "spreading activation" of related words in a neural network. But what counts as a related word? Clearly words can be related to each other in several ways including semantically (vow/pledge) or morphologically (vow/vowed) or merely orthographically (vow/vowel). (These distinctions are observed in rhetorical stylistics in the figures *synonymy, polyptoton* and *paronomasia*.) But researchers using the illustrative pairs offered in the previous sentence have demonstrated that the strongest priming occurs among morphologically related sets of words (Feldman and Prostko 23). They attribute this effect to the combination of orthographic and semantic simiarlities; in other words, these words both look alike and share related meanings (25).

This phenomenon of the relatedness of words that look or sound alike is investigated from an entirely different frame of reference in neurolinguistics: as errors in verbal processing or slips of the tongue (Crystal 261–63). Since these slips follow certain patterns, they, too, are thought to provide evidence of how language is organized in the brain. The fact that people can mistakenly say "pig" for "dig," for example, presumably shows the need to recruit separate phonemes in the construction of a word. Such errors also suggest that the mental lexicon may, at some level, be organized phonetically since it is words that sound alike that are usually mistaken for one another, and it is certainly the case that words that sound alike require similar motor instructions for their articulation.

Many figures of speech in the early modern catalogs draw attention to sound similarities and differences, to aural play, to the potential confusion of pairs of words and the resolution of that confusion. In his 1577 edition of *The Garden of Eloquence* Peacham specified fourteen devices for morphing one word into another by, for example, adding or subtracting a letter or syllable from the beginning, middle or end of a word, changing one letter for another, or transposing letters, and so on (Peacham, E1–E2; Peacham's list of tactics represents virtually all the contrastive features a modern linguist could catalog). Under several different figures *(agnominatio, allusio, paranomasia, polyptoton)* Peacham and other classical and early modern rhetoricians recommended the usefulness of words that closely resemble each. The findings of the neuroscientists, outlined above, suggest a rationale for their advice. In recommending word play with key terms, rhetorical stylistics exploits the brain's grouping of words as they are processed by their phonetic or morphological similarities. This linguistic feature is certainly the basis in, for example, Peacham's recommendation of paronomasia.

Paranomasia is a figure which declineth into a contrarie by a likelihood of letters, either added, changed, or taken away. Added thus, be sure of his sword, before you trust him of his word. Another: so fine a launderer, should not be a slanderer. Changed thus, More bold in a butterie then in a batterie. A fit witnesse, a fit witlesse. Taken away, thus. This is no stumbling, but plaine tumbling.

The Use of This Figure

This figure is commonly used to illude [sic] by the Addition, change and taking away. (56)

An example of using a pair of related and potentially confusable words to great argumentative effect occurs in Glenn Loury's recent study, *The Anatomy of Racial Inequality*. Loury analyzes race relations in the United States as the result not of continuing institutional inequality but of a persistent stigma imputed to blacks by whites. He figurally expresses his point as a difference between what he calls "discrimination in contract" and "discrimination in contact" (95–96). Here in the service of a book-length argument is a serious and intentional use of the verbal "play" recommended frequently in rhetorical manuals. The near and potentially confusable "contract" and "contact" together represent a distinction that, as Loury hopes to convince his audience, has been unappreciated by social theorists and politicians in the United States, namely, that racism endures less as a legal institution than as set of behaviors based on deep-seated stereotypes. Loury's language choices underwrite his argument. Just as his two key terms are phonemically close and hence potentially confusable, so are these two sources of discrimination; the more easily remedied institutional source with the more pervasive social cause. It is doubtful that Loury looked up this device in a sixteenth-century figure manual, but he nevertheless draws on the same feature of language and of the mental construal upon which it is based.

CONCLUSION

A complete rhetorical theory of language incorporating the detailed parser and functional insights of the great style manuals has never been worked out. Nor is anything like a complete account of language processing in the brain available from cognitive neuroscientists. But there are clearly intriguing correspondences between specific elements in these very different regimes. Many of the formal devices identified in rhetorical stylistics have been given psychological reality in brain research, providing mutual ratification. The brain is uniquely attuned, for example, to sound units of similar duration or to words that are minimally different, and these linguistic features were singled out by rhetoricians in the classical and early modern tradition.

The rhetorical devices have also been identified in terms of function as well as form. That makes it possible to connect rhetorical stylistics with actual language practices as they are embodied in real situations. At the next level of integration, rhetorical choices such as Roosevelt's or Loury's represent the intersection of the formal (the features available in the language) and the historical (including the exigence, audience, and constraints the individual rhetor faces). The formal possibilities, identified ultimately in both rhetoric and neurolinguistics, and the historical particulars together constitute the "available means of persuasion."

Though historians of rhetoric sometimes deplore the early modern period's fascination with style, thinking that it somehow detracts from substance and demeans the discipline, they do so without appreciating that a rhetorical perspective requires explanations in terms of means and ends. The elaborate attention to language in the early modern period also offers the most promising source for a rhetorical theory of language that might inform research into brain processes in the way that an arhetorical linguistics has in the past. Such a theory would emphasize the importance of sound patterns in effective language, whether at the passage, sentence, or word level, particularly as these constitute the affective content of a text, spoken or written. A rhetorical theory of language would also emphasize the importance of communicating and deciphering intentions in linguistic exchanges and hence would never factor out the human source of an utterance. At the same time, a neurolinguistics based on rhetorical principles would try to study language as it is normally used through research protocols that mimic real situations. Experiments could also be designed to investigate other features identified as significant in rhetorical stylistics.

Rhetoricians themselves need not and should not imitate cognitive neuroscientists. As humanists, they should continue to concentrate on historically situated texts and the political, social, and cultural events and trends they embody. But rhetorical scholars should not be hostile to potential scientific grounding either. In the days of Campbell, rhetoricians did predict that their discipline could be made compatible with then current scientific explanations of the mind; in the late eighteenth century, that desire also amounted to an attempt to ground the laws of persuasion in the laws of perception. The prospects for such convergence are perhaps better now than they were two hundred years ago, thanks to the impressive functional characterization of the brain coming from neuroscientists. This characterization should enrich rhetorical theory in the long run. For no matter how sophisticated our studies of culturally situated, planned, or spontaneous rhetorical acts, they all come down to human brains acting on human brains.

NOTES

1. A surprising number of major theoretical positions in cognitive science have been offered in the form of books presumably intended for general readers. This prac-

tice of conducting disciplinary arguments in public allows proponents of a particular view to present their premises as established to a degree of certainty that their peers would not acknowledge. (See for example on this issue Michael Tomasello's review, "Language Is Not an Instinct," of Steven Pinker's *The Language Instinct*.)

2. In his history, Gardner gave the "cognitive" disciplines five distinguishing features: constructing a level of representation in the mind that is neither neurobiological or cultural (e.g., mental constructs such as schema or images); emphasizing computer modeling of mental processes; removing anything to do with affect, culture, context or history; seeking interdisciplinary connections; and revisiting the major issues of epistemology long of interest in Western philosophy (Gardner 38–45). A recent issue of *Science*, published since this article was written (27 February 2004), features research showing the current importance of an evolutionary perspective on language.

3. The discontinuity of cognitive science from the rhetorical tradition, its very different modeling of the purpose of language, has historical origins. Gardner gave cognitive science roots in the disciplines of linguistics, psychology, and anthropology, as well as in the post–World War II boom in computers and artificial intelligence. Psychology, linguistics, and anthropology formed themselves as disciplines in the late nineteenth century, at the time of rhetoric's decline as an academic subject. Yet the directions of study partitioned in these disciplines, a division that cognitive studies seeks to overcome, were once combined in the rhetorical tradition where language, mental habits and social behavior were combined objects of study in pursuit of the principles of persuasion.

4. This emphasis on information processing and other computer constructs in the discourse of cognitive studies has been frequently criticized, especially by John Searle. But in a recent exchange in this long-sustained contention, Steven Pinker crowed that "Searle's eccentric decree [against the computer analogy] has not kept thousands of cognitive scientists and neuroscientists from invoking signals, codes, rules, representations, neural computation, parallel distributed processing, and other information-theoretic constructs" (Pinker, "'Words and Rules'" 50). In a very recent work (*Wider than the Sky*, 2004), Gerald Edelman has been extremely critical of the computer/brain analogy.

5. Elsewhere I have argued at length against a two-domain theory of language that separates the figures from supposedly unfigured usage. In my view, the traditional figures are especially effective ways of achieving certain functions in a language. The *antithesis*, for example, is the clearest and most succinct way to express an argument from opposites. But the figures listed in manuals are by no means the only linguistic forms that have specifiable functions (see Fahnestock, *Rhetorical Figures* 15–40 and especially 23, 37–38).

6. It is interesting that prosodic differences are not the same as the tonal differences involved in a language that uses pitch differences to make semantic distinctions, such as Chinese. A Chinese speaker distinguishing among three variants of a phoneme on the basis of pitch in order to construe the meaning of a word uses the same area of the left hemisphere involved in phonemic distinctions (Dubin 54).

7. Research has shown that the right hemisphere is not uninvolved in many other aspects of language construal, and in extreme cases, such as children who have lost their entire left cerebral cortex due to Sturge-Weber syndrome, it is possible for the right hemisphere to provide the physical substrate of language abilities (Calvin and Ojemann 189). More intriguing is research that suggests right-brain specialization for comprehending larger language patterns such as narratives (Deacon 311–16), but such ability may also be tied ultimately to prosodic construal.

8. A potential connection between this observation and Aristotle's recommendation of *energeia* is intriguing though admittedly far-fetched. In the little understood third member of the set of the "Asteia" or Urbanities, which also includes metaphor and antithesis, Aristotle recommends visualization through actualization (Kennedy 247); "I call those things 'before the eyes' that signify things engaged in an activity" (248). He praises Homer especially for his ability to make the lifeless living and create activity, concluding, "He makes everything move and live, and *energeia* is motion" (249). It is tempting to credit Aristotle with an intuitive awareness of this stimulation of the motor cortex that can come about with the language of motion.

WORKS CITED

Borod, Joan C., Ronald L. Bloom, and Cornelia Santschi-Haywood. "Verbal Aspects of Emotional Communication." In *Right Hemisphere Language Comprehension: Perspectives from Cognitive Neuroscience.* Ed. Mark Beeman and Christine Chiarello. Mahwah, NJ: Lawrence Erlbaum, 1998.

Burke, Kenneth. *A Rhetoric of Motives.* Berkeley: U of California P, 1950.

Calvin, William H. *How Brains Think: Evolving Intelligence, Then and Now.* New York: Basic Books, 1996.

Calvin, William H., and George A. Ojemann. *Conversations with Neil's Brain: The Neural Nature of Thought and Language.* Reading, MA: Perseus Books, 1994.

Chomsky, Noam. *Knowledge of Language.* New York: Praeger, 1985.

———. "Chomsky's Revolution: An Exchange"[Letter to the Editor]. *New York Review of Books* 18 July 2002: 64.

[Cicero]. *Rhetorica ad Herennium.* Trans. Harry Caplan. Cambridge, MA: Harvard UP, 1954.

Coltheart, Max, Robyn Langdon, and Michael Haller. "Computational Cognitive Neuropsychology and Acquired Dyslexia." In *Evaluating Theories of Language: Evidence from Disordered Communication.* Ed. Barbara Dodd, Ruth Campbell, and Linda Worrall. San Diego, CA: Singular, 1996. 9–36.

Crystal, David. *The Cambridge Encyclopedia of Language.* Cambridge: Cambridge UP, 1987.

Damasio, Antonio R. *Emotion, Reason, and the Human Brain.* New York: Avon Books, 1994.

Deacon, Terrence W. *The Symbolic Species: The Co-evolution of Language and the Brain.* New York: W. W. Norton, 1997.

Dubin, Mark Wm. *How the Brain Works*. Malden, MA: Blackwell Science, 2002.

Fahnestock, Jeanne. *Rhetorical Figures in Science*. New York: Oxford UP, 1999.

———. "Verbal and Visual Parallelism." *Written Communication* 20.2 (April 2003): 123–52.

Faust, Miriam. "Obtaining Evidence of Language Comprehension from Sentence Priming." In *Right Hemipshere Language Comprehension: Perspectives from Cognitive Neuroscience*. Ed. Mark Beeman and Christine Chiarello. Mahwah, NJ: Lawrence Erlbaum, 1998. 285–307.

Feldman, Laurie Beth, and Brendon Prostko. "Graded Aspects of Morphological Processing: Task and Processing Time." *Brain and Language* 81 (2002): 12–27.

Freedman, David J., Maximilian Riesenhuber, Tomaso Poggio, and Earl K. Miller. "Categorical Representation of Visual Stimuli in the Primate Prefrontal Cortex." *Science* 291 (12 January 2001): 312–16.

Gardner, Howard. *The Mind's New Science: A History of the Cognitive Revolution*. New York: Basic Books, 1985.

Just, Marcel Adam, Patricia A. Carpenter, Timothy A. Keller, William F. Eddy, and Keith R. Thulborn. "Brain Activation Modulated by Sentence Comprehension." *Science* 274 (4 October 1996): 114–16.

Kennedy, George A., trans. *Aristotle on Rhetoric: A Theory of Civic Discourse*. New York: Oxford UP, 1991.

Klepousniotou, Ekaterina. "The Processing of Lexical Ambiguity: Homonymy and Polysemy in the Mental Lexicon" *Brain and Language* 81 (2002): 205–23.

Lakoff, George. "The Contemporary Theory of Metaphor." In *Metaphor and Thought* 2nd ed. Ed. Andrew Ortony. Cambridge: Cambridge UP, 1993.

Lamb, Sydney M. *Pathways of the Brain: The Neurocognitive Basis of Language*. Amsterdam: John Benjamins, 1998.

Lieberman, Philip. *Human Language and Our Reptilian Brain: The Subcortical Bases of Speech, Syntax and Thought*. Cambridge, MA: Harvard UP, 2000.

Loury, Glenn. *The Anatomy of Racial Inequality*. Cambridge, MA: Harvard UP, 2002.

McCormack, Paul. "From Snarks to Boojums: Why Are Prosodic Disabilities So Rare?" In *Evaluating Theories of Language: Evidence from Disordered Communication*. Ed. Barbara Dodd, Ruth Campbell, and Linda Worrall. San Diego, CA: Singular, 1996. 37–54.

Peacham, Henry. *The Garden of Eloquence* (1577/1593). A facsimile reproduction, with an introduction by William G. Crane. Gainesville, FL: Scholars' Facsimiles and Reprints, 1954.

Perelman, Chaim, and Lucie Olbrechts-Tyteca. *The New Rhetoric: A Treatise on Argumentation*. Trans. John Wilkinson and Purcell Weaver. Notre Dame, IN: U of Notre Dame P, 1969.

Pinker, Steven. *Words and Rules: The Ingredients of Language*. New York: Basic Books, 1999.

———. "'Words and Rules': An Exchange" [Letter to the Editor]. *New York Review of Books* 27 June 2002: 49–50.

Safire, William. *Lend Me Your Ears: Great Speeches in History*. New York: Norton, 1997.

Searle, John. "'Words and Rules': An Exchange" [Letter to the Editor]. *New York Review of Books* 27 June 2002: 50–52.

Thorpe, Simon J., and Michele Fabre-Thorpe. "Seeking Categories in the Brain." *Science* 291 (12 January 2001): 260–63.

Tomasello, Michael. "Language Is Not an Instinct." *Cognitive Development* 10 (1995): 131–56.

Zatorre, Robert J., Alan C. Evans, Ernst Meyer, and Albert Gjedde. "Lateralization of Phonetic and Pitch Discrimination in Speech Processing." *Science* 256 (8 May 1992): 846–49.

AFTERWORD

Using Traditions

A Gadamerian Reflection on
Canons, Contexts, and Rhetoric

Steven Mailloux

Academic disciplines are institutionalized sets of practices, theories, and traditions for knowledge production and dissemination. Each element in the set
can be defined in terms of the others: Theories are metapractices within traditions of disciplinary thought. Practices are theories performed in actions
embedded in disciplinary traditions. Traditions are interpreted canons and
interpretive contexts for disciplinary practices and theories; and as canons and
contexts, traditions are constituted through the paradigmatic practices and
metapractices of a disciplinary formation. In the preceding essays, rhetorical
study is sometimes referred to as a discipline and at other times assumed to be
an interdiscipline. As an interdiscipline—a field between and within disciplines such as English and communication—rhetoric is currently practiced,
theorized, and historicized in different ways at different times within different places in the American academy.[1] The present volume foregrounds the
opportunities of such interdisciplinarity, especially as those varied possibilities
become actualized in the forms and contents of specific traditions and in
deliberations on the concept of 'tradition' itself. In what follows I explore some
of these (inter)disciplinary uses of tradition through a consideration of Hans-
Georg Gadamer both as a candidate for the textual canon within the rhetorical tradition and as a theorist for understanding what "the rhetorical tradition" can mean.

We can begin again with the two notions of tradition already mentioned: tradition as a textual canon within a discipline and tradition as the historical context for disciplinary work. In the first sense, tradition is the object of a discipline's research and teaching; and in the second, it is the concrete situation for understanding and practicing those activities. Gadamer captures something of both senses in developing the concept of 'the classical' to explain the pivotal role of tradition in his philosophical hermeneutics. In *Truth and Method* he historicizes "the classical," commenting on how it "came to be used in modern thought to describe the whole of 'classical antiquity' when humanism again proclaimed the exemplarity of this antiquity" (288). The modern use of the concept revived "an ancient usage, and with some justification, for those ancient authors who were 'discovered' by humanism were the same ones who in late antiquity comprised the canon of classics" (288). In being canonized, these authors were judged "the culmination of the norm" of the particular literary genre of which each was considered representative (289). Such idealization took place retrospectively through critical reception: "What gives birth to the classical norm is an awareness of decline and distance. It is not by accident that the concept of the classical and of classical style emerges in late periods" (288). For Gadamer, then, "the classical" is both normative and descriptive: It is a normative concept prescribing what is most valued and thus to be preserved; it is also a historical concept describing a period (with a before and after) and a style (based on repetition and difference).

The concept of the classical, of course, plays a crucial role in the establishment of rhetorical studies within the academic humanities and is central to most considerations of the rhetorical tradition, as illustrated again and again throughout the present collection. As the purported origin of rhetorical theory and a valued model for rhetorical practice, classical antiquity overdetermines the configuration of the rhetorical tradition and its alternatives. Classical rhetoric represents the authoritative period of initial conceptual development; it serves as an unsurpassed resource for theoretical frameworks and practical genres in rhetorical study; and it is a privileged object of both admiring imitation and critical displacement for reproducing and transforming the rhetorical tradition as canon and history.

Throughout the present volume, the classical figures the rhetorical tradition in just these synecdochal ways. For instance, the introduction offers classical rhetoric as an example of how, in one view, the rhetorical tradition continues to function "as a perhaps outmoded but still convenient label," noting that rhetoricians can "accept references to 'the classical tradition' of rhetoric, while at the same time recognizing that the label actually yokes together several distinct, often competing perspectives, each of which may be the source of its own 'tradition.'" But the classical is also central to more thorough-going critiques of the rhetorical tradition understood as the standard history of rhetoric and its textual canon. Both of the essays cited in the introduction as

representing this more critical view depend upon "classical rhetoric" as a recognized starting point for the tradition they wish to revise. S. Michael Halloran's 1976 essay "Tradition and Theory in Rhetoric" argues that there is a significant discontinuity between classical rhetoric's production model for
employing established conventions and modern rhetoric's theoretical models
for understanding the rhetorical process (239); while Thomas Miller's 1993
"Reinventing Rhetorical Traditions" begins its argument for an expansion of
the traditional canon with the usual references to the "practical political
speeches by Isocrates and Demosthenes" and the "theories of Aristotle." The
rhetorical tradition, as Miller suggests, might indeed be a "fiction that has just
about outlasted its usefulness" (26) but only if that tradition is understood as
a closed canon privileging the classical narrowly defined. In fact, as the present collection testifies, the rhetorical tradition is alive and well and living in
what might be called the "various rhetorics of traditions" (cf. Miller 27), and
reference to the classical remains a nearly unavoidable rhetorical tactic in any
discussion of the tradition and its alternatives. Whether seen as a heritage
organized around teaching practices (Graff and Leff), an alternative reconstruction based on theoretical refinement (Gross), a source and object of
hermeneutic perspectives (Ceccarelli), a sustainable pedagogical philosophy
(Walzer), or an enabling ground for contemporary democratic politics
(Atwill; Jarratt; Kinney and Miller; Hart-Davidson, Zappen, and Halloran),
the rhetorical tradition continues to be viable in these chapters and the classical remains that tradition's defining moment. Even when the tradition is
simply assumed and used as a complementary model for investigating language processing (Fahnestock) or when the tradition as canon is completely
rejected as a disciplinary focus (Gaines), classical rhetoric serves as an
unavoidable signpost along contemporary rhetorical paths of thought.
Throughout this volume, then, we see the importance of the classical to
rhetorical studies as a period within its canonical history and as an intellectual
touchstone for its theoretical development as an (inter)discipline.

The classical period preoccupies discussions of the rhetorical tradition
and its alternative definitions and configurations; the classical touchstone is
repeatedly praised for its ongoing relevance or criticized for its exclusionary
narrowness; and the classical canon is continually championed, expanded,
reinterpreted, or challenged. However, there is another sense in which, from
Gadamer's perspective, these notions of classical period, touchstone, and
canon are much less important for helping us understand how the rhetorical
tradition works than is the fact that the classical is exemplary of disciplinary
interpretation as such. Gadamer writes, "the classical epitomizes a general
characteristic of historical being: preservation amid the ruins of time" (*Truth*
289). The classical is most profoundly the articulation of past and present
within a rhetorical tradition that is not just a canon of texts, practices, principles, or ideologies but rather, the interpretive context of all disciplinary work

wherever and whenever it takes place. As Gadamer says of understanding more generally, disciplinary understanding *"is to be thought of less as a subjective act than as participating in an event of tradition,* a process of transmission in which past and present are constantly mediated" (*Truth* 290). I will return to this point below.

But first let me comment a bit further on the predominant way the rhetorical tradition is used within the disciplinary debates of rhetorical studies: tradition as textual canon and its standard history.[2] Several of the preceding chapters focus on the definition, function, form, and content of tradition as canon. In the one case where the concept of 'canon' is explicitly rejected, I find it difficult to see how in both theoretical and practical terms the notion of 'corpus' can replace canon as a disciplinary understanding of tradition. When Robert Gaines argues for this replacement, he provides a very useful elaboration of what the (inter)discipline of rhetoric should attend to when it researches and teaches the classical tradition. However, I think most rhetoricians will question the theoretical justification and practical usefulness of putting corpus in place of canon as an alternative disciplinary object of study. Instead, we might see the corpus, under Gaines's capacious description, as the interpreted historical context of which the canon (as text and history) is the interpretive focus. That is, for rhetorical studies, Gaines's definition of the classical corpus is the disciplinary world out of which emerges the canon of texts (objects of interpretation and evaluation) that students of rhetoric research and teach. To think otherwise is to act as if the whole corpus was an undifferentiated set of objects that could be addressed neutrally without prejudices, without valuing some objects more than others for particular purposes. Certainly Gaines is not advocating any such fictional objective methods or impossible disinterested attitudes, but at least in this argument he does not seem to acknowledge (what Gadamer sees as) the necessity of positive prejudice in the human sciences.[3] Without such hermeneutic forestructures of prejudice (enabling assumptions, initial questions, shared exemplars, valued criteria, etc.) interpretive activity could not get started. That is to say, if the rhetorical tradition as canon did not exist, rhetorical studies would simply have to invent it.

And, of course, that is what it did (and continues to do). To be an academic discipline or interdiscipline, rhetoric needed practices, theories, and traditions (as canons and histories) that it could call its own. But that is not quite the right way to put it. Humanistic disciplines do not form and then find distinctive practices, paradigmatic theories, and canonical traditions. Rather, emergent sets of practices, theories, and traditions constitute what counts as a discipline and interdiscipline. In this sense, as an (inter)discipline we do not really have much choice about *whether* we will have the rhetorical tradition as canon and history but only about *how* we will have it, with what content, in what configuration, through which criteria, for what purposes.

In his contribution to the present volume, Alan Gross criticizes this "how" as it is currently conceived. Of a recent rhetoric anthology, Gross asks rhetorically, "What field of study is it that can comfortably accommodate Cicero, Nietzsche, and Bakhtin?" To remedy this incoherence, Gross proposes using W. B. Gallie's notion of "essentially contested concepts" to give the discipline a coherent intellectual core that can be employed for academic legitimation. But if we understand "contested concepts" not ahistorically but rhetorically, then we can say that such concepts are already in place. They form a crucial part of the discursive dynamic loosely holding any discipline together; and insofar as this intradisciplinary rhetoric can be redescribed and re-presented as a part of a discipline's identity, such concepts can be used to explain and "justify" the field's academic legitimacy as a separate area of study with its own practices, theories, and traditions for constructing and distributing knowledge. That is, historically contested concepts are not disciplinary options that can be embraced or not; rather, they are necessary parts of any discipline's rhetorical dynamic. Furthermore, coherence is not an outcome of recognizing contested concepts as the basis of a tradition; coherence is one hermeneutic criteria used in the ongoing rhetorical exchanges in order to recognize the relevant contested concepts. The rhetorical hermeneutics of any field requires some shared concepts and some internal contestation for that field to function and develop as an academic discipline; and in such a dynamic, coherence is as much a part of what is shared and what is contested as any other criteria of disciplinary identity. In still other words, the coherence of a tradition is the result of interpretive work applied within a discipline's rhetorical exchanges and not a regulative idea situated outside the dynamic independently controlling its activity. Whether Cicero, Nietzsche, and Bakhtin are canonical for rhetorical studies depends on several historically specific aspects of the (inter)discipline, one of which is the available arguments for including these figures in the canon. To explore this point further, let me pose the question of Gadamer's canonical status: Does Gadamer belong in the rhetorical tradition, and how might one decide the issue?

Two recent anthologies of rhetoric do not include Gadamer in their selections: Brummett's *Reading Rhetorical Theory* (2000) and Bizzell and Herzberg's *The Rhetorical Tradition* (2001). Both books by necessity must limit their twentieth-century selections given their attempts to be historically comprehensive. However, Foss, Foss, and Trapp's *Contemporary Perspectives on Rhetoric* (2002) and their companion volume *Readings in Contemporary Rhetoric* (2002) also ignore Gadamer. He is not included in a standard history of rhetoric such as Golden, Berquist, and Coleman's *Rhetoric of Western Thought* (1997), and he rates no separate entry in Moran and Ballif's *Twentieth-Century Rhetorics and Rhetoricians* (2000). However, Gadamer does receive attention in Sloane's *Encyclopedia of Rhetoric* (2001) and Jasinski's *Sourcebook on Rhetoric* (2001) and a separate entry in Enos's *Encyclopedia of Rhetoric and*

Composition (1996). Significantly, many articles have been published on Gadamer in the major journals of rhetorical studies over the last decade.

Let me begin an argument here for including Gadamer as an important part of the rhetorical tradition. I do this less to add to the case already made by others than to use the making of the case as a framework for further examining how the rhetorical tradition works in today's (inter)disciplinary formation of rhetorical studies. The most relevant question to ask regarding Gadamer's inclusion in the canon is this: What is rhetorical about his philosophical hermeneutics? The question already begs some other questions, such as, What counts as rhetorical? Here I will use the term *rhetoric* simply to mean our use of language in a context, or perhaps (to be more Gadamerian from the outset) language's contextual use of us. Contextual language use involves effects on audiences, effects that are figurative and suasory; that is, rhetoric involves troping and persuading, two practices with long histories of theoretical discussion. In other places, I have taken to expanding this definition further: rhetoric is the political effectivity of trope, argument, and narrative in culture.[4] With these definitions in mind, I turn to Gadamer.

Gadamer's philosophical hermeneutics is rhetorical in (at least) four ways, and it is those ways and their intersections I would like to explore to help us better understand what the rhetorical tradition is and how it functions in rhetorical studies. First and most important, Gadamer follows Heidegger and posits the fundamental linguisticality of our hermeneutic being-in-the-world. "*Language is the universal medium in which understanding occurs.* . . . All understanding is interpretation, and all interpretation takes place in the medium of a language that allows the object to come into words and yet is at the same time the interpreter's own language" (Gadamer, *Truth* 389). Gadamer does not ignore nonlinguistic aspects of our experience:

> Of course, the fundamental linguisticality of understanding cannot possibly mean that all experiencing of the world takes place only as language and in language. . . . There are such things as hunger and love, work and domination, which themselves are not speech and language but which circumscribe the space within which speaking-with-each-other and listening-to-each-other can take place. ("On the Origins" 179–80)

Nevertheless, for Gadamer understanding and thinking are saturated with language and this rhetorical saturation takes a particular shape in his hermeneutics, both in terms of its theoretical argument (for tradition) and its practical figuration (as dialogic conversation).

The primacy of tradition in Gadamer's hermeneutic account has been the source of much discussion in the reception of his work, most famously in his exchanges with Jürgen Habermas. As I have already noted, Gadamer argues for the centrality of tradition to interpretive activity, both in our everyday lives and in such specialized contexts as disciplinary activities. "We are always situated within traditions, and this is no objectifying process—i.e., we do not conceive of what tradition says as something other, something alien. It is always part of us, a model or exemplar, a kind of cognizance that our later historical judgment would hardly regard as a kind of knowledge but as the most ingenuous affinity with tradition" (*Truth* 282). Tradition in Gadamer is rhetorically articulated: we address and are addressed by tradition. "Our historical consciousness is always filled with a variety of voices in which the echo of the past is heard. Only in the multifariousness of such voices does it exist: this constitutes the nature of the tradition in which we want to share and have a part" (*Truth* 284). Indeed, the very "essence of tradition is to exist in the medium of language" (*Truth* 389; cf. 358).

In regard to textual interpretation, Gadamer gives tradition a special role: "Hermeneutic work is based on a polarity of familiarity and strangeness." It involves a "tension," which "is in the play between the traditionary text's strangeness and familiarity to us, between being a historically intended, distanciated object and belonging to a tradition. *The true locus of hermeneutics is this in-between*" (*Truth* 295). Gadamer claims further that since tradition is "essentially verbal in character," the interpretation of the "verbal tradition retains special priority over all other traditions" (*Truth* 389). Might we not say, then, that for Gadamer's hermeneutics, rhetoric as verbal tradition is both the universal medium of understanding and the primary target of interpretive attention?

But the rhetoricality of Gadamer's notion of tradition does not stop there. For Gadamer, thinking is "the unending dialogue of the soul with itself" ("On the Origins" 189), and understanding resembles dialogic conversation with others (cf. *Truth* 387–88). At the center of Gadamer's own hermeneutic thinking is this metaphor of conversation, which appears again and again in his account of understanding in general and in particular. Not only is hermeneutic activity troped as conversation in Gadamer's description of our everyday being-in-the-world, but also in his accounts of various specialized tasks within our ken. For example, Gadamer tropes all theoretical activity as extensions of conversations involving dialogic answers to the questions of specific historical contexts. Each theory is a particular answer to a particular historical question; and, one might add, each historical interpretation of a specific question-answer scene is itself simultaneously a response to a question of its own historical context. The trope of conversation appears again in Gadamer's characterization of philosophical interpretation: "[E]very dialogue with the thinking of a thinker—which we seek to conduct because we strive to understand—is in itself an unending conversation. The conversation is real insofar as we seek to find our own language as the common one" ("On the Origins" 188). I take this last sentence to mean that though it is the case that in dialogue the fusion of horizons is always within our own vocabulary, within our own communal set of beliefs, practices, and desires, we should always emphasize the commonality between ourselves and our partner in conversation. As Gadamer puts it: "In conversation . . . we attempt to open ourselves to [the conversation partner], and this means holding fast to our common ground" ("On the Origins" 188).

But now, I think, we have moved to another rhetorical dimension of Gadamer's philosophical hermeneutics. The first two dimensions are Gadamer's Heideggerian claim for the fundamental linguisticality of understanding and his own distinctive figuration of that linguisticality as conversation. When that description of how understanding actually does work turns into a prescription about how it should work, we move on to a related but different mode of rhetorical preoccupation in Gadamer's thought. Effective understanding of the other only occurs through a dialectical openness, openness to the other's claims and presuppositions *and* openness to a questioning of our own claims and presuppositions. In this prescriptive way of rhetorical theorizing within his hermeneutics, Gadamer himself uses the term *rhetoric* explicitly and goes on to distinguish philosophical rhetoric from sophistic rhetoric, true dialectic from false sophism. "Where . . . but to rhetoric should the theoretical examination of interpretation turn?" Gadamer asks in "Rhetoric, Hermeneutics, and Ideology-Critique" (318). Indeed, Gadamer turns many times to the canonized rhetorical tradition as a useful resource for developing his philosophical hermeneutics, especially because of what he sees as that tradition's built-in anti-Cartesian, antimethod antiscientism. But Gadamer views that tradition in a fairly conventional way: as the standard account of good philosophy versus dangerous sophistry.

> Rhetorical theory was a long-prepared-for result of a controversy that represented the breaking into Greek culture of an intoxicating and frightening new art of speaking and a new idea of education itself: that of the Sophists. . . . From Protagoras to Isocrates, the masters of rhetoric claimed not only to teach speaking but also the formation of a civic consciousness that bore the promise of political success. Yet it was Plato who first created the foundations out of which a new and all-shattering art of speaking . . . could find its limits and legitimate place. ("Rhetoric" 316)

Gadamer, however, puts his own distinctive stamp on this standard account, as he shows through a series of remarkable readings the specific configuration of the storied opposition between a Platonic dialectic (good philosophical rhetoric) and eristic sophistry (bad rhetoric or sophism), between working cooperatively to find truth and battling sophistically to win arguments, between a radical openness to a conversational partner's questions about our own assumptions and a technically clever defense and advocacy of our beliefs.

This view accepts and champion's Plato's and Aristotle's attacks on the Sophists, which is a major difference between Gadamer and thinkers such as

Nietzsche, Heidegger, and many recent poststructuralists. However, my way of putting the case here is somewhat misleading because Gadamer rejects Platonism as thoroughly as these other thinkers. It is just that he does not reject Plato. More exactly, he rejects the Platonist interpretation of the Platonic text, and it is the Platonist interpretation that much pre- and poststructuralist thought accepts as accurate and then proceeds to attack as metaphysical (Heidegger), foundationalist (Rorty), or worse. In his early work Gadamer teaches a very different reading of Plato than is usually assumed by revisionist historians of the rhetorical tradition. Gadamer's Plato might still be the antisophist, but his aim was not to defend philosophy as a set of metaphysical doctrines (as antiphilosophers from Nietzsche to Rorty would have it) but rather dialectically to perform it as a way of being and acting. What is rhetorical about Gadamer's hermeneutics is closely tied to this anti-Platonist reading of Plato.

In his earliest publications and throughout his career, Gadamer distanced himself from Heidegger's critique of Plato. Rather than interpreting Plato as the beginning of the forgetfulness of Being within Western metaphysics, Gadamer claimed that such a Platonistic interpretation ultimately read the Platonic text as dogmatic statement rather than dialectical conversation. Early Gadamer emphasized that Plato's dialogues dialectically performed the particular way that truth was concealed and unconcealed. That is, Gadamer agreed with Heidegger of the 1920s that we should read Plato through the eyes of Aristotle, but he disagreed with what we see when we do so.[5] Heidegger saw Plato as ignoring truth as unconcealment and as leading to the forgetfulness of being in founding metaphysics through his dialectical search for eternal ideal forms of Truth, Goodness, and Justice. Though elsewhere claiming that Aristotle continued this establishment of metaphysical thinking by reducing logos to statement and truth to an attribute of logos,[6] Heidegger early on reinterpreted Aristotle in a way that stunned and captivated the young Gadamer: Heidegger saw Aristotle's critique of Plato's theory of Ideas not just as the first in a long line of metaphysical revisions of Plato, but in certain places as an explicit formulation (later called "a last glimmer"[7]) of pre-Socratic notions of truth as unconcealment.

Though he too reads Plato through Aristotle, Gadamer sees Aristotle as misreading Plato's dialectic. For Gadamer, what is important in the dialogues is not philosophical doctrine but rhetorical form, not Idealistic theory but dialectical performance. From Gadamer's earliest writings forward, this distinction is crucial. In his 1931 *Habilitationsschrift, Plato's Dialectical Ethics,* supervised by Heidegger, Gadamer argues that Aristotle turned "Platonic dialectic" into "Aristotelian conceptual investigation," ignoring, as did the Platonist tradition to follow, the rhetorical fact that the concepts asserted were part of a dialogue not a treatise. "Aristotle projected Plato onto the plane of conceptual explication. The Plato who presents himself in this explication is the object of Aristotle's critique. What makes this critique problematic is that

this projection cannot also catch the inner tension and energy of Plato's phi-
losophizing as they speak to us, with such incomparable convincingness, in his
dialogues" (Gadamer, *Plato's Dialectical Ethics* 7).

Almost half a century later, Gadamer continued to argue for this anti-
Aristotelian and partially anti-Heideggerian interpretation of Plato's dialogues: "Certainly it is none other than Plato, with his doctrine of ideas, his
dialectic of ideas, his mathematization of physics, and his intellectualization
of what we would call ethics, who laid the foundation for the metaphysical
conceptualization of our tradition. But simultaneously he limited all his pronouncements by means of mimicry" ("On the Origins" 184). Gadamer
encourages us to "first learn to read Plato's writings as mimicry." To do so consists "in taking the conceptual pronouncements that are encountered in conversation and relating them with exactness to the dialogical reality out of
which they grew." To read Plato as mimic means to see his "art of dialogue-
poetry" achieving a conversational goal similar to Socrates with his "customary irony." In the dialogues "is confided for the first time what Socrates actually intends with an art of refutation that too often works sophistically."
Human wisdom does not "pass from one to the other as water can be led from
one vessel to another over a strand of wool [*Symposium,* 175d]." Rather, "a
knowledge of our own ignorance is what human wisdom is. The other person
with whom Socrates carries on his conversation is convicted of his own ignorance by means of his 'knowledge.' This means that something dawns upon
him about himself and his life of illusions." Socrates leads his interlocutor to
this realization, according to Gadamer, just as Plato's dialogues "strip his
reader of his supposed superiority," leading the reader to accept the mode of
dialectical conversation as the way to the unconcealment of truth in dialogue.
Gadamer remarks further that "obviously it is not a specialized knowledge
that is in question here. It is another mode of knowing beyond all the special
claims and competences of a knowing superiority, beyond all of the otherwise
known *technai* and *epistemai*" ("On the Origins" 184–85).

We can use these passages to move on to the final rhetorical dimension
of Gadamer's philosophical hermeneutics I want to examine: Above, Gadamer
alludes negatively to sophistry and positively to alternatives to *technē* and
epistēmē. In Gadamer's attack on Cartesian method, *technē* is associated with
sophistic rhetoric and *phronēsis* (practical wisdom) with philosophical rhetoric
and hermeneutics. For example, in *Truth and Method* Aristotle's treatment of
phronēsis becomes a useful analogy for Gadamer in explaining his own philosophical hermeneutics (*Truth* 312–24). But even more important for
Gadamer's hermeneutics and for my analysis is that *phronēsis* is the basis for
the practical philosophy Gadamer advocates in his rereading of the Platonic-
Aristotelian legacy; and, Gadamer claims, the distinction between this over-
looked practical philosophy and its dominant other, theoretical philosophy,
has been preserved only in the "weak afterglow of the rhetorical tradition."[8]

But today that very rhetorical tradition is currently being transformed in such a way that it now reemerges in solidarity with (not set against) a revisionist sophistry that is context specific, practically oriented, and community based. It is precisely in recent debates over the older Greek Sophists that we can see one of the most important contemporary uses of the rhetorical tradition: as a topic and medium for cooperative work across disciplinary divides.[9] One might even extend these revisionist readings of sophistic rhetoric to ask: Would it not be more consistent with Aristotelian *phronēsis* and rhetoric to see Platonic dialectic and eristic sophistry simply as two alternative conversational strategies more or less appropriate depending on the time and place of the conversation? That is, since Gadamer sees *phronēsis* as practical wisdom within particular situations and rhetoric as reading specific cases for appropriate means of persuasion, would it not be more consistent with his situation-oriented notion of hermeneutic application to suggest that Platonic dialectic and sophistic rhetoric each has a practical utility in different situations rather than prescribing that dialectic should always be employed and sophism opposed? Is it not the case that dialectic could function sophistically and sophistic rhetoric dialectically given certain rhetorical conditions? Making the right judgment concerning what to use when and where is what phronetic rhetoric is all about and would seem to be what Gadamer's rhetorical hermeneutics should promote.[10]

Still, and this is my concluding point, it might be more useful for the current (inter)discipline of rhetorical studies to have dialectic be the default rhetorical strategy in most situations. Contrast this to the negative eristic that is certainly the default tactic within most academic contexts today. Whether the scene is a panel at a professional conference, a curricular discussion at our home institutions, a faculty seminar anywhere: the default rhetorical strategy is to argue against, react negatively, promote and defend our own assumptions and not to listen, examine our beliefs in light of what we hear, work with rather than against the ideas of others. What traditional humanists and the most radical posthumanists have in common is this default strategy to oppose eristically rather than work with dialectically. It is the latter rhetorical strategy that I find most admirable about what Gadamer so consistently advocated for over sixty years.[11]

It is no easy task, of course, to maintain a strong commitment to this rhetorical strategy of cooperative intellectual engagement, especially across disciplinary boundaries. But I would like to suggest, again, that the rhetorical tradition is precisely one of those topics that can be used to encourage such cooperative cross-disciplinary discussion among rhetoricians institutionally housed in different departments. Indeed, the present volume testifies to the viability of the topic for this very purpose. I have tried to indicate how Gadamer's work, at least in its rhetorical hermeneutic dimension, offers significant resources for this ongoing discussion. Through his theoretical practice, we can see how in important ways aspects of the rhetorical tradition—as interpreted canonical history and as interpretive rhetorical context—ultimately blend into each other: we do disciplinary work within a rhetorical tradition even as we debate and revise that tradition. Thus, to say it once more, the question is not whether we should have a tradition in rhetorical studies but how we will have it. Continuing to ask that question, as this volume demonstrates, remains a promising opportunity for cross-disciplinary work in rhetorical studies, not only today but also for the foreseeable future.

NOTES

1. On disciplinarity and interdisciplinarity, see Klein; Moran; and Mailloux, "Practices."

2. For an influential recent discussion of canonicity along with relevant background, see Guillory; also see Condren; Gorak; Kolbas; and Weinsheimer 124–57.

3. "If we want to do justice to man's finite, historical mode of being, it is necessary to fundamentally rehabilitate the concept of prejudice and acknowledge the fact that there are legitimate prejudices" (Gadamer, *Truth* 277).

4. See Mailloux, *Rhetorical Power* and *Reception Histories*; see also Cain, *Reconceptualizing*.

5. On the effect of Heidegger's reading of Aristotle on Gadamer, see Gadamer, *Heidegger's Ways* and "On the Origins." For Heidegger's use of Aristotle to read Plato, see Heidegger's 1924–25 Marburg lecture course, which Gadamer attended (Heidegger, *Plato's Sophist* 8).

6. In Aristotle, "the truth becomes the correctness of the logos" (Heidegger, *Introduction* 186).

7. See Heidegger, *Introduction* 190.

8. Gadamer, *Idea* 169. For further discussion of Gadamer and Aristotelian *phronēsis*, see Mailloux, "Rhetorical Hermeneutics" and Hariman.

9. For bibliographies of these debates, see Mailloux, *Rhetoric, Sophistry, Pragmatism* 236–42; Schiappa and Enos 324–25.

10. See Gadamer's declaration: "I oriented myself expressly to rhetoric in *Truth and Method*, and I found confirmation for this from many sides but above all in the work of Chaim Perelman, who looks at rhetoric from the point of view of law" ("On the Origins" 182). Perelman's New Rhetoric develops a theory of argumentation that is similar to Aristotle's dialectical reasoning, which "seeks through argumentation the acceptance or rejection of a debatable thesis" (*Realm of Rhetoric* 4). Perelman admits that Aristotle opposed rhetoric to dialectic in his *Topics*, but then Perelman finesses the issue by emphasizing that Aristotle's *Rhetoric* calls rhetoric the *"antistrophos"* or counterpart of dialectic. For Aristotle, "dialectic is concerned with arguments used in a controversy or discussion with an individual, while rhetoric concerns the orator's technique in addressing a crowd gathered in a public square. . . . In contrast to ancient rhetoric, the new rhetoric is concerned with discourse addressed to *any sort of audience*" (4–5).

The New Rhetoric thus "amplifies as well as extends Aristotle's work" (4). And, of course, Aristotle's *Rhetoric* famously defines rhetoric as an ability to see the available means of persuasion in each particular case *(peri hekaston)* (1355b). The situation-specific nature of this seeing is underlined in George Kennedy's gloss that *peri hekaston* "refers to the fact that rhetoric deals with specific circumstances (particular individuals and their actions)" (Kennedy 36–37, n. 34).

11. Of all the figures in the rhetorical tradition I might here cite as support for my point, I can think of none as relevant as Wayne Booth in *Modern Dogma and the Rhetoric of Assent*.

WORKS CITED

Bizzell, Patricia, and Bruce Herzberg, eds. *The Rhetorical Tradition: Readings from Classical Times to the Present.* 2nd ed. Boston: Bedford/St. Martin's, 2001.

Booth, Wayne C. *Modern Dogma and the Rhetoric of Assent.* Chicago: U of Chicago P, 1974.

Brummett, Barry, ed. *Reading Rhetorical Theory.* Fort Worth: Harcourt, 2000.

Cain, William E., ed. *Reconceptualizing American Literary/Cultural Studies: Rhetoric, History, and Politics in the Humanities.* New York: Garland, 1996.

Condren, Conal. *The Status and Appraisal of Classic Texts: An Essay on Political Theory, Its Inheritance, and the History of Ideas.* Princeton: Princeton UP, 1985.

Enos, Theresa, ed. *Encyclopedia of Rhetoric and Composition: Communication from Ancient Times to the Information Age.* New York: Garland, 1996.

Foss, Sonja K., Karen A. Foss, and Robert Trapp. *Contemporary Perspectives on Rhetoric.* 3rd ed. Prospect Heights: Waveland P, 2002.

———, ed. *Readings in Contemporary Rhetoric.* Prospect Heights: Waveland P, 2002.

Gadamer, Hans-Georg. "On the Origins of Philosophical Hermeneutics." In *Philosophical Apprenticeships.* Trans. Robert R. Sullivan. Cambridge, MA: MIT P, 1985. 177–93.

———. *The Idea of the Good in Platonic-Aristotelian Philosophy.* Trans. P. Christopher Smith. New Haven: Yale UP, 1986.

———. *Plato's Dialectical Ethics: Phenomenological Interpretations Relating to the Philebus.* Trans. Robert M. Wallace. New Haven: Yale UP, 1991.

———. *Truth and Method.* 2nd ed. Trans. Joel Weinsheimer and Donald G. Marshall. New York: Crossroad, 1991.

———. *Heidegger's Ways.* Trans. John W. Stanley. Albany: State U of New York P, 1994.

———. "Rhetoric, Hermeneutics, and Ideology-Critique." Trans. G. B. Hess and R. E. Palmer. In *Rhetoric and Hermeneutics in Our Time.* Ed. Walter Jost and Michael J. Hyde. New Haven: Yale UP, 1997. 313–34.

Golden, James L., Goodwin F. Berquist, and William E. Coleman. *The Rhetoric of Western Thought.* 6th ed. Dubuque: Kendall/Hunt, 1997.

Gorak, Jan, ed. *Canon vs. Culture: Reflections on the Current Debate*. New York: Garland, 2001.

Guillory, John. *Cultural Capital: The Problem of Literary Canon Formation*. Chicago: U of Chicago P, 1993.

Halloran, S. Michael. "Tradition and Theory in Rhetoric." *Quarterly Journal of Speech* 62 (1976): 234–41.

Hariman, Robert, ed. *Prudence: Classical Virtue and Postmodern Practice*. University Park: Pennsylvania State UP, 2004.

Heidegger, Martin. *An Introduction to Metaphysics*. Trans. Ralph Manheim. New Haven: Yale UP, 1959.

———. *Plato's Sophist*. Trans. Richard Rojcewicz and Andre Schuwer. Bloomington: Indiana UP, 1997.

Jasinski, James. *Sourcebook on Rhetoric: Key Concepts in Contemporary Rhetorical Studies*. Thousand Oaks: Sage, 2001.

Kennedy, George A., trans. and ed. *Aristotle, On Rhetoric: A Theory of Civic Discourse*. New York: Oxford UP, 1991.

Klein, Julie Thompson. *Interdisciplinarity: History, Theory, and Practice*. Detroit: Wayne State UP, 1990.

Kolbas, E. Dean. *Critical Theory and the Literary Canon*. Boulder: Westview, 2001.

Mailloux, Steven. *Rhetorical Power*. Ithaca and London: Cornell UP, 1989.

———. *Reception Histories: Rhetoric, Pragmatism, and American Cultural Politics*. Ithaca and London: Cornell UP, 1998.

———. "Practices, Theories, and Traditions: Further Thoughts on the Disciplinary Identities of English and Communication Studies." *Rhetoric Society Quarterly* 33 (2003): 129–38.

———. "Rhetorical Hermeneutics Still Again: or, On the Track of *Phronēsis*." In *A Companion to Rhetoric*. Ed. Walter Jost and Wendy Olmsted. Oxford: Blackwell. 457–72.

———, ed. *Rhetoric, Sophistry, Pragmatism*. Cambridge: Cambridge UP, 1995.

Miller, Thomas P. "Reinventing Rhetorical Traditions." In *Learning from the Histories of Rhetoric*. Ed. Theresa Enos. Carbondale: Southern Illinois UP, 1993. 26–41.

Moran, Joe. *Interdisciplinarity*. London: Routledge, 2002.

Moran, Michael G., and Michelle Ballif. *Twentieth-Century Rhetorics and Rhetoricians*. Westport, CT: Greenwood, 2000.

Perelman, Chaim. *The Realm of Rhetoric*. Trans. William Kluback. Notre Dame: U of Notre Dame P, 1982.

Schiappa, Edward, and Richard Leo Enos. "Reviewing the Sophists Rhetorically." *Rhetoric Review* 22 (2003): 318–25.

Sloane, Thomas O., ed. *Encyclopedia of Rhetoric*. Oxford: Oxford UP, 2001.

Weinsheimer, Joel. *Philosophical Hermeneutics and Literary Theory*. New Haven: Yale UP, 1991.

Contributors

JANET M. ATWILL is professor of English at the University of Tennessee. She is the author of *Rhetoric Reclaimed: Aristotle and the Liberal Arts Tradition* (Cornell University Press, 1998), coauthor of two composition textbooks, and coeditor with Janice Lauer of *Perspectives on Rhetorical Invention* (University of Tennessee Press, 2002). She is presently completing a book to be published by the State University of New York Press, entitled *New Civic Rhetorics: The Classical Tradition and the Global Polis.*

LEAH CECCARELLI is associate professor in the Department of Communication at the University of Washington. Her publications include one book, *Shaping Science with Rhetoric* (University of Chicago Press, 2001), and several articles, book chapters, and book reviews on rhetorical criticism and the rhetoric of science. Professor Ceccarelli serves on the editorial boards for three journals.

JEANNE FAHNESTOCK is professor of English at the University of Maryland, College Park. She is the author of *Rhetorical Figures in Science* (Oxford University Press, 1999) and, with Marie Secor, *A Rhetoric of Argument* (2nd ed., McGraw-Hill, 1990), as well as numerous articles on rhetorical analysis and the rhetoric of science.

ROBERT N. GAINES is associate professor of communication, University of Maryland, College Park. His research is principally concerned with the individuals and intellectual forces that shaped rhetorical theory in ancient times. His publications on ancient rhetoric have appeared in *Advances in the History of Rhetoric, Hermes, Philosophy and Rhetoric, Rheinisches Museum für Philologie, Rhetoric Society Quarterly, Rhetorica, Transactions of American Philological Association,* and *Transactions of the Canadian Society for the Study of Rhetoric.* He is a past president of the American Society for the History of Rhetoric, has served in the Council of the International Society for the History of Rhetoric, and currently serves as a member of the Board of Directors for the Rhetoric Society of America. He is editor of *Advances in the History of Rhetoric* for 2002–05.

RICHARD GRAFF is assistant professor in the Department of Rhetoric, University of Minnesota-Twin Cities. His research focuses on classical rhetoric, oral performance and literate practices in antiquity, and ancient and modern theories of prose style.

ALAN G. GROSS is professor of rhetoric at the University of Minnesota-Twin Cities (grossalang@aol.com, http://rhetoric.umn.edu/agross/). He is author of *The Rhetoric of Science* (Harvard University Press, 1996), *Communicating Science* (with Joseph Harmon and Michael Reidy, Oxford University Press, 2002), and *Chaim Perelman* (with Ray Dearin, State University of New York Press, 2002).

S. MICHAEL HALLORAN is professor emeritus in the Department of Language, Literature, and Communication at Rensselaer Polytechnic Institute, where he has taught since 1967. He was recently named a fellow of the Rhetoric Society of America.

WILLIAM HART-DAVIDSON (hartdw@rpi.edu) is assistant professor of technical communication and human-computer interaction at Rensselaer Polytechnic Institute. His research and teaching bridge technical communication and information technology, with a particular emphasis on technologies for supporting literate activity.

SUSAN C. JARRATT is campus writing coordinator and professor of English and comparative literature at the University of California, Irvine. Formerly professor of English and director of the Women's Studies program and of college composition at Miami University in Oxford, Ohio, she has published on ancient Greek rhetoric and issues of social difference in contemporary composition studies. She is author of *Rereading the Sophists* (Southern Illinois University Press, 1991) and coedited *Feminism and Composition Studies: In Other Words* (Modern Language Association, 1998) with Lynn Worsham. She coedits (with Susan Romano) *Peitho,* the newsletter of the Coalition of Women Scholars in the History of Rhetoric and Composition, and is currently writing a book about the rhetoric of the Second Sophistic, memory, and public space.

THOMAS J. KINNEY is a PhD candidate in the Rhetoric, Composition, and the Teaching of English program at the University of Arizona, where he studies the history and theory of rhetoric, critical theory, and cultural studies. He also teaches courses in composition, advanced composition, and rhetoric. Currently, he is working on his dissertation, which is a Marxist and postcolonial critique of the traditional cognitive map of rhetoric and its civic republican (or proprietarian) assumptions.

MICHAEL LEFF is professor and chair of the Department of Communication, University of Memphis. He has published extensively in the areas of rhetorical criticism and history of rhetoric and is former editor of the journal *Rhetorica*.

STEVEN MAILLOUX is professor of English and comparative literature at the University of California, Irvine. He is the author of *Interpretive Conventions: The Reader in the Study of American Fiction* (Cornell University Press, 1982), *Rhetorical Power* (Cornell University Press, 1989), and *Reception Histories: Rhetoric, Pragmatism, and American Cultural Politics* (Cornell University Press, 1998) and is editor of the volume *Rhetoric, Sophistry, Pragmatism* (Cambridge University Press, 1995).

THOMAS P. MILLER is professor at the University of Arizona, where he directs the writing program. In 1999, he was awarded the Administrator of the Year from the university's Graduate and Professional Student Council, and in 1998 he received the Mina Shaughnessy Prize from the Modern Language Association for his most recent scholarly book, *The Formation of College English: Rhetoric and Belles Lettres in the British Cultural Provinces* (University of Pittsburgh Press, 1997). In 2002, he received an NEH fellowship to work on the second volume of this project, "The Formation of College English: From the American Republic of Letters to the Information Economy."

ARTHUR E. WALZER is professor of rhetoric, University of Minnesota-Twin Cities. He is the author of *George Campbell: Rhetoric in the Age of Enlightenment* (State University of New York Press, 2002) and editor (with Alan Gross) of *Rereading Aristotle's Rhetoric* (Southern Illinois University Press, 2000).

JAMES P. ZAPPEN is associate professor in the Department of Language, Literature, and Communication at Rensselaer Polytechnic Institute. He is author of *The Rebirth of Dialogue: Bakhtin, Socrates, and the Rhetorical Tradition* (forthcoming from State University of New York Press), and series editor for the State University of New York Press Studies in Scientific and Technical Communication. Currently he is designing a youth-services information system for Troy and Rensselaer County, New York, with colleagues from Rensselaer Polytechnic Institute and the State University of New York-Albany and with funding from the National Science Foundation, the 3Com Urban Challenge Program, and other organizations.

Index

Made in the USA
Lexington, KY
28 May 2013